TEACHING GIFTED
AND TALENTED LEARNERS
IN REGULAR CLASSROOMS

TEACHING GIFTED
AND
TALENTED LEARNERS
IN
REGULAR CLASSROOMS

Edited By

ROBERTA M. MILGRAM

WITHDRAWN

CHARLES C THOMAS • PUBLISHER

Springfield • Illinois • U.S.A.

Published and Distributed Throughout the World by

CHARLES C THOMAS • PUBLISHER
2600 South First Street
Springfield, Illinois 62794-9265

© *1989 by* CHARLES C THOMAS • PUBLISHER

ISBN 0-398-05557-2

Library of Congress Catalog Card Number: 88-39250

Printed in the United States of America
SC-R-3

Library of Congress Cataloging-in-Publication Data
Teaching gifted and talented learners in regular classrooms / edited
  by Roberta M. Milgram.
      p.   cm.
   Bibliography: p.
   Includes index.
   ISBN 0-398-05557-2
   1. Gifted children—Education.   2. Mainstreaming in education.
I. Milgram, Roberta M.
LC3993.T33   1989
371.9′046—dc19   88-39250
                                                                          CIP

CONTRIBUTORS

Margaret A. Anderson is Director of the Rio Grande School, Sante Fe, New Mexico.

Ken Bareford is a teacher in the Educational Enrichment Program for Gifted and Talented Students, Summit, New Jersey. He is co-author (with Shillenberg, P.M., Pacigia, J.A., and Townsend, J.L.) of *The Teacher's Computer Book* (1987, Teachers College Columbia Press).

Gary A. Davis is Professor, Department of Educational Psychology, University of Wisconsin.

Rita Dunn is Professor, Division of Administrative and Instructional Leadership and Director, Center for the Study of Teaching and Learning Styles, St John's University.

Sandra N. Kaplan is Associate Director of the National/State Leadership Training Institute on the Gifted and the Talented, Los Angeles, California.

C. June Maker is Professor and Coordinator of Graduate Programs in Education for the Gifted, Division of Special Education, University of Arizona.

Nancy Chezar Milgram is a teacher in the Educational Enrichment Program for Gifted and Talented Students, Summit, New Jersey. She received her B.A. from Barnard College, and her Ed.M. from Harvard Graduate School of Education.

Roberta M. Milgram is Associate Professor, School of Education, Tel-Aviv University, Israel.

Margaret A. Thomas, Department of Educational Administration, University of Wisconsin.

Dina Tirosh is Lecturer, School of Education, Tel-Aviv University, Israel.

S. Samuel Shermis is Professor, Department of Education, Purdue University.

Judith L. Shrum is Associate Professor, Division of Curriculum and Instruction, College of Education, Virginia Polytechnic Institute and State University.

Robert E. Yager is Professor, Science Education Center, University of Iowa.

נח אִישׁ צַדִּיק ...

בְּדֹרֹתָיו...

בראשית ו:ט

"Noach was a righteous and decent person in his generation . . . "
Genesis 6:9

This book is dedicated to
my husband,
Noach
because he deserves it. . . . and more.

Thank you for sharing with me the joys of life: marriage,
children, grandchildren, career and living in Israel.

PREFACE

For more than 20 years I have been conducting research and teaching courses on topics of giftedness and creativity. On the basis of this experience it seems to me that two main problems merit more attention. The first problem is that the literature devotes too little attention to gifted learners in regular classrooms, and the second is that many significant research findings do not reach teachers in the field. This book is designed to address both of these problems by focusing specifically on the teaching of gifted children in regular classrooms, and by contributing to the wider dissemination of research findings. I have, moreover, an additional goal: to propose a new model of giftedness that will generate research on the topic of giftedness and encourage systematic development, implementation, and evaluation of curriculum materials and teaching strategies.

In the last two decades we have witnessed major increments in the quantity and quality of empirical research and modest increments in theoretical developments in the field. Progress in these areas has provided the impetus for the most dramatic change of all during the period, the steep rise in the number and variety of special education programs developed for gifted and talented learners in the United States and around the world. Theoreticians and educators have developed many effective approaches and innovative materials in a variety of subject matter areas. In many instances, unfortunately, well-established research findings and reports of highly successful, innovative advances in teaching strategy and curriculum materials fail to reach those actively engaged in teaching gifted children. By the same token, researchers rarely consider knowledge and experience gleaned from the field. This book is designed to present knowledge that has accumulated from empirical research and from experience in the field to teachers in regular classrooms, i.e., to the "end-of-the-line-user."

The choice of topics and the structure of the book reflect its goals. The book is divided into two sections. The first is devoted to presentation of the 4 × 4 model of giftedness that I have developed, the three guiding principles for teaching gifted and talented children in regular classrooms, computer application programs in gifted education, and a unique administrative arrangement that combines the pull-out and mainstreaming approaches. In the second section of the book the emphasis shifts from general principles to research and practice in specific subject matter areas: the language arts, science, mathematics, social studies, and foreign languages.

I realized that the material is so rich and complex that the quality of the end product would be greatly enhanced if each topic were presented by an expert. I searched the literature on the topic of each chapter and invited the person who had the requisite background and experience to write an original chapter on the topic of his or her expertise. The authors were selected because they combined excellent research credentials with respect for and, in many instances, practical experience in gifted education. With few exceptions, the authors whom I approached agreed to prepare original papers and expressed warm support for the conceptualization and plan of the book. I was delighted with the warm response of these authors at the onset of our project and have been very pleased with the chapters that resulted. I am especially grateful to them for providing me with the opportunity to broaden and deepen my own knowledge of giftedness and talent. It has been gratifying to correspond with the authors whose work is included in the current volume and to meet with many of them in person. I have learned a great deal from each author. I thank them for their creative efforts, cooperation, and patience. I especially appreciate the flexibility demonstrated by them as we worked together to make a contribution to gifted education.

I appreciate the warm interest and encouragement of the publisher of this volume, Payne E. L. Thomas. His vision in appreciating the value of the topic and his efficiency in guiding it to completion is gratefully acknowledged. I thank the School of Education of Tel Aviv University for their support.

My interest in the topic of giftedness and the inspiration for the theoretical model of giftedness that I have developed has come from my family. I am in very good company, considering the number of psychologists whose ideas were based upon observations of their own children. In watching my children and grandchildren grow and develop, I saw that giftedness and talent come in many forms. I thank my children Shoshana and Raymond Knapp, and Wendy and D. Jonathan Rimon (Milgram), and grandchildren Avinoam Rimon, Rachel Heather Knapp, Nadav Moshe Rimon, Dashiell Ari Knapp, Talia Sara Rimon, Assaf Daniel Rimon, Genevieve Ilana Knapp, and Yael Rimon for sharing with me their gifts and talents. I acknowledge with respect and gratitude the wise advice and editorial assistance that I received from my husband, Noach Milgram, and from my daughter, Shoshana Knapp.

This book is written for educators of the gifted and talented—teachers, counselors, educational specialists, and administrators—and for college and university students who plan to work in this field. It may be read with profit by professional workers in other specialized areas of special education, by the parents of gifted and talented children, and by those interested in education in general. I invite readers to respond to this volume by sending me their comments, criticisms, and/or recommendations. I promise to read and respond to all comments and to incorporate appropriate suggestions in a second edition of this book several years hence.

CONTENTS

Page

Preface   ix

Part I: Customizing the Teaching-Learning Process for Gifted and Talented Children in Regular Classrooms

Chapter 1:   Teaching Gifted and Talented Children in Regular Classrooms: An Impossible Dream or a Full-Time Solution For a Full-Time Problem
Roberta M. Milgram 7

Chapter 2:   Curriculum Content for Gifted Students: Principles and Practices
C. June Maker 33

Chapter 3:   Individualizing Instruction for Mainstreamed Gifted Children
Rita Dunn 63

Chapter 4:   Teaching Gifted Children for Creative Growth
Gary A. Davis and Margaret A. Thomas 113

Chapter 5:   Using Computer Application Programs With Gifted Learners
Ken Bareford 129

Chapter 6:   The SEEK (Summit Educational Enrichment for Kids) Pull-Out Program: A Boon and not a Bane to Teaching Gifted Children in Regular Classrooms
Nancy Chezar Milgram 147

Part II: Customizing Curriculum Content for the Gifted and Talented in Regular Classrooms

Chapter 7:   Language Arts for Gifted Learners
Sandra N. Kaplan 169

Chapter 8:   Assessing and Providing for Gifted Children with Special Needs in Reading and Library Skills
Margaret A. Anderson 179

Chapter 9:   Teaching Mathematically Gifted Children
             Dina Tirosh 205
Chapter 10: Teaching Science to Gifted Science Students
             Robert E. Yager 223
Chapter 11: Teaching Students Gifted in Social Studies
             S. Samuel Shermis 249
Chapter 12: Challenging Linguistically Gifted Students in the Regular
             Foreign Language Classroom
             Judith L. Shrum 269
Index 295

TEACHING GIFTED
AND TALENTED LEARNERS
IN REGULAR CLASSROOMS

PART I
CUSTOMIZING THE
TEACHING LEARNING PROCESS
FOR GIFTED AND TALENTED CHILDREN
IN REGULAR CLASSROOMS

INTRODUCTION

ROBERTA M. MILGRAM

This book is designed to give regular classroom teachers an understanding of the need to provide special education for their gifted and talented students, awareness that they themselves can meet this need in the regular classroom, and the tools with which to meet this formidable challenge. Many important issues associated with teaching gifted and talented children in regular classrooms are raised and discussed in depth. In addition to the real-world examples and practical suggestions included in each chapter, authors refer to a wide variety of books, films, and other curriculum materials that will be of help to teachers.

The major theme of this book is that the educational teaching-learning process should be customized for each gifted and talented child. To customize the educational process means to tailor it to match the unique needs of each learner. The process of customizing education for gifted children is accomplished by differentiating the curriculum, individualizing the instructional process, and developing a creative classroom environment. The book is divided into two sections, the first dealing with customizing the teaching-learning process for gifted and talented children in regular classrooms and the second with customizing curriculum content for them.

The first section opens with the presentation of a comprehensive model of giftedness developed by the editor. Giftedness is conceptualized in terms of four cognitive categories, two having to do with intelligence and two with creativity or original thinking. Each of the four categories is manifested in the individual at one of four ability levels in one or more of the three major learning environments—home, school, and community. The model emphasizes individual differences associated with age, sex, socioeconomic status, culture, subculture, and selected personality characteristics. It postulates that children may be gifted by one criterion and not by another, and directs attention to the need to tailor curriculum and instructional strategies for a specific gifted child according to his or her profile of assets. The model is designed to help teachers in regular classrooms understand the wide range of individual differences in gifted learners and to guide school administrators and school boards in their discussions and policy decisions about special education for gifted learners.

The remainder of Section One is devoted to the presentation and elaboration of the following three principles for teaching gifted and talented children in regular classrooms:

(1) Differentiation of curriculum (Maker, Chapter 2);

(2) Individualization of instruction (Dunn, Chapter 3); and

(3) Development of a creative classroom atmosphere (Davis & Thomas, Chapter 4).

Maker stresses the critical importance of providing a curriculum for gifted learners that is qualitatively different from the one usually included in the basic curriculum for all children. She specifies adjustments in the amount, variety, and complexity of curriculum material as well as in its level of abstraction and complexity. She recommends that the curriculum be comprehensive, organized around key concepts, and relevant to a future world that will be very different from the present.

Dunn discusses individualization both theoretically and practically. First, she defines learning style as the conditions under which each person begins to concentrate, absorb, process, and retain new and difficult information and skills. Second, she describes the administration and scoring of her own Learning Style Inventory, a well-established instrument that yields an individual profile of each student's learning style characteristics. Third, Dunn summarizes and integrates relevant findings and reports that higher school achievement and more positive attitudes toward school have consistently resulted when learning style and instructional environment match, and the opposite results when they do not. The kinds of practical arrangements deemed necessary for this individualization are well within the scope of the teacher in a regular classroom.

The call for individualization of instruction in order to provide for the wide range of individual differences found in regular classrooms is not new. The problem has been how to individualize in a classroom with 30 or more students. The Contract Activity Packages (CAPS) developed by Dunn and described in detail in her chapter are of particular importance. These materials provide a practical and inexpensive way to implement individualization of instruction according to learning style.

In Chapter Four, Davis and Thomas deal with the question of how to develop a creative classroom atmosphere. They review some of the major concepts developed in research on creative thinking as well as the techniques used in enhancing creative problem-solving and explain how these ideas and techniques can be applied to teaching. Two categories of gifted learners will derive special benefit from a creative classroom environment, i.e., children with overall original/creative thinking ability and children with specific creative talent.

In Chapter 5, Bareford explains that teachers can use personal computers to differentiate curriculum, to individualize instruction, and to develop a creative atmosphere. He suggests that the focus on acquiring skill in computer programming and in learning computer languages has been misguided. It did not lead to the widespread computer literacy but rather to computer anxiety and avoidance in many teachers and pupils, even among some gifted and talented learners. While not denigrating the value of acceleration and enrichment in computer science when appropriate for an individual or small group of learners, Bareford proposes that all learners, especially the gifted, will benefit more from acquiring familiarity and experience with application programs such as word processing, data bases, communication packages, and spreadsheets. He cites a number of real-world projects that have been used successfully with gifted learners of different types and levels and recommends their implementation. Classroom teachers should view the computer as a tool to be used creatively and selectively based on the needs of the individual learner. The various uses arranged hierarchically include: simple drill and practice, complex individualized tutorial lessons, games, problem-solving exercises and simulations, application programs, and programming. The chapter clarifies how personal computers make it possible for regular classroom teachers to provide a wide variety of learning experiences for gifted and talented students in a manner and at a level that was hitherto impossible.

The N. Milgram chapter represents a unique approach to teaching gifted and talented learners in regular classrooms. It is a variation of the ubiquitous "pull-out" program but solves many of the problems most frequently associated with it. The SEEK program described in the chapter reflects in practice a number of the most important ideas that are suggested in this book: open admission for all interested children, activities anchored in the regular classroom, fruitful gifted education specialist-regular classroom teacher collaboration. Since the administrative arrangements for pull-out programs are in place in so many school districts, the SEEK approach can be implemented easily and rapidly, thus serving the needs of gifted and talented children in regular classrooms more fully.

Chapter 1

TEACHING GIFTED AND TALENTED CHILDREN IN REGULAR CLASSROOMS: AN IMPOSSIBLE DREAM OR A FULL-TIME SOLUTION FOR A FULL-TIME PROBLEM?

ROBERTA M. MILGRAM

Stephen Wozniak, who as a young man made the first Apple® computer and later founded a multimillion dollar corporation, would qualify by any definition as gifted—in retrospect. Yet he was not identified in his high school as gifted. In fact, he was a dropout. He built the first Apple computer as an out-of-school project, on his own leisure time in his garage. One might imagine that Wozniak lived in a small, isolated community that offered few opportunities to children who demonstrate remarkable abilities at an early age. Interestingly enough, the opposite was true. He grew up in California, a state that has pioneered special education for the gifted and continues to invest heavily in these programs. This book is designed to provide teachers in regular classrooms with an understanding of how such a situation occurred and to help them recognize and enhance remarkable abilities, such as those of Stephen Wozniak.

In a national survey conducted by the Richardson Foundation, Cox, Daniel, and Boston (1985) reported that the overwhelming majority of gifted children spend most of their time in regular classrooms. They found that among gifted children who received any special education at all, the most frequently used program option is the "pull-out" model. In this model, gifted children are in regular classrooms most of the school week and are "pulled-out" for a period of time ranging from an hour to a full day a week to study with other gifted learners in a setting other than the regular classroom. The second and third most common programs—enrichment and independent study—are also implemented within the regular classroom. Given that most gifted children and youth spend

7

most of their time in regular classrooms, the major opportunities for enhancing their abilities are in this setting. If regular classroom teachers do not provide appropriate learning experiences for these children, then it is quite likely that most gifted students will not receive these experiences at all.

Teaching gifted and talented learners in the regular classroom is, in the opinion of many educators, one of the best ways to provide for the special needs of these children. Many believe, however, that this is an impossible dream. Because teachers do not have qualitatively different curricula available to them and because they don't know and haven't used individualized teaching strategies, they frequently have difficulty in challenging gifted and talented learners. Most of the literature on innovations and adjustments in curriculum and teaching strategy for gifted children fails to specify what is most useful in regular classrooms versus special education settings. This confounding is unfortunate because some materials and strategies are useful in homogeneous classes, but inappropriate in heterogeneous classrooms, while other approaches are better suited to the latter and not the former. The chapters that follow, each prepared with the mainstreamed gifted child in mind, are designed to help teachers make the impossible dream possible.

Teachers frequently raise three basic questions:

1. *Who* are the gifted and talented children in my classroom? How shall I recognize them?
2. *How* shall I teach them?
3. *What* shall I teach them?

Systematic scientific knowledge and practical experience have accumulated in response to these questions over the years. It is unfortunate that this knowledge is not readily available to regular classroom teachers, who are in the best position to use it. This book is an effort to reduce the gap between the existence of knowledge and its implementation.

The book is divided into three parts, each devoted to one of the three questions cited above. The present introductory chapter, which answers the question *Who*, provides information about the nature of giftedness and how to identify gifted learners in regular classrooms. The second section, which answers the question *How*, describes teaching strategies that help teachers in regular classrooms meet the special needs of gifted and talented learners. The third section, which answers the question *What*, describes the specific curriculum areas, such as mathematics, science, social studies, foreign language, and language arts, as customized for gifted and talented learners.

I. DEFINITION OF GIFTEDNESS

The meaning of giftedness is a topic of continuing discussion in the literature. Terman (1925), Terman, and Oden (1947, 1959), and others in the early part of the century used the Stanford-Binet IQ of 140 or higher as an operational definition of giftedness. For many years the field was dominated by this unidimensional, IQ-oriented view of giftedness. In the 1950s the definition of giftedness was expanded by Guilford (1956) to include creativity and educators began to speak of the gifted and talented. In the 1970s Marland (1972), then United States Commissioner of Education, proposed a multifaceted definition of giftedness that was adopted by the United States Office of Education, and enacted into law by the Congress of the United States in the Gifted and Talented Children's Act of 1978.

The definition read as follows:

> The term gifted and talented children means children and whenever applicable, youth, who are identified at the preschool, elementary, or secondary level as possessing demonstrated or potential abilities that give evidence of high performance capability in areas such as intellectual, creative, specific academic, or leadership ability, or in the performing and visual arts, and who by reason thereof, require services or activities not ordinarily provided by the school. (Sec.902)

With the prestige of federal law behind it, Marland's (1972) omnibus definition of giftedness became widely accepted. By 1980, 39 states had enacted legislation based upon this definition. The definition is advantageous because it defines giftedness broadly rather than in terms of IQ alone, and justifies the provision of services to different kinds of gifted and talented children. Unfortunately, it lacks conceptual clarity, and the diverse abilities referred to have been difficult to define operationally and assess reliably.

A 4 × 4 Structure of Giftedness Model

To overcome these shortcomings, the author has developed a 4 × 4 model of the structure of giftedness (see Fig. 1-1). Giftedness is conceptualized in terms of four categories, two having to do with aspects of intelligence (general intellectual ability and specific intellectual ability) and two with aspects of original thinking (general original/creative thinking and specific creative talent). Each category of giftedness may be viewed as a cognitive process with a corresponding product or performance. Each of the four processes is manifested in the individual at one of four ability levels (profoundly gifted, moderately gifted, mildly gifted, and nongifted), hence the name 4 × 4.

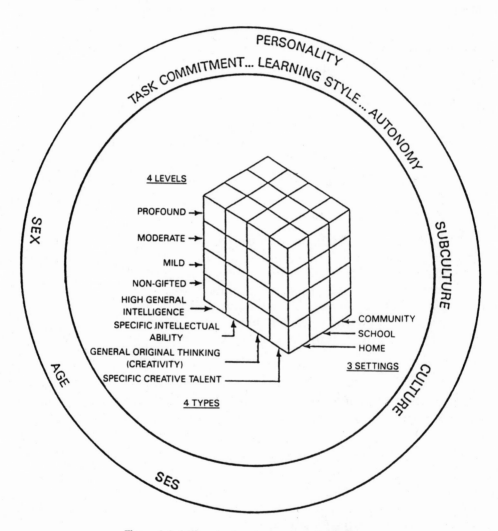

Figure 1-1. Milgram: 4 × 4 structure of giftedness

There are two other aspects to the model. First, there is the dimension of learning environment. Gifted and talented children and youth grow up in three interrelated learning environments—the home, the school, and the community. Second, giftedness is depicted as embedded in a solid circle of individual differences associated with age, sex, socioeconomic status, culture, subculture, and personality characteristics (e.g., task commitment, learning style, and autonomy). The 4 × 4 model is designed to compare and contrast the different kinds of giftedness among children and within the same child. It directs attention to the need to tailor curriculum and instructional strategies to groups of children gifted by one criterion and not by another, and facilitates planning for a specific gifted child according to his or her profile of assets.

Four Categories of Giftedness

The first category, *general intellectual ability* or *overall general intelligence*, refers to the ability to think abstractly and to solve problems logically and systematically. This ability is measured in adults and children by performance on psychometric tests and is frequently reported as IQ scores. Intelligence in adults is related to successful performance of a wide variety of vocational and academic tasks and in children by high-level performance in the school work, in general. This category of giftedness in children has received the most attention over the years. It has been clarified conceptually, clearly defined, and efficiently measured. Most school programs for gifted children are designed with these learners in mind.

The second category, *specific intellectual ability,* refers to a clear and distinct intellectual ability in a given area, such as mathematics, foreign languages, art, music, science, social science, literature, or drama. For example, a person characterized by a specific intellectual ability in mathematics demonstrates outstanding computational ability, knowledge of mathematical principles, and deep understanding of mathematical concepts. In art it is reflected in aesthetic appreciation and/or technical ability; in science by mastery of scientific information and principles, and in music by auditory discrimination (a "good ear") and musical memory.

Specific intellectual abilities in adults are reflected in real-world performance and accomplishment in any one of a number of specific areas. Their performance may be highly competent, but not necessarily highly original. Specific intellectual abilities in children and adolescents are often, but not invariably, expressed in superior academic performance in school subjects as reflected in specific school grades and achievement tests. Programs designed to serve the educational needs of children in this category exist in many communities (e.g., Stanley, 1977, 1979). They are, however, far less common than those designed for children in the first category.

The third category, *general original/creative thinking,* may be defined as a kind of problem-solving by means of which original, i.e., unusual, solutions of high quality are generated (Guilford, 1967; Mednick, 1962). The ideas and solutions that result from the process of creative problem-solving in adults and children are imaginative, clever, elegant, or surprising.

A large number of cognitive and other abilities have been cited in comprehensive literature surveys as implicated in creative or original thinking (e.g., Barron & Harrington, 1981). Among the abilities mentioned most frequently are ideational fluency, curiosity, fantasy, imagery, problem-finding, metaphoric production, and selective attention deployment. Most of the research, however, has focused on one cognitive capacity postulated by numerous investigators to be an essential component of creativity—the quantity and quality of ideational production. This general ability has been referred to by Barron and Harrington (1981) as "raw creative ability," as distinguished from "effective creativity," and is implicated in the fourth category of giftedness discussed below.

Original thinking people are different from others not only at the output stage as reflected in ideational production but also at the input. They perceive and define problems differently and notice things that others ignore (Wallach, 1970). They probably store and retrieve information differently as well. As a consequence of these basic differences, they produce unique and imaginative solutions.

The fourth category *specific creative talent,* refers to a clear and distinct creative ability in one area. Talent is manifested in both children and adults in the generation of socially valuable, novel products in science, mathematics, art, music, social leadership, business, politics, or any other important human endeavor. The realization of potential talent often requires time to incubate and develop as a result of life experience. It is, therefore, more fully manifested in adults, but may be in evidence long before adulthood, especially if one knows where to look. One way to identify specific creative talent in children before these abilities become fully realized in one's vocation, is by examining leisure time and out-of-school activities.

Gifted children and adolescents frequently use their leisure time in a way that is very different from the way it is used by their less gifted peers.

Many read voraciously in their area of special interest. Children with special talent in music, science, or art, for example, may spend long hours practicing and perfecting techniques on their own initiative. The enormous investment of time and effort over an extended period of time that frequently characterizes the development of talent (Bloom, 1985) makes it clear that the actualization of talent is not only a gift but an achievement.

We generally think of leisure time activities such as watching television or playing games with friends as nonintellectual or frivolous. While many gifted children certainly spend time in these activities, it may be that what they do out-of-school is as unusual as what they do in school or perhaps even more unusual. The activities that gifted children engage in are often highly intellectual in nature and, moreover done to satisfy their own curiosity and interests, rather than to achieve high grades and satisfy the needs of teachers and parents.

Out-of-school activities of gifted children and adolescents have received scant attention in the literature (Holland, 1961; Milgram & Milgram, 1976a; Milgram, Yitzhak, & Milgram, 1977; Terman, 1925). I consider leisure activities an excellent indicator of early talent and will suggest later in this chapter that much more attention be focused on them.

Levels of Giftedness

Gifted behavior may be found in children and adults at mild, moderate, and profound levels (see Fig. 1-2). These levels are hierarchical in organization and become increasingly infrequent in occurrence as one moves from nongifted to profoundly gifted. It is extremely rare for programs to differentiate among gifted learners by level. We sometimes find special programs or schools for profoundly gifted children, but almost never encounter practical consideration of the distinction between the mild and moderate levels of giftedness.

This situation is surprising when one considers the enormous attention and importance devoted to the levels of ability in children and youth at the other end of the ability continuum—the mentally retarded. Until the early part of this century, admittedly, there was no distinction between the various levels of mental retardation. With the advent of modern measurement techniques, however, the theoretical and practical importance of the different levels of mental retardation were strongly emphasized (American Psychiatric Association, 1980). Four levels of

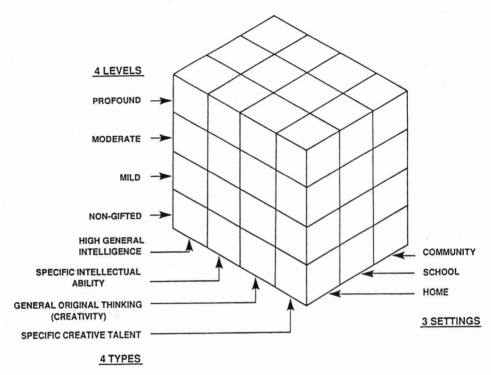

Figure 1-2. Milgram: 4 × 4 structure of giftedness

retardation have been defined—mild, moderate, severe, and profound. Professional and lay terminologies have been developed to reflect these levels. Parents and teachers are informed about these levels and their educational implications in a clear and definitive manner. Each level reflects a distinct range of expectations with respect to short- and long-term accomplishments that is different from those of the other levels.

Most educators agree that the concept of levels is highly important in understanding and educating mentally retarded children and youth. In planning educational programs, all agree that level of intellectual functioning is a prime consideration. No one would suggest that mildly retarded individuals learn the same curriculum material, in the same way, and in the same setting as profoundly retarded. By contrast, in conceptualizations of giftedness and in educational programming for gifted learners the concept of levels has, for the most part, been ignored. This is unfortunate. Educators should strive to match the gifted child's special educational program with his/her specific needs as determined by the category and level of giftedness.

In research, as well as in educational practice, most studies define giftedness as above a certain cutoff point on IQ score with no further distinction among gifted individuals above the cutoff. A few investigators, however, have focused attention on profoundly gifted learners. In one of the earliest studies of gifted children, Hollingworth (1942) highlighted the differences between profoundly gifted children, defined by her as those with IQ of 180 or higher and their less gifted peers. More recently, Feldman (1986) investigated child prodigies in academic subjects and in the arts. Albert (1983, in press), Albert, and Runco (1986, 1987) and Bloom (1985) described eminent people in a wide variety of fields who presumably are at the profound level of one or more of the four cognitive categories. Some participants in the Study of Mathematically Precocious Youth (SMPY) conducted at Johns Hopkins University by Stanley (1977, 1979) are profoundly gifted in mathematics, with specific creative talent in the discipline.

Differentiation by levels is a unique feature of the proposed model. Failure to differentiate conceptually among gifted children by level results in failure to provide appropriate programs for children at each level. The same curriculum and administrative arrangement cannot meet the needs of the 16 different groups of learners (category × level) identified by the model. A major reason for the failure of many full-time special education settings to meet the needs of their pupils is the failure to distinguish between the four categories of giftedness and their levels. All category × level combinations cannot be served adequately in the same classroom at the same time. No group is serviced adequately, even if all the children in the classroom are gifted. We contend that a gifted child who is profoundly gifted in mathematics, moderately gifted in music, and/or mildly gifted in science is more likely to have her or his needs met in a regular classroom in which the curriculum is differentiated and the teaching-learning process individualized than in a full-time special setting operating without a differentiated curriculum and individualized instruction. In order to teach each child appropriately, we must consider the interrelationships of the categories and levels of giftedness.

The Interrelationship of the Categories and Levels. The first two categories, general and specific intellectual ability are moderately correlated (Tannenbaum, 1983). Neither, however, is substantially correlated with the other two categories of giftedness. Considerable evidence has accumulated confirming that neither general nor specific intellectual ability is related to overall creative thinking, operationally defined as ideational fluency (Kogan, 1983; Milgram, 1983; Milgram & Arad, 1981; Milgram & Feingold, 1977; Milgram & Milgram, 1976b; Milgram, Milgram, Rosenbloom, & Rabkin, 1978; Milgram & Rabkin, 1980; Milgram, Moran, Sawyers, & Fu, 1987; Wallach, 1970; 1971; 1985). By the same token, no relationship has been found between the two categories of intellectual ability and specific talent in a wide variety of spheres ranging from mathematics and science to sports, music, and social leadership. Even specific creative activities that are regarded as highly intellectual in nature, are unrelated to scores on measures of general intelligence when allowance is made for a minimal baseline level of intellectual ability (Holland, 1961; Milgram & Milgram, 1976a; Wallach & Wing, 1969; Wing & Wallach, 1971).

Categories three and four, general creative thinking and specific creative talent, are moderately related to each other (Amabile, 1983; Milgram & Milgram, 1976a; Wallach & Wing, 1969; Wing & Wallach, 1971). In an extensive review of the literature, Barron and Harrington (1981) cited 70 studies in which a positive relationship obtained between measures of ideational fluency and nontest real-world indices of creative behavior. This issue is still open, however, since Wallach (1985) summarized results of a number of studies indicating that general original/creative thinking is not related to any significant degree with specific real-world creative performance.

Investigators in a variety of specific fields have grappled with the problem of the interrelationships of the categories and levels cited here. Some researchers view high general intelligence as a necessary, but not sufficient, condition for the development of giftedness in mathematics (Humphreys, 1985; Ridge & Renzulli, 1981). These investigators, however, did not distinguish between the two kinds of mathematical giftedness, computational ability and what is referred to in the mathematics education literature (Leder, 1986) as mathematical excellence. Tirosh (Chapter 9 of the present volume) summarizes the work of a number of researchers who distinguish between these two kinds of mathematical giftedness. These researchers view mathematical excellence as the ability to produce a large number of possible solutions to a problem and of generating problems as well as solutions, and insist that such excellence is not necessarily related to intelligence.

In Chapter 10 of the current volume, Yager examines the relationship of overall intellectual ability, high scholastic achievement in scientific subjects, and excellence in science. He also views the three as not necessarily related to one another. He points out that the far-reaching changes in curriculum materials and teaching methods that accompanied the introduction of exemplary science programs to American high schools resulted in a major change in the distribution of school grades among these students. Learners characterized by high general intelligence previously received high grades in high school science courses because the requirements for achieving those grades were highly similar to the requirements of most IQ tests. With the improvement of science courses to include the requirement for experimentation and innovative thinking, many of these learners no longer received high grades.

Excellence

Excellence is a term that is currently receiving much attention in the educational literature. Concern is expressed over the lack or loss of excellence in our schools. Unfortunately, excellence is an elusive concept that has many different meanings. Excellence is defined in the dictionary as superiority of performance and implies a creative or original attainment so high that comparison is hardly possible. According to the 4 × 4 Model, excellence is reflected at the profound level of the fourth category, specific creative talent. Excellence is eminent accomplishment that includes original thinking, and problem-finding or generating at the profound level. Such talent is the hallmark of great artists, composers, architects, inventors, engineers, computer scientists, mathematicians, educators and psychologists. We occasionally see it in children as well, for example, in prodigies in music, chess, and mathematics.

The exact relationship of excellence—that is, profound level creative talent in a specific domain—to the other three categories remains to be investigated. It probably requires more than just a specific creative talent, even at the profound level, to attain true excellence. It seems reasonable to assume that excellence represents a combined effect of specific talent with one or more of the other three categories. A threshhold phenomenon may operate in such a way that only beyond a certain level of the other three abilities can profound specific creative ability or excellence emerge. The interactions and threshhold effects of the four processes remain to be investigated.

Three Settings

It has become increasingly clear that the realization of potential abilities is dependent on the complex interaction of environmental opportunities with cognitive abilities and personal-social characteristics. A major finding of the classic Terman longitudinal study of gifted children was that high IQ alone does not guarantee academic or vocational success (Burks, Jensen, & Terman, 1930; Terman, 1925; Terman & Oden, 1947, 1959). Many investigators have reported that beyond a certain intelligence level, academic and vocational success are determined not by further increments of intelligence but by other factors—personal-social and environmental (Matarazzo, 1972; McClelland, 1973; Tannenbaum, 1983). The proposed Model reflects this understanding by citing three settings (school, home, and community) that affect giftedness, and emphasizing that giftedness must be viewed as embedded in a circle of a wide variety of genetic and environmental influences. Let us look now at each of the three settings—school, home, and community—in terms of the positive and negative influences that each may have on the developing gifted child.

The School Setting

Schools operate under the questionable assumptions that they can identify and develop giftedness in children. The considerable evidence that schools have difficulty in identifying gifted learners will be discussed later in this chapter. Similarly, there is little evidence that schools succeed in developing giftedness and what evidence exists is weak. In a recent meta-analytic study, Goldring (1987) reported that gifted children of the high overall intelligence category, who receive their education in homogeneously grouped classes, reach higher levels of academic achievement in some subjects than their gifted mainstreamed peers. She cautioned, however, against drawing conclusions based upon this finding because of the weak research design of the majority of the studies included. The influence of school experience, special or regular, on the other three kinds of giftedness described above has, to the best of my knowledge, never been examined.

When interviewed after having achieved eminence in their fields, very few gifted adults mention their schools and teachers as important influences in the development of their giftedness (Bloom, 1985). Here we have an example of a producer-consumer difference of opinion with serious implications. School teachers and administrators think that they can provide for the special needs of gifted learners and that they are doing so in many districts. Gifted individuals, however, do not see schools as having contributed to their development in a significant way.

In the light of the earlier discussion on the types and levels of giftedness, it is clear that schools meet the needs of only a small number of gifted learners. Even school districts that spend large amounts of money on programs for gifted children are not meeting the needs of the large majority of mild, moderately, and profoundly gifted youngsters. This failure can be attributed largely to undifferentiated (one-size-fits-all) education. One way to improve the situation is to *customize* the school experience for each gifted child. To customize means to tailor to the unique needs of each child. The process of customizing the education of gifted children is guided by following three principles:

1. Differentiate the curriculum
2. Individualize the instructional process
3. Develop a creative classroom environment

The remaining sections of this book are devoted to in-depth treatment of the three principles and how they may be applied to each subject matter area in regular classrooms in order to customize the teaching-learning process.

The Family Setting

Genetics and Giftedness. We are becoming increasingly aware of the critical contribution of "the family" to the occurrence of potential giftedness and its realization. Although everyone accepts the role of both heredity and environment in shaping the developing child, the relative contribution of each is the topic of considerable ongoing controversy. It is, therefore, surprising that our search for understanding of giftedness has, for the most part, focused exclusively on environment. The 4 × 4 Model reflects the conceptual position that both genetic and environmental factors determine the occurrence and realization of giftedness.

Albert and Runco (Albert, 1983; Albert, in press; Albert & Runco, 1986, 1987) have focused their work on family influences in giftedness and have done much to clarify the complex nature of this influence. Of particular importance is their authoritative summary of the evidence for the influence of heredity on variables that contribute to giftedness such as temperament, cognitive style, and other personality differences. Albert and Runco acknowledge that early infant and twin studies and especially longitudinal research are required in order to confirm genetic determinants of giftedness, but they, nevertheless, conclude:

> Yet there are studies (see Galton, 1869, 1874; Greenacre, 1957; McCurdy, 1983; Roe, 1952; Scarr, Webber, Weinberg, & Wittig, 1981) pointing to a similarity of interest and aptitudes among biological family members which suggest biological bases for them. I remind the reader that since Galton (See, for example, Goertzel & Goertzel, 1962) there has been a steady volume of data, empirical and literary, showing high parent-child and sibling similarities in interests, general vocational pursuits, talents, and career attainments. Successful (eminent) performers in the arts and sciences very often have aptitudes, talents, and values quite similar to one or both biological parents regardless of the parents' own level of achievement (Goertzel & Goertzel, 1962; MacKinnon, 1962; McCurdy, 1983; Roe, 1952). A recent empirical work from the point of view of economics and occupational choice (Laband & Lentz, 1985) confirms the high degree of constitutional and psychological similarities among pairs of fathers and sons (and some daughters and mothers) within elective politics, a variety of professional sports, and some businesses (Albert & Runco, 1987).

Patterns of Family Socialization. The behavior and attitudes of parents and the quantity and quality of their interest in the gifted child, as well as their interaction with him or her, is a critical influence on the development of giftedness. Many profoundly gifted adults cite the efforts of parents and other mentors in stimulating and directing their developing talents (Albert & Runco, 1987; Bloom, 1985; Cox, Daniel, & Boston, 1985). The range of attitudes and behaviors that parents demonstrate with reference to their gifted children is far wider than many imagine. Meckstroth (Meckstroth, in press; Webb, Meckstroth, & Tolan, 1982) describes the wide variety of emotions and attitudes that parents demonstrate toward their gifted children. For example, parents are frequently overinvolved with their gifted children, identify with their achievements, and display too much interest in every aspect of the child's life. Some parents devote no special attention to their gifted child, thus making it less likely that he or she will receive appropriate enrichment or acceleration. Some highly gifted children are born into disadvantaged environments in which their special abilities are not perceived at all, or are misperceived and regarded as more of an annoyance than a blessing. Although many parents are delighted to have their child identified as gifted, many are not. They feel cheated in that their child is not "normal."

Some parents find it hard to cope with their child's constant barrage of questions and demands for attention. Others balk at the financial burden frequently required in order to help the gifted child realize his or her potential. These examples demonstrate that family influence is a complex rather than simple phenomenon, one that has yet to be examined systematically.

The Family As a Complex Concept. Albert and Runco (1987) wisely point out the tendency in the literature of giftedness to treat the concept of "the family" simplistically and globally. They assert that it is necessary to distinguish among the influences of the various persons within the immediate and extended family, and summarize their view as follows: "In a study of the antecedents, it is critical to be very specific as to the factors, the persons, and the variety of interactive processes one refers to as 'the family' (Albert & Runco, 1987). When we consider the realities of modern life in which a child may be part of more than one family, i.e., single parent families, stepparents, "blended families," then the importance of a more sophisticated understanding of the term "family influences" becomes critical.

Cornell adds another hitherto ignored dimension to the investigation of family influences. He points out that in addition to the influence of family on gifted children, these children frequently have a strong influence on their parents and siblings (Cornell, 1984). The nongifted sibling of a gifted child faces a unique set of adjustment challenges. This writer has observed another source of family influence that has received no attention in the literature, namely the influence of grandparents. It is reasonable to conclude that in some instances, grandparents play a critical role in the realization of their grandchild's giftedness.

Finally, and most important for the current discussion, both genetic and environmental family influences probably operate somewhat differently on each of the types and levels of gifted people depicted in the 4 × 4 Model. Albert and Runco (1987) cited the need to investigate family influences on different types and levels of giftedness separately. They report dramatically different family backgrounds and developmental paths to eminence for children and adults highly gifted in mathematics or science, versus those with exceptionally high IQ, or profoundly gifted in the arts, social sciences, or politics (Albert, in press; Albert & Runco, 1987). Gifted behavior must be understood from genetic and familial environmental perspectives in complex interactions that require empirical validation.

The Community Setting

Communities influence the specific opportunities of special education that will be available to gifted learners in three ways: (1) by policy decisions that determine the resources available for special education of gifted and talented learners; (2) by creating opportunities for gifted children and adolescents to broaden the scope and depth of the educational experiences available to them, i.e., by providing interaction with community leaders and access to community institutions such as universities, museums, and businesses; and (3) by advocacy on behalf of gifted education.

Public policy on special education for the gifted has been changeable indeed (DeLeon & VandenBos, 1985; Gallegher, 1979). The ambivalence that many people feel toward gifted children is reflected in some ill-advised educational policy (Tannenbaum, 1983). Sometimes the special needs of gifted learners are ignored for long periods of time. At other times the same communities show extraordinary interest in the identification of gifted learners and the enhancement of educational opportunities for them. Communities are more likely to adopt policies that allocate resources to the development of materials to be used to differentiate and individualize curriculum within regular classrooms and to train teachers to use approaches that will benefit all children than they are to fund special education for gifted learners in segregated settings.

The role of communities in the development of giftedness is also evident in the fact that the number of programs for gifted learners that reach into the community is continuing to grow. Many profoundly gifted adults cite the efforts of mentors in stimulating and directing their developing talents (Albert & Runco, 1987; Bloom, 1985; Yager, in press). Cox, Daniel, and Boston (1985) cite as especially promising programs those that provide real-world experiences such as internships or mentor programs. By the same token many universities and museums are increasingly providing facilities and services for gifted and talented learners.

The far-reaching influence of family on the individual gifted learner is also expressed at the community level. Many parents of gifted children organize to promote special education for gifted children as a group. It is not uncommon for the parents of gifted children to be themselves gifted and successful professionally and economically. In many communities these parents provide powerful and highly effective advocacy for the benefit of their children that is reflected in a more equitable allocation of resources for special education.

The Circle of Individual Differences

Since the intellectual abilities of gifted children are often so remark- able, the cognitive aspects of giftedness receive most attention. In the 4 × 4 model the important role of individual differences among gifted learners is highlighted by presenting the categories, levels, and settings in a solid circular boundary. In the circle of individual differences we find variables of age, sex, culture, subculture, and especially personality characteristics. The solid circle design depicts the postulated interac- tions between the dimensions within the boundaries of the circle (i.e., the 4 × 4 Model) and those included in the solid circle. The exact nature of the effects of these solid-circle variables in shaping the development of gifted learners is discussed in later chapters of the current volume and in a companion volume to appear shortly (Milgram, in press).

Little attention has been given in the past to building a comprehensive theory of giftedness. We, therefore, find in the literature many empirical findings about giftedness, but far fewer explanatory models of the phenomenon. A notable exception is the recent book by Sternberg and Davidson (1986). By presenting a wide variety of conceptions of giftedness in one volume, the authors have made a singular contribution to the literature of giftedness. The practical implications of these different approaches remain to be spelled out.

The 4 × 4 model can serve to provide in readable form a general frame of reference to be used by teachers and counselors in their work with gifted learners and their families. For example, Susan, who is profoundly gifted in foreign languages, and David, who is mildly gifted in music, require different curriculum materials and teaching methods, as well as teachers with different training and experience. By the same token, Jonny, who is profoundly gifted in overall original thinking with a strong interest in business, and Joy, who is moderately gifted in science, have different educational needs. The parents and siblings of a child moderately gifted in social science may be quite different from those of a child profoundly gifted in art or computer science. Communities should consider after school, summer, and vacation enrichment programs for mildly and moderately gifted children in the different categories, but they should also recognize that profoundly gifted learners require internships, mentorships, and other special out-of-school experiences. In addition to the 16 category × level combination, each child presents an intricate combination of personal-social and cultural characteristics that contribute to determining one's level of academic achievement and nonacademic accomplishments.

The 4 × 4 Model is not, however, merely a convenient way to organize information about gifted children. It can explain excellence in children and adolescents and eminence in adults. The 4 × 4 Model of Giftedness as presented here is not considered to be in final form. It requires empirical validation and is designed to generate and to guide further research.

II. THE PROBLEM OF IDENTIFICATION

We now turn to the second question teachers ask, how to recognize gifted learners. In the light of the discussion about the nature of giftedness above, it is clear that the idenntification of gifted and learners is a complex and intricate procedure.

Two Assumptions of Traditional Identification

In using conventional and traditional procedures to identify gifted learners, we may well provide special education to some nongifted and deny it to some gifted. This risk constitutes excellent reason for delaying "tagging" young children as gifted based upon psychometric evidence. We should instead identify gifted children on the basis of real-world evidence of abilities as demonstrated over a long period of time in regular classrooms.

In the vast majority of school districts, the procedure used to select children for participation in programs for the gifted is based mainly upon initial screening by means of group-administered IQ tests, followed by further clarification of other cognitive and personal-social character-istics on an individual basis. In some instances, in the interest of economy, a prior initial screening based upon teacher recommendations is conducted.

This process of identification is based mainly upon two overlapping assumptions. The first is a general assumption about gifted individuals and the second, a specific assumption about the tests most frequently used to identify gifted individuals. The first assumption is that giftedness is a stable human characteristic, that is, something that you are or are not as a child and will continue to be as an adult. Once gifted, always gifted, and the converse: if not gifted as a child, there is no chance of being gifted as an adult. The second assumption is that psychometric test scores are valid predictors of gifted life achievement.

Considerable evidence based on experience in the field and research data indicates that both assumptions are untenable. On the basis of their professional experience, educational administrators and teachers seriously question the stability of the phenomenon of giftedness and the validity of the tests currently used to identify it. They stress the need to retest and reevaluate children identified as gifted because the performance of many children does not appear to merit their continued participation in programs for the gifted. With reference to the second assumption, experienced educators are disturbed by the fact that many children identified as gifted on the basis of their psychometric test scores and given special educational opportunities to nurture their gifts do not attain notable life achievements, whereas some children who were not identified as gifted and were not given special educational opportunities attain outstanding accomplishments in school subjects and subsequently make major contributions to society.

Formal research findings also lend little support to the above assumptions of the stability of the phenomenon of giftedness and the validity of the test scores. The predictive validity of IQ/achievement test scores with reference to gifted behavior in adults is modest at best. Academic achievement test scores in the earlier years are only modest predictors of academic achievement in the adult years due in part to the fact that above a certain threshold of intelligence, other factors determine academic achievement (Matarrazo, 1972). There is little evidence that children identified as gifted on the basis of IQ and/or achievement test scores invariably reach the highest occupational levels, achieve outstanding vocational success, or provide professional and community leadership (McClelland, 1973; Tannenbaum, 1983; Terman & Oden, 1959; Wallach, 1976; Wallach & Wing, 1969). Similarly, research evidence strongly indicates that given proper nurturing experiences, older children, adolescents, and even adults may demonstrate gifted behavior even if they were not identified as gifted as children. Renzulli (1978) surveyed studies of gifted and talented people conducted over the last hundred years and concluded,

An examination of this research clearly and unequivocally tells us that gifted behaviors can be developed in persons who are not necessarily those individuals who earn the highest scores on standardized tests.

Intrinsically Motivated Behavior as a Predictor of Giftedness

If IQ and school grades are not valid predictors of professional eminence and social leadership, we must consider alternative predictors. I suggest that teachers consider intrinsically motivated domain-specific behavior, both in and out of school, as additional indices of potential eminence. Children who spend many hours reading, practicing an instrument, painting, or working in their "laboratories" reflect not only intellectual abilities but task commitment, and other cognitive and personal-social attributes that determine strongly life outcomes. One could argue that projects in school and leisure activities outside of school are more stable and valid indicators of giftedness than IQ scores.

In a number of studies, high school and college students described their intrinsically motivated out-of-school activities. They reported the quantity and quality of their creative performance, i.e., nonacademic talented accomplishments in a wide variety of areas such as science, music, fine arts, social leadership, writing, community service, drama, sports, and dance (Holland, 1961; Holland & Austin, 1962; Holland & Nichols, 1964; Milgram & Milgram, 1976a; Richards, Holland, & Lutz, 1967; Wallach & Wing, 1969; Wing & Wallach, 1971). The findings indicate that creative accomplishments in high school are associated with continuing creative performance in college. This finding is hardly surprising. It seems entirely reasonable that the best predictor of one's future interest and activity in a given realm would be the record of one's past attainments in that area. When it comes to academic achievement, past performance has been clearly demonstrated to be the best indicator of future achievement. The findings to date seem to indicate that a similar situation obtains in the realm of creative performance.

The finding that intrinsically-motivated, out-of-school activities in high school are associated with continuing creative activity in the later years provides the basis for recommending that opportunities for intrinsically-motivated activities be provided in school as well. An important benefit of this policy is that schools will expose children from disadvantaged backgrounds to opportunities for the development of domain-specific, leisure-time activities similar to those frequently made available to advantaged students.

This book is designed to help teachers customize in-school learning experiences for gifted learners in regular classrooms in terms of their abilities and interests. To customize is defined as "to alter to the tastes of the buyer." Custom-made means "made according to the specifications of an individual purchaser." We suggest that, beginning at the elementary school level, all children should be given the opportunity to demonstrate individual domain-specific special interests and abilities. These would be manifested in individual or small-group projects that result in products to be evaluated by the teacher and in some instances to be shared with peers. The projects would become increasingly comprehensive and complex in the course of the school years. The products would reflect a continuing trend in the direction of development of abilities and interests.

The approach that has been described above may seem to the reader to be an impossible dream. The chapters that follow are designed to justify and exemplify in a wide variety of curriculum areas customizing the teaching-learning process for gifted learners in regular classrooms. In the second section of the book, authorities in each subject matter area present approaches and techniques that provide classroom teachers with the tools required to customize specific school subjects for gifted learners.

I will sum up by returning to the example with which I opened, Stephen Wozniak, the high school dropout from California who invented the Apple personal computer. We said that in this chapter we would try to come to an understanding of how such a talented person could move through the educational system without being noticed. How did it happen? There could be many explanations, but I will discuss only two.

The first is that the young man's giftedness was not recognized because it took a form that was different from what many people think of as gifted. If this is the case, then applying the 4 × 4 Structure of Giftedness Model as a guide to identifying gifted students and providing them with special education in and out of the classroom would make it more likely that we would meet the needs of learners with a specific creative talent, like Steven's.

A second possible explanation is that the young man's giftedness was not recognized because of the methods most frequently used to identify gifted learners. If we were to use multidimensional identification procedures, and not screen initially on the basis of general intelligence or teachers' recommendations, we are more likely to identify the Stevens in our classes. In identifying potential eminence we should place heavy emphasis on real-world indicators of remarkable accomplishments, both in and out of school. For example, had Vozniak been asked, "What do you do on your own time, not for grades or assignments but for your own pleasure and enjoyments?" From his answer we would have recognized his exceptional ability.

There is a lot to learn from the story of Steven Vozniak, but there is also a danger in it. Why? Because his is the story of a person who made it, his story has a happy ending. Recognized authorities in the field, however, assert that the failure of many gifted children to realize their potential abilities is a major problem (Tannenbaum, 1983). Their views clearly contradict the popular prejudice that gifted children will realize their potential without special education of any kind. Being a gifted child in no way guarantees that one will automatically grow up to be a responsible, achieving member of society. The Marland Report (1972) reported: " ... disturbingly, research has confirmed that many gifted children perform far below their intellectual potential. We are increasingly being stripped of the notion that a bright mind will make its own way." Some have estimated that as many as 15–30 percent of high school dropouts are gifted and talented. Many highly gifted and talented children and adolescents are clearly underachieving in the school setting.

A National Commission on Excellence in Education (1983) summarized its findings in a volume whose title, "A Nation At Risk," reflected their ominous conclusion: "The educational foundations of our society are presently being eroded by a rising tide of mediocrity that threatens our very future as a nation and as a people."

We can prevent this rising tide of mediocrity from enveloping our society (1) by expanding our theoretical formulation of giftedness to include the many different kinds of talent that society requires; (2) by broadening our operational definition of the predictors of giftedness to include a wide variety of academic and nonacademic attainments in and out of school; and (3) by seeking ways to enhance giftedness in its many forms with the framework of the regular classroom. Interestingly enough, performing these tasks will answer the three questions teachers ask.

REFERENCES

Albert, R.S. (1983). Family positions and the attainment of eminence: A study of special family positions and special family experiences. In R.S. Albert (Ed.), *Genius and eminence: The social psychology of creativity and exceptional achievement.* Oxford: Pergamon Press.

Albert, R.S. (in press). People and processes: Developmental paths to eminence. In R.M. Milgram (Ed.), *Counseling gifted and talented learners in regular classrooms.* Springfield, IL: Charles C Thomas.

Albert, R.S. & Runco, M.A. (1986). The achievement of eminence: A model based upon a longitudinal study of exceptionally gifted boys and their families. In Robert J. Sternberg and Janet E. Davidson (Eds.), *Conceptions of giftedness* (pp. 323–357). New York: Cambridge University Press.

Albert, R.S. & Runco, M.A. (1987). The possible personality dispositions of scientists and nonscientists. In D.N. Jackson and J.P. Rushton (Eds.), *Scientific excellence: Origins and assessment.* Beverly Hills: Sage Publications.

Amabile, T.M. (1983). *The social psychology of creativity.* New York: Springer-Verlag.

American Psychiatric Association (1980). *The diagnostic and statistical manual of mental disorders* (3rd Edition). Washington, DC: Author.

Barron, F., & Harrington, D.M. (1981). Creativity, intelligence and personality. *Annual Review of Psychology, 32,* 439–476.

Bloom, B.S. (1985). *Developing talent in young people.* New York: Ballantine Books.

Burks, B.S., Jensen, D.W., & Terman, L.M. (1930). *Genetic studies of genius: Vol. 3 The promise of youth: Follow-up studies of a thousand gifted children.* Stanford, CA: Stanford University Press.

Cox, J., Daniel, N. & Boston, B.O. (1985). *Educating able learners: Programs and promising practices.* Austin, TX: University of Texas Press.

DeLeon, P.H. & VandenBos, G.R. (1985). Public policy and advocacy on behalf of gifted and talented children. In F.D. Horowitz & M. O'Brien (Eds.), *The gifted and talented: Developmental perspectives* (pp. 409–435). Washington, DC: American Psychological Association.

Feldman, D.H. (1980). *Beyond universals in cognitive development.* Norwood, NJ: Ablex.

Feldman, D.H. (1986). *Nature's gambit: Child prodigies and the development of human potential.* New York: Basic Books.

Fox, L.H. & Washington, J. Programs for the gifted and talented: Past, present, and future. In F.D. Horowitz & M. O'Brien (Eds.), *The gifted and talented: Developmental perspectives* (pp. 197–221). Washington, DC: American Psychological Association.

Gallegher, J.J. (1979). Issues in education for the gifted. In A.H. Passow (Ed.), *The gifted and the talented: Their education and development* (pp. 28–44). Chicago: University of Chicago Press.

Galton, F. (1869). *Hereditary genius.* New York: Macmillan.

Galton, F. (1874). *English men of science: Their nature and nurture.* New York: Macmillan.

Goldring, E. (1987). A meta-analysis of classroom organizational frameworks for gifted education students. Paper presented at the annual meeting of the American Educational Research Association, Washington, DC.

Goertzel, V., & Goertzel, M. (1962). *Cradles of eminence.* Boston: Little, Brown.

Greenacre, P. (1957). The childhood of the artist. In R. Eissler et al., (Eds.), *The psychoanalytic study of the child, Volume 12* (pp. 47–72). New York: International Universities Press.

Guilford, J.P. (1956). The structure of intellect. *Psychological Bulletin, 53,* 267–293.

Guilford, J.P. (1967). *The nature of human intelligence.* New York: McGraw-Hill.

Holland, J.L. (1961). Creative and academic performance among talented adolescents. *Journal of Educational Psychology, 52,* 136–147.

Holland, J.L., & Austin, A.W. (1962). The prediction of the academic, artistic, scientific, and social achievement of undergraduates of superior scholastic aptitude. *Journal of Educational Psychology, 53,* 132–143.

Holland, J.L., & Nichols, R.C. (1964). Prediction of academic and extracurricular achievement in college. *Journal of Educational Psychology, 55,* 55–65.

Hollingworth, L.S. (1942). *Children above 180 IQ Stanford-Binet: Origin and development.* Yonkers, NY: World Book.

Humphreys, L.G. (1985). A conceptualization of intellectual giftedness.In F.D. Horowitz & M. O'Brien (Eds.), *The gifted and talented: Developmental perspectives* (pp. 99–123). Washington, DC: American Psychological Association.

Kogan, N. (1983). Stylistic variation in childhood and adolescence: Creativity, metaphor, and cognitive styles. In J.H. Flavell & E.M. Markham (Eds.), *Handbook of Child Psychology: Vol.3. Cognitive Development* (pp. 630–706). New York: Wiley.

Leder, G. (1986). (Guest Editor). Special Issue: Mathematically able students. *Educational Studies in Mathematics, 17.*

MacKinnon, D.W. (1962). The nature and nurture of creative talent. *American Psychologist, 17,* 484–495.

Marland, S.P., Jr. (1972) *Education of the gifted and talented.* Washington, DC: U.S. Government Printing Office.

Matarrazo, J.D. (1972). *Wechsler's measurement and appraisal of adult intelligence.* (5th edition) Baltimore, MD: Williams and Wilkins.

McClelland, D.C. (1973). Testing for competence rather than for "intelligence." *American Psychologist, 28,* 1–14.

McCurdy, H.G. (1983). The childhood pattern of giftedness. In R.S. Albert (Ed.), *Genius and eminence: The social psychology of creativity and exceptional achievement.* New York: Pergamon Press.

Mednick, S.A. (1962). The associative basis of the creative process. *Psychological Review, 69,* 220–232.

Milgram, R.M. (in press) (Ed.). *Counseling gifted and talented learners in regular classrooms.* Springfield, IL: Charles C Thomas.

Milgram, R.M. (1983). A validation of ideational fluency measures of original thinking in children. *Journal of Educational Psychology, 75,* 619–624.

Milgram, R.M., & Arad, R. (1981). Ideational fluency as a predictor of original problem-solving. *Journal of Educational Psychology, 73,* 568–572.

Milgram, R.M., & Feingold, S. (1977) Concrete and verbal reinforcement in creative thinking in disadvantaged children. *Perceptual and Motor Skills, 45,* 675–678.

Milgram, R.M. & Milgram, N.A. (1981). Ideational fluency as a predictor of original problem-solving. *Journal of Educational Psychology, 73,* 568–572.

Milgram, R.M., & Milgram, N.A. (1976a). Creative thinking and creative perform-ance in Israeli children. *Journal of Educational Psychology, 68,* 255–259.

Milgram, R.M., & Milgram, N.A. (1976b). Group versus individual administration in the measurement of creative thinking in gifted and nongifted children. *Child Development, 47,* 563–565.

Milgram, R.M., Milgram, N.A., Rosenbloom, G., & Rabkin, L. (1976). Quantity and quality of creative thinking in children and adolescents. *Child Development, 49,* 385–388.

Milgram, R.M. & Rabkin, L. (1980). A developmental test of Mednick's associative hierarchies of original thinking. *Developmental Psychology, 16,* 157–158.

Milgram, R.M., Moran, J.D. III, Sawyers, J.K., & Fu, V. (1987). Original thinking in Israeli preschool children. *School Psychology International, 8,* 54–58.

Milgram, R.M., Yitzhak, V., & Milgram, N.A. (1977). Creative activity and sex-role identity in elementary school children. *Perceptual and Motor Skills, 45,* 71–376.

National Commission on Excellence in Education. (1983). *A Nation at risk: The imperative for educational reform.* Washington, DC: U.S. Government Printing Office.

Perkins, D.N. (1981). *The mind's best work.* Cambridge, MA: Harvard University Press.

Richards, J.M., Jr., Holland, J.L., & Lutz, S.W. (1967). The predictions of student accomplishment in college. *Journal of Educational Psychology, 58,* 343–355.

Renzulli, J.S. (1978) What makes giftedness? Reexamining a definition. *Phi Delta Kappan, Vol. 60,* 180–261.

Ridge, H.L., & Renzulli, J.S. (1981). Teaching mathematics to the talented and gifted: An interdisciplinary approach. In V.J. Glennon (Ed.), *The mathematical education of exceptional children and youth* (pp. 191–266). Reston, VA: National Council of Teachers of Mathematics.

Roe, A. (1952). *The making of a scientist.* New York: Dodd, Mead.

Scarr, S., Webber, P.L., Weinberg, R.A., & Wittig, M. (1981). Personality resemblance among adolescents and their parents in biologically related and adoptive families. *Journal of Personality and Social Psychology, 40,* 885–898.

Stanley, J.C. (1979). The study and facilitation of talent for mathematics. In A.H. Passow (Ed.), *Seventy-eighth yearbook of the National Society for the Study of Educa-tion* (pp. 169–185). Chicago: University of Chicago Press.

Stanley, J.C. (1977). Rationale of the study of mathematically precocious youth (SMPY) during its first five years of promoting educational acceleration. In J.C. Stanley, W.C. George, & C.H. Salano (Eds.), *The gifted and the creative: A fifty-year perspective* (pp. 75–112). Baltimore: Johns Hopkins University Press.

Tannenbaum, A.J. (1983). *Gifted children: Psychological and educational perspectives.* New York: Macmillan.

Terman, L.M. (1925). *Genetic studies of genius: Mental and physical traits of a thousand gifted children.* Stanford, CA: Stanford University Press.

Terman, L.M. & Oden, M.H. (1947). *Genetic studies of genius: Vol. 4. The gifted child grows up: Twenty-five years follow-up of a superior group.* Stanford, CA: Stanford University Press.

Terman, L.M. & Oden, M.H. (1959). *Genetic studies of genius: Vol. 4. The gifted child at mid-life: Thirty-five years follow-up of the superior child.* Stanford, CA: Stanford University Press.

Wallach, M.A. (1971). *The intelligence/creativity distinction.* Morristown, NJ: General Learning Press.

Wallach, M.A. (1985). Creativity testing and giftedness. In F.D. Horowitz & M. O'Brien (Eds.), *The gifted and talented: Developmental perspectives* (pp. 99–123). Washington, DC: American Psychological Association.

Wallach, M.A. (1970). Creativity. In P.H. Mussen (Ed.), *Carmichael's manual of child psychology, Vol.1* (3rd ed., pp. 1211–1272).

Wallach, M.A. & Wing, C.W., Jr. (1969). *The talented student: A validation of the creativity-intelligence distinction.* New York: Holt, Rinehart, & Winston.

Webb, J.T., Meckstroth, E.A., & Tolan, S.S. (1982). *Guiding the gifted child.* Columbus, OH: Ohio Publishing Company.

Wing, C.W., Jr. & Wallach, M.A. (1971). *College admissions and the psychology of talent.* New York: Holt, Rinehart, & Winston.

Chapter 2

CURRICULUM CONTENT FOR GIFTED STUDENTS: PRINCIPLES AND PRACTICES[1]

C. JUNE MAKER

The purpose of this chapter is to present, define, and provide examples of principles that should be used to guide the selection, development, and presentation of curriculum content for gifted students. The focus is on the regular classroom setting, but the principles apply to any situation in which gifted students learn. The chapter is divided into three sections. In the first section the overall principle that curriculum content for gifted learners must be qualitatively different is presented and explained. In the second section, curriculum content is defined and the manner in which seven basic principles (Abstractness, Complexity, Variety, Organization, Economy, Comprehension, Relevance for Future) can be used by regular classroom teachers in their efforts to customize curriculum content for their gifted students is discussed. Information on each principle is presented in the following sequence: (1) definition of the principle, (2) statement of a typical topic from the basic curriculum, followed by an example of how the treatment of that topic could be modified so that the resulting differentiated curriculum content reflects the principle being explained, and (3) specific suggestions to teachers in regular classrooms about how to implement the principle under discussion. In the third section, I use the real-life stories of five children to illustrate how curriculum content can be modified to match individual differences in learners.

---

[1]General principles described in this chapter were first presented by the author and explained in depth in two books: *Curriculum Development for the Gifted* and *Teaching Models in Education of the Gifted*, both published in 1982 by Aspen Publishers, 1600 Research Blvd., Rockville, Maryland.

I. QUALITATIVE DIFFERENCES IN CURRICULUM CONTENT

According to most experts and practitioners in the field of education for gifted students, the most important principle underlying the selection of curriculum for gifted students is that *curriculum content designed for gifted learners must be qualitatively different from that usually included in the basic curriculum for all children.* Several corrolaries follow from this major principle of "qualitative difference."

First, increasing quantity of curriculum content is not in and of itself a way of providing gifted children with qualitatively different learning experiences. Simply "covering more material or learning more ideas" is inappropriate differentiation. In regular classroom situations, when students complete their assignments early, for example, teachers often respond by giving them additional work such as writing another story, completing ten more math problems, drawing another picture. More of the same work is appropriate only if the child is interested and herself chooses such an activity, if certain needed skills are developed by the activity, and especially, if an added challenge is provided, e.g., "use a different perspective, "try to complete these new problems without any mistakes."

A second related idea is that qualitative differences in the curriculum should match as closely as possible the qualitative differences in gifted learners. In other words, the content selected for gifted students should build upon, allow the development of, and encourage the growth of, the positive cognitive and personal-social characteristics that make gifted students different from others. In an earlier chapter in this book Milgram described her 4 × 4 model of the structure of giftedness. She conceptualizes gifted behavior in terms of four categories (overall intellectual ability, specific intellectual ability, overall original or creative thinking, and specific creative talents) interacting with four levels (profoundly, moderately, mildly gifted, and nongifted). Teachers should bear these differences in mind in customizing curriculum content to meet the needs of the individual gifted child.

For every principle used in describing differentiated curriculum content, one should be able to identify the learner characteristics on which it is based. One implication of this idea for regular classroom teachers is that the content of the curriculum will have certain common elements for all gifted students in a particular class as well as for gifted students in classes from year to year. However, certain elements of the content must be different from child to child and year to year because each year's gifted students will have different characteristics.

A third idea related to the principle of "qualitatively different" and to the second idea above is appropriateness. Content for gifted students can be different from the content included for all students, yet be inappropriate. As stated above, one way to judge the appropriateness of content is to determine its relationship to the unique characteristics of each student. Other criteria for judging appropriateness are outlined in a later section of this paper.

One could argue that designing a differentiated curriculum based upon the individual needs and characteristics of gifted children in regular classrooms can result in a significant advantage for their nongifted classmates. In any classroom situation other learners have certain interests, abilities, and personal-social characteristics in common with gifted students. Thus, content selected because of its value for a gifted student may be of great interest and value to several other students. In the interest of providing more appropriate, qualitatively different curriculum content for the gifted, the regular content can be selected or modified. At least some other learners in that classroom can benefit from these changes.

Finally, the principle of differentiated curriculum and the concept of relating the curriculum to learner characteristics has a fourth element. Because content for gifted students is designed to enable and encourage growth and development of positive learning characteristics found in gifted students (learn rapidly, develop understanding of relationships between ideas), it must allow participation at the student's current level of understanding, but encourage responses at the highest level possible. A metaphor I have employed before (Maker, 1987) is that curricula for the gifted must provide a floor, but not a ceiling—a foundation for learning, but no restrictions on development. If content is selected and taught in a lock-step manner, gifted students cannot learn as rapidly as their capabilities allow, and they cannot make connections among ideas that can, potentially, change the direction or character of a field of study. All students can benefit when restrictions are removed from the learning process. The major caution for teachers when using such open approaches is that these approaches may be frustrating to students who are not gifted or who have had no prior experience with such techniques. In bringing this discussion to a close, I want to emphasize that the principles advocated for selecting and presenting content for gifted learners *may be* appropriate for all children, are *definitely* appropriate for certain other children, but they are *essential* for gifted students.

II. QUALITATIVE DIFFERENCES IN CURRICULUM CONTENT: SEVEN PRINCIPLES

Definition of content. Content is the specific information, the concepts, abstract principles, skills, and attitudes students are expected to learn. Many different definitions and classifications of content exist. Guilford (1967) defines content as information, and recognizes four distinct types: figural, symbolic, semantic, and behavioral. Bloom (1967), when describing categories of educational objectives, includes knowledge or information as the basic level, and defines three types. The category of *specifics* includes terminology and particular facts. The next type, *ways and means of dealing with specifics* includes characteristic ways of presenting or treating phenomena, trends and sequences, classifications and categories, criteria, and methodology. Methodological and thinking skills usually would be included in this category. *Universals and abstractions* in a field, the third category of knowledge, consists of principles, generalizations, theories, and structures. Bruner (1960) includes in content what he calls the basic structure of a discipline, including certain key concepts, the relationships among them, and specific examples of these concepts and relationships. Content, then, is defined by these writers and this author as the information that is taught or learned by students. This information ranges from figures with no meaning other than their visual properties to symbols with certain meanings; to letters, words, and other semantic information; and to behaviors of people or animals. Various levels of information also can be defined, and range from specific to general. All levels of information are found within most category types. For example, within the category of behavioral information, an action such as smiling is a specific fact, interpretation of a smile as friendliness or happiness is a "way of dealing with specifics," and a generalization such as "people who smile more than they frown are usually happy and well-adjusted" is a generalization or abstraction about behavior.

In the following pages seven basic principles (Abstractness, Complexity, Variety, Organization, Economy, Comprehension, Relevance for Future) that should guide regular classroom teachers in their efforts to customize curriculum content for their gifted students are explained and illustrated.

1. Abstractness

Definition. The focus of learning for gifted students should be on understanding "big ideas," themes, and general principles rather than on remembering facts, specific data, and isolated ideas for their own sake. Certainly, specific information is important, but specific data should be learned because it is an example of a bigger idea or concept, and should be chosen because of its value in helping gifted students develop an abstract idea.

Basic Curriculum Content. Students are studying countries of the world. They are making reports about the customs, history, geography, and language of certain countries.

Differentiated Content for Gifted Students. The focus of discussions and reports should not be limited to describing each country and remembering specific data about the geography of the country. Important ideas that can be applied to all countries need to be developed:

1. Cultures never remain static, although the context of change (political, social, and technological), the speed of change, and the importance of change vary greatly (Cultural Change).

2. The solution of important human problems requires human beings to engage in joint effort. The more complex is the society, the more cooperation is required (Interdependence).

3. The survival of a society is dependent upon agreement on some core of values by a majority of its members (Values).

Implementation. The basic curriculum is seldom organized around big ideas, themes, or principles; and often the identification of principles underlying the teaching of certain facts is impossible. If textbooks or curriculum guides do not contain generalizations, key concepts, or themes, the teacher will need to develop them. One way is to examine the content being taught to determine what themes or concepts can be identified as unifying principles. Another approach would be to select themes or ideas from generalizations and key concepts related to the subject(s) being taught. Specialists in content areas also could be called upon to identify principles important in their area, and these could be used to focus the content on abstract ideas.

After big ideas or principles have been identified, a variety of approaches can be used. One approach is to have gifted students participate in the same activities as other students, but ask them to focus their efforts on general principles rather than specific facts. Using the example above, they could write about one of the three principles identified (rather than about a country), and cite examples of how these principles operate in at least three countries. Another approach would be to have gifted students participate in different activities. In the example above, rather than writing a report about a country, they might participate in discussions in which they identify similarities and differences between various countries that relate to the general principles. Another approach is to have gifted students participate in the same activities as other students, with the same focus, and then involve the entire class in discussions of the underlying ideas that develop relationships between ideas being studied. Using the example already discussed, gifted students would write reports about countries, then all students would participate in discussions in which they identified similarities and differences in the countries studied. These similarities and differences could then be related to the general principles listed above.

2. Complexity

Definition. Content that is complex represents an integration of information from a variety of disciplines and a variety of sources. The more different the disciplines and sources are from each other, the more complex are the ideas derived from the integration of principles from the disciplines.

Basic Curriculum Content. Students in a high school biology class are studying classification of plants and animals. They are learning the various categories and what animals or plants are included in each.

Differentiated Content for Gifted Students. Students should focus upon the development of various systems for classification, and the general principles underlying these systems. Statements expressing complex content related to classification of animals are the following:

1. Systems are developed to classify elements found in all disciplines. Some examples of classification systems are periodic tables of the elements (chemistry), types of social institutions (sociology), types of literature (language arts), types of measurement data (mathematics).

2. Systems of classification have similar purposes, underlying principles, and results.

3. Patterns of regularity exist in our social, physical, and living environment. Discovering, measuring, describing, and classifying these patterns is necessary to the understanding of our environment.

Implementation. Because of the usual compartmentalization of the curriculum, especially at the high school level, integration of concepts and information from a variety of academic disciplines is difficult. However, because gifted students often learn the basic content being taught much more rapidly than do other students, they can investigate related ideas from other disciplines while other students are learning basic content. Using the example above, gifted students could develop descriptions of classification systems from other disciplines and share these with the class. This sharing could be followed by a discussion of the similarities and differences between the various classification systems.

Another approach teachers can take is to coordinate the teaching of similar content in several disciplines. At the elementary level, this coordination is much easier, since only one teacher is responsible for most of the content areas. In this case, the order in which particular topics are taught can be decided based on their potential for integrating several disciplines. At the secondary level, coordination with other teachers is necessary, but can be very exciting for both students and teachers. Using the example of classification, a discussion could be added to the activities in biology class, English class, or chemistry class in which students discuss all the classification systems they know, list the similarities and differences, and construct general statements about the development and use of classification systems.

3. Variety

Definition. The content for gifted students should include material different from that usually found in the basic curriculum for all students. However, choosing content simply because it is *different* is inappropriate. Content that is both different and appropriate will meet four conditions: (a) relevance to the understanding of abstract principles or concept being taught, (b) relevance to the interests of the students, (c) potential for contributing depth and breadth of understanding of principles and concepts, and (d) relevance to the future needs of gifted students.

Basic Curriculum Content. In language arts, students are studying literature, focusing on the elements of drama in plays, both ancient and modern.

Differentiated Content for Gifted Students. To differentiate the content for gifted students, if the underlying principle the teacher is trying to develop is "Understanding the techniques used by print and nonprint mass media gives an awareness of its impact and influence on the individual and on society, both past and present," appropriate content for the gifted would be (a) elements of drama in movies or media, analysis of drama from past to present (relevant to principle being developed); (b) student choice of media in which they would like to study elements of drama, student selection of a time period in which to analyze elements of drama in all forms of print and nonprint media (relevant to student interest and to principles being developed); and (c) elements of drama in literature from a variety of cultures, with specific cultures chosen by students (relevant to principles being developed, relevant to student interest, potential for contributing depth and breadth of understanding of principles and concepts). All the examples above are relevant to the future needs of gifted students because they are designed to develop the ability to analyze a variety of forms of media, and to develop an awareness of the impact of media on their lives. Concepts can be applied immediately as well as in the future.

If the underlying principle to be developed through a study of the elements of drama in plays were different, for instance, "Written composition is a process of discovering the message, determining the most appropriate format, considering the audience, and revising the writing before achieving a final product," the content focus and options should be different. Appropriate content includes the following: (a) differences in "dramatic" techniques used by a variety of authors, differences in "dramatic" techniques used in various media, and the reasons for difference in writing techniques and dramatic techniques in various media (relevant to principle being taught); (b) student choice of authors or types of media with sharing of final results of studies (relevant to principle and student interest); and (c) study of a wide variety of authors (based on time period, styles, media), with student selection of authors and sharing of final results of analysis. All the examples above are relevant to the future needs of gifted students if one believes that from their ranks will come the creative writers and producers of the future.

Implementation. The teacher's first step in implementing the principle of variety is to determine the big idea(s) or underlying principle(s) that provide a reason for teaching certain information or skills. Next, the teacher can consider requiring or making optional certain types of content as in the examples above. When abstract ideas provide the "thread" that ties together basic content and varied content, the usefulness of the varied content is assured. What teachers need to avoid is the addition or substitution of content that just seems interesting (to them or to the students), but does not achieve other purposes as well. The best content to include meets all four conditions outlined in the definition of variety.

Methods that can be used to implement the principle of variety include individual student research or exploration of topics of interest that are related to the content focus (underlying focus) with sharing and group discussion of individual research. Individuals or small groups can choose topics from lists identified by the teacher, or can select topics not identified by the teacher if they can provide a reasonable description of the connection between their interest and the major content focus. Students can develop creative ways to present the results of their studies, and can develop statements that demonstrate synthesis of the various examples provided by others through a variety of methods such as group discussions, simulation games, role-playing, and essays or other creative writing assignments.

4. Organization

Definition. Learning, memory, and understanding are facilitated if the facts, ideas, concepts, and skills to be taught are organized around key concepts and big ideas rather than haphazardly, for convenience in teaching, chronologically, or other usual ways.

Basic Curriculum Content. Science topics include the study of various animals and their habitats, and often animals are studied one at a time or in functional groups such as zoo animals, insects, animals used as helpers, extinct animals, animals found in certain habitats.

Differentiated Content for Gifted Students. The study of animals should be organized differently, depending upon the underlying principle providing the focus. For example, if the major idea to be developed is "Living things are interdependent with one another and with their environment," animals studied at a particular time would be chosen because they illustrate particular aspects of the principle: (a) they live in certain habitats, thus their characteristics are similar; (b) they became extinct because of dramatic changes in the environment (e.g., dinosaurs); (c) they are the target of efforts to control numbers, or are extinguished because of man's attempts to interfere with the natural food chain through introduction of certain plants or animals, or elimination/extinction of natural predators.

If the major idea to be developed is different, for example, "Living things are in a process of continual change," other groupings of animals would be appropriate. Animals might be studied because they demonstrate certain techniques for learning as they develop from babies to adults (e.g., share child-rearing tactics). Also appropriate would be to group animals together for study because they illustrate a particular evolutionary history, or because they illustrate certain principles of evolutionary history, or because they illustrate certain principles of evolution. Grouping according to type of current habitat, for instance, would not be as appropriate as grouping according to types of *changes* of habitat (e.g., sudden, dramatic change versus slow, gradual change).

Implementation. Full implementation of the curriculum differentiation principle of organization around key concepts is sometimes simple and sometimes very difficult. If, for example, the content teachers wish to teach as illustrations of a particular principle, is usually taught at different grade levels, and other teachers are extremely protective of their "turf," a different organization may be difficult. Often, however, content can be chosen from that usually developed at a particular grade level, but simply organized differently and presented in a different sequence. Although teachers often believe that students learn better if they read their textbooks in the order in which they are written, absolutely no evidence exists to support this assumption! Much evidence is available to demonstrate the need for conceptually-organized content, especially for gifted students (Goldberg, Passow, Camm, & Neill, cited in Gallagher, 1975; Grobman, 1962; Lowman, 1961; Wallace, 1962). Such organization also facilitates the learning of other students as long as sufficient examples of the concept are provided.

To develop principles and concepts that can be used to provide an organizing thread for content, teachers can employ a method such as Hilda Taba's teaching strategy named "Concept Development" (Institute for Staff Development, 1971). Using this technique, a teacher would list the topics to be studied, being as specific as possible, in a certain content area or across all content areas for which he/she is responsible. After these are itemized, the list should be analyzed to determine general groupings of topics based on common ideas or principles. Several different groupings should be developed, and need not be discrete. Next, each grouping of topics should be reviewed, and labels or titles developed for each grouping, based on the similarities between items in the group. At the next step, groups of topics are analyzed to determine whether topics already contained in one group could fit under a different label. Following an analysis of topics in each group, labels can be examined to ascertain which of the labels is (are) more inclusive, i.e., can be used to subsume other titles and topics from many groups. These inclusive labels usually constitute the most abstract concepts that unify the material or topics to be taught. Deviating from the Taba strategy at this point, the teacher could then develop statements of principles based on each of the abstract labels or based on combinations of these labels. After this exercise, effective organization of the material is clear. One simply needs to refine the groupings of topics that have already been made.

Teaching approaches that can be used, once the sequences for introducing content have been determined, can be similar to those listed in discussing other principles above: (a) individual or small-group investigations of similar topics, with sharing and discussion of individual research; (b) creative presentations of results; (c) simulation games; (d) role-playing; and (e) essays or other creative writing assignments. The common element in all these methods, however, is that students must be asked questions or be involved in activities in which they are asked to consider how all topics are similar, are asked to identify the underlying common principles in the examples, and are expected to demonstrate synthesis of the material taught during a particular period of time.

5. Economy

Definition. Content needs to be selected, organized, and presented in ways that will achieve economy in the learning process. Irrelevant and unnecessary learning needs to be eliminated, or at least minimized as does forgetting and relearning. Implementation of other principles described in this chapter will facilitate economy, and are necessary but not sufficient conditions for achieving the goal of economy. In addition to focusing on abstract, complex ideas, selecting a variety of content to illustrate these ideas, and organizing material to be taught on the basis of underlying principles perceived to be important, teachers should apply the following criteria in the decision-making process: (a) the ideas to be taught can be understood in an "intellectually honest" form by children at a particular developmental level (i.e., do not have to be re-learned in a more correct form at a later date); (b) the specific examples or illustrations of a principle are related, but varied enough that gifted students need all of the examples to develop the idea or concept being taught; (c) the ideas taught at a particular level are important foundations for later learning and/or development; and (d) collectively, the ideas or principles developed in a particular academic area are essential to the understanding of that academic area or related areas of scholarly activity.

Basic Curriculum Content. A topic often included in social studies is the American Revolution, including names, dates important battles, causes, and results.

Differentiated Content for Gifted Students. The American Revolution is studied as an example of a particular type of conflict—one that illustrates certain significant principles:

1. As a strong motivating factor in individual and group action, the desire for power often leads to conflict (power, conflict).

2. The historical past influences the present. The present cannot be understood adequately without knowledge of the past (historical analysis). These two principles, and others as well, can be developed through study of the American Revolution. However, depending on the principle considered most important to the learners, teachers would make different choices of content to achieve the goal of economy.

For example, the first principle, illustrating power and conflict, might be best understood by preschool and primary children if they examine conflicts in which they have been involved—events that illustrate the use of or need for power. At a later time, students could focus on aspects of the American Revolution in which individuals or groups were in conflict because of a desire for power. Similar aspects of other revolutions could be analyzed, but chosen carefully because they illustrate different dynamics of the relationship between need for power and conflict between groups and individuals. Studying many revolutions would not be necessary because gifted students could understand with a few examples the concept as applied to revolutions, and should then extend their learning by analyzing power/conflict relationships in situations other than revolutions—such as in current political situations like the presence of United States military forces in the Mideast.

The second idea, the value of historical analysis, can be understood at an individual and family level by primary age children, but few children ages 6 to 8 would understand the significance of the American Revolution in shaping our daily lives. They can, however, grasp the significance of their mother's anger over one broken cup (a family heirloom) and this same person's easy forgiveness and lack of anger when three cups (bought recently at a yard sale) were broken. Even intermediate age students may find the historical significance of the American Revolution difficult to comprehend. To develop the important concept of historical analysis, then, personal experiences, family events, or experiences of their peers, such as moving from city to city or country to country (because a parent is involved in military service) versus living in the same small town all one's life can be the focus of attention, or the facts to be examined. Moving from one city or neighborhood to another also is an experience that can be used to illustrate how past events help to interpret the present.

Students at secondary levels can study the American Revolution as an example of an event that helps them understand the present. Other events, such as the bringing of slaves to this country, changes in immigration laws, and other wars, need to be analyzed to develop full understanding of the uses (and value) of analysis of past events.

Implementation. In each of the examples provided above, the focus is on development of understandings that can be applied in students' lives now as well as serving as foundations for later learning in an academic area. Even though students may be expected to analyze the American Revolution in detail and know certain facts about it, the specific facts are not learned simply for the sake of knowing them, but for the more important purpose of using them to support a generalization or hypothesis with applicability *beyond* the specific instance of the American Revolution. Knowledge of what facts to use to support an opinion and where to obtain those facts is much more important than being able to impress others with the volume of information known but not used (except in a "Trivial Pursuit" competition). A well-known fact is that all of us forget many of the specific facts we memorize, but remember the context in which we learned them.

Educators responsible for teaching the basic curriculum to a variety of learners can get assistance in choosing important principles and varied examples of those principles from scholars, local school district curriculum experts, former students, university professors, and graduate students. Various "experts" can be asked to review content plans, rank them in order of significance, and explain their rankings. These differing perceptions can be compared, the reasons for rankings examined, and content selected to teach based on the criteria outlined in the definition above. Current students also can participate in decision-making when given choices of different examples to investigate in depth.

6. Comprehensiveness

Definition. Four different types of content exist in every discipline or academic area: (a) conclusions and ideas resulting from thought and empirical study, (b) significant individuals who have contributed to the advancement of a field or altered its course, (c) methods of study and problem solving, and (d) attitudes and values that shaped the field and continue to influence it in the future. Gifted students need exposure to all these types of content.

Basic Curriculum Content. In math, students are studying different number bases.

Differentiated Content for Gifted Students. To achieve comprehensiveness in curriculum content related to number bases, students could be introduced to a variety of base systems and the uses of these systems (conclusions and ideas), could study individuals who developed particular systems of numeration in a variety of cultures and historical periods (significant people), could analyze the methods for testing these systems (e.g., use of a binary system with early computers, value in various practical settings) and compare the methods to determine commonalities (methods of study and problem-solving), and could examine the reasons why particular number systems were developed (attitudes and values).

Implementation. Since the basic curriculum usually contains ideas and conclusions, the teacher needs to supplement the study of these ideas with an analysis of people, methods, and ideas. These other types of content can be integrated easily through a focus on significant people and their ideas. For example, when students are introduced to the binary system, they can discuss the development of this system—the person(s) responsible, the events leading up to its development, the struggles involved in getting the idea accepted, and the similarities/differences between developers of mathematical theories and developers of social theories. Students can interview scholars and practitioners from the community, write letters and send questionnaires to leading individuals in particular fields, and listen to guest speakers who are willing to talk about their lives and their work in a particular field of study.

7. Relevance for the Future

Definition. Content chosen for inclusion in the curriculum for gifted students should be relevant to the future of individuals who are quite likely to become significant people in their fields, and to the future of those who will live in a society radically different from our own or that of our parents. Many past and current trends can, and have been, used to predict what will happen to our world in the future. Educators must not ignore such realities as those cited by Naisbitt (1984) and applied to a world community rather than one society:

1. Many developed nations are changing from industrial bases to information bases.

2. The economic status of most, if not all, nations is dependent on worldwide factors in addition to (and perhaps to a greater degree than) national factors.

3. Long-term planning and a future orientation are necessary to our economic, physical, emotional, and political survival on this planet.

Other realities have been identified by the Task Force on Economic Growth (1983):

1. Most individuals graduating from high schools now will not retire 35 years later from the same job.

2. Of the jobs available to today's and tomorrow's graduates, at least half will require "learning to learn" skills and adaptability to change rather than (or to a much greater degree than) specific skills that can be learned and practiced for many years.

Basic Curriculum Content. A variety of examples has been presented in this chapter: countries of the world, classification of animals, elements of drama in plays, study of animals, the American Revolution, number bases.

Differentiated Content For Gifted Students. Each of the topics above that often are included in the basic curriculum contains both past and present-oriented aspects and future-oriented aspects. Examples of both these aspects are included in Table 2-1. Others certainly could be generated.

Implementation. In the examples given above, the past and present aspects of topics are not considered irrelevant to the understanding of the topic in the future. However, they are designed as examples of an overemphasis on the past and of the "status quo" without taking the next step to develop skills and understandings necessary in a changing world. Some tips for the teacher in implementing a curriculum relevant for the future of gifted students are the following:

1. Examine the differences between the environment where you attended school and that same environment today. Develop a list of the differences and similarities. Use these to help you decide what may be relevant to teach your students.

Table 2-1.
Past, Present, and Future Orientations of Selected Content Topics

Past & Present Orientation	*Future Orientation*
1. *Countries of the World*	
• languages, customs, and geography of neighboring countries	• influences of close and distant neighboring countries on our society
• differences between countries	• interdependence of nations
• knowledge of factual information about countries	• ability to understand the interrelationships among facts about various countries and use this understanding to recommend positive changes in our society
2. *Classification of Animals*	
• memorization of categories and the animals included in each	• understanding of the basis for classification systems and the principles for developing new ones
• knowledge of the most acceptable and most respected classification systems	• exposure to many classification systems and the advantages/disadvantages of each
• learning about classification of animals	• classifying animals
3. *Elements of Drama in Plays*	
• reciting plays and dialogues	• writing plays
• remembering writers and names of plays	• identifying periods of history, social events, and other aspects of the context and how they influenced the dramatic elements of the play
• study of drama limited to written plays	• study of drama including dramatic elements in both print and nonprint media
4. *Study of Animals*	
• ability to identify parts of animals accurately when dissected	• development of improved techniques for dissection
• knowledge of extinct animals and where they lived	• analysis of factors leading to or contributing to extinction of certain animals
• ability to identify predators and prey in the food chain	• understanding of the complex relationships involved in a food chain, the harmful effects of man's interference, and development of ways to correct past mistakes

Table 2-1. Continued

Past & Present Orientation	Future Orientation
5. *The American Revolution*	
• knowledge of key people, dates, and outcomes of battles	• understanding of the reasons why certain people, dates, and battles were significant
• focus on the effects of the revolution on American society	• focus on the effects of the revolution on all the countries involved, both indirectly and directly, and the reasons for these effects
• focus on who was "right" in the conflict	• focus on the effects of differing values and experiences on people's perceptions of right and wrong
6. *Number Bases*	
• practice in making conversions from one base to another	• analysis of the methods for converting from one base to another, and development of more efficient methods
• knowledge of various number systems and bases and the historical period in which they were used	• understanding of the historical development of number systems and bases, the factors influencing their creation, and the reasons they became outmoded or were changed
• knowledge of situations in which certain number systems or bases are considered most appropriate	• understanding and development of criteria for deciding which numeration systems or bases are most appropriate

2. Focus on the *use* of information to solve problems rather than the *acquisition* of information.

3. Always remember the sophisticated technology available to adults to make their jobs easier (e.g., calculators, word processors, computer software programs) and examine the skills you emphasize to determine whether the time necessary to develop proficiency in the use of these skills is worthwhile. Although development of proficiency in certain skills such as spelling, handwriting, and computation may be useful, understanding of the concepts involved and knowledge of ways to develop such skills in the future may be a more important use of the students' limited instructional time.

4. As residents of a particular country and members of a certain society, our perception of situations in our own country may be (and

probably are) very different from the perceptions of people from other countries. The perceptions of those in other countries are equally important, and in some instances, more important, in determining the future of our country than are our "inside" views.

III. ALANA, CLAUDIA, FREELAND, JEANNIE, JOHN: NO TWO ALIKE

A regular classroom teacher needs to differentiate curriculum content to match individual learning styles, levels of ability, and interests. In this section brief vignettes of real children with differing levels and types of abilities developed by Maker (1987) are presented. Specific examples of classroom activities are given to demonstrate how the curriculum content principles cited earlier can be implemented by regular classroom teachers to the benefit of children like these.

Descriptions of Children

Alana. Alana is a 5-year-old black child in kindergarten. She was reading at the fourth-grade level after being in school for only six months, so her teacher recommended that she be tested by the school psychologist. On the Stanford-Binet, she scored in the very superior range, with an IQ of 170. The psychologist and her teacher recommended that she be sent to a special school for the gifted or be accelerated to first or second grade. Her mother, who is a waitress at an expensive restaurant and her father, who owns a very successful cleaning business, saw no reason why she should be singled out as different and put into a higher grade. They would not even consider a special school. They "made it" on their own without any special help and believed Alana should do the same.

Alana is interested in many subjects but has become entranced with a neighbor's computer and word processor. She doesn't care about being friends with children of her own age but spends hours with the neighbors, who are in the fourth and fifth grades, and her older brother, who is in the fifth grade. She and her brother and their neighbors enjoy playing computer games and experimenting with the word processor.

In school, Alana gets bored very quickly with the activities of her classmates but enjoys working at her own pace in the individualized language arts program. She was very excited when her teacher suggested that she could go to the computer lab when she finished her work.

Claudia. A seventh grader, Claudia is a beautiful brown-haired girl who is well liked by everyone. She has many friends with whom she spends a great deal of time listening to music, dancing, and talking. She considers her friends more important than school and is often late with her homework because she is busy with her friends. However, Claudia makes good grades in all her classes and achieves at an average or slightly above-average level in all subjects. She enjoys working on special projects with her friends. After she and several of her friends took a drama class together and enjoyed putting on two plays, they decided to join the drama club and continue with these activities. Claudia spends hours planning plays and drawing sketches of sets to share with her friends. In one of the plays for class, she designed all the costumes, sketched the scenery, and supervised the painting of the backdrops.

School has not always been easy for Claudia, however. From the time she was an infant, Claudia lived with her grandparents, who spoke only Spanish. Her parents were migrant workers and did not want her to move from place to place with them. Because she was a shy, quiet youngster, Claudia's teachers did not realize she was having problems with English, and she fell behind in achievement, especially reading. Claudia's artwork was beautiful, and she loved to please her teachers by drawing or painting for them. As a young child, Claudia had always been interested in drawing, painting, and crafts. She was not encouraged by her parents or grandparents, but her teachers saw this as a strength in such a quiet girl and encouraged her to continue.

In the third grade, things began to change for her. She had learned to speak English well and began to catch up in reading. Her grades improved throughout elementary school, as did her achievement. She continued to make beautiful illustrations for stories and to draw and paint for her friends. When she entered school, Claudia's IQ was 89, when tested again in third grade, her scores had risen to 115 on tests administered to the class as a group.

Freeland. Freeland is a high school junior who loves athletic activities, clubs, and debate. He plays basketball, is captain of the debate team, and can be counted on to be at all meetings of the clubs. He is running for vice president of the student council this year but also is very interested in his studies. He is in advanced placement classes in math and science and in honors classes in English. Last year Freeland won top honors in the state science fair for his design of a solar energy collector. He is highly motivated and will work on projects alone or with a group.

Freeland always has been a good student. He participated in special enrichment programs for gifted students whenever they were available at his school. Teachers loved to have him in class because he always knew the answers, was well behaved, and was willing to complete extra assignments. Students respected him and asked him to help with their projects and assignments. They often chose him as group leader.

Freeland's parents, both from a white, middle-class background, are interested in his education and have provided him with many opportunities to pursue his interests. His father, a science professor at a university, would like to see him major in engineering at an Ivy League school in the East, but Freeland is more interested in going to school at the local university where many of his friends already are enrolled. He has participated in the precollege program there and knows his way around campus. Although his mother, a freelance writer, also would like him to attend a well-known university, she believes that he should be allowed to choose his school and that he needs to spend more time narrowing his interests and deciding on a career before he decides where to go.

When tested by the school psychologist in fifth grade, Freeland scored in the superior range (IQ 132) on an intelligence test and showed achievement one and a half to two grade levels above his grade placement in most academic subjects. His achievement continues to be in approximately this range, and his interests are varied.

Jeannie. Jeannie, a fourth grader, is a difficult child with whom to work. She seems to be bright but hates school. When the teacher asks a question, her answers are completely offbeat. She is always asking questions that annoy the teacher and that take the discussion away from the central issue. Her work is sloppy and incomplete and always shows a different perspective. She completes assignments only when they are in an area in which she is interested. She hates arithmetic and refuses to learn her math facts. Her stories, which are interesting and imaginative, are seldom punctuated correctly, and her spelling is atrocious. Jeannie often distracts the other children with her funny anecdotes.

Jeannie's third-grade teacher, who was very concerned about her apparent ability and her poor performance, referred her for testing because she thought Jeannie might have a learning disability. She showed no signs of learning problems, but she did demonstrate that she was capable of achieving at a much higher level than her performance showed (IQ 115). Her parents, however, did not evidence concern because her achievement was average or only slightly below average in most areas.

Jeannie is the second child in a large family and spends a great deal of time taking care of the younger children. Her mother, who takes in ironing, and her father, who paints houses and does other odd jobs, are struggling to make enough money to support the family and have little time to be concerned about her education. However, they want all their children to have the opportunities they did not have as youngsters. Since Jeannie seems to be a happy child at home, they see no cause for concern. Her stories and drawings are amusing to the family.

John. John is a sixth grader who recently transferred to a boarding school near the Navajo reservation. His parents, who live in a rural area 50 miles from the nearest grocery store, had been concerned about the four hours a day he was spending riding a bus to and from school. They miss his help with the sheep but feel that he needs to make friends and continue his studies. John's father is a sheepherder, and his mother weaves rugs. His younger brothers and sisters still live in the family's one-room hogan and ride a bus to school.

In school, John is very quiet and has few friends. He prefers to work alone and would rather be given a structured task with clear guidelines than an open-ended one. He seems to study all the time and completes all assignments conscientiously. His teachers are pleased with his dedication but wish he had more friends. Even though he works very hard, John's performance is not outstanding. His achievement is high in math and science, low in reading and language arts, and average in social studies. However, his teacher was surprised at his ability to operate equipment, since he had not seen most of it before coming to school, and surprised at his willingness to attempt to repair anything broken. His teacher requests his help whenever she shows a film or uses any audiovisual equipment in class. She was amazed when John completely took apart the clock that was not working and put it back together. She was even more surprised when it worked!

When John was tested by the school psychologist, his scores on the Wechsler Intelligence Scale for Children-Revised were surprising. His verbal scores were average or slightly below, but his scores on the performance scale were superior, especially on the Block Design subtest.

Although not all of these five students fit the traditional profile of academically gifted students, they all would be considered gifted by certain definitions. When the classroom teacher encourages and develops the abilities of children like these, the classroom climate is improved for all students. The ideas used for the development of the abilities of these

Table 2-2.

Examples of Content Representing Principles and Selected to Meet Interests and Needs of Individual Gifted Students

Student	Abstractness	Complexity	Variety	Organization	Economy	Comprehensiveness	Relevance for the Future
Alana	Suggest that she read fairy tales and fables from different countries, and write a paragraph or short essay about how they are alike and different.	If the topic is classification, she can develop as many different ways as possible to categorize a group of concrete objects. Other grouping tasks could follow, such as words, animals, emotions.	Interviews with different people who have recently seen a certain movie could focus on how they reacted to the movie. Hold a class discussion of the kinds of movies, books, and television programs preferred by members of the class, and the reasons for these preferences.	Suggest observation of mother animals and their babies in a zoo to see how they are alike and different. Give her picture books about animals and ask her to tell what similarities she observes about the characteristics of animals that live in (a) the desert, (b) the city, (c) the jungle, (d) a cold climate.	Hold a group discussion of personal experiences in which someone's behavior could not be explained without knowing about their personal history. Suggest that she write a story about one of the experiences she has had or was described by a student in the class.	Suggest that she read 2 short plays and discuss how they are alike and different. Suggest that she interview local writers about their use of drama and try one of their methods in the next story she writes.	Provide opportunities for developing skills using the word processor for writing. Introduce a variety of writing programs and software.
Claudia	Encourage the writing and presentation of a play about cultural changes in 3 countries by her small group. Allow sketches and drawings as	Encourage her to design a way to classify various pieces of art or a group of paintings by artists of a certain time period. Suggest drawing dia-	Give small groups of students the task of developing a videotape, poem, or play illustrating the elements of drama studied. Hold a class dis-	She may be interested in interviewing her friends and family, focusing on the people (animals, plants) on whom they depend. An	Interviews with relatives and friends who live in Mexico or who lived there in the past, focusing on their perceptions of significant events in the his-	Include in interviews questions about Mexican individuals significant in the various academic areas and reasons they are considered significant.	As a group, solve the problem of how to improve long-range planning in developed and underdeveloped countries. Focus on the reciprocal

a substitute for a written report. Encourage her to develop examples of the handicrafts characteristic of countries being studied, and suggest that she explain their development and influence in the culture.

grams of various classification systems familiar to her, and as a further challenge, develop a drawing of a new system for classifying something (e.g., costumes worn during certain rituals or on special occasions).

cussion of the role of set design and costumes to the elements of drama in a play. As an extension, she could design costumes and scenery for the plays written by other students.

extension of this idea would be to examine interdependence from several points of view (physical, emotional, social) and analyze the answers people give according to these factors.

tory of their country would allow her to involve her family and others of her background in her education, showing that learning comes from interactions with people as well as from reading books. She could use her Spanish language skills by conducting all interviews in her native language, translating her results and her presentation if she wishes, or give it to the teacher in Spanish (the teacher could identify someone proficient in Spanish to read the report and make comments, if the teacher does not know Spanish).

Present interview results to the class, and follow presentation with a discussion of the differences and similarities between Americans and Mexicans considered significant in their academic fields. A related focus could be on a comparison of the methods of research and problem solving used in social science (for example) in Mexico and the United States. Study the lives of famous and not-so-well-known artists focusing on how they developed their talent.

relationships necessary for both countries to develop because of their interdependence. Claudia and her friends can be encouraged to focus on Mexico and the United States if interested.

Table 2-2. Continued

Student	Abstractness	Complexity	Variety	Organization	Economy	Comprehensiveness	Relevance for the Future
Freeland	Suggest a study of leaders and their styles of leadership in the countries analyzed by him or his group. Have him organize the presentations of various groups and the discussion following the presentations.	Assist him in organizing an investigation of the different types of classification systems used in math, science, and English; and in involving groups of students from other classes.	Encourage him to investigate dramatic techniques used in political campaigns and speeches. Hold a class discussion emphasizing commonalities in dramatic techniques used in different media, and as a follow-up, challenge him to develop a campaign speech using these methods.	He could study the process of change in societies and social institutions. To incorporate his interest in alternative sources of energy such as solar, he could study the impact of development of particular forms of energy on technological advancements in certain cultures. Designing methods for using solar energy that would be most acceptable in certain cultures would also be an interesting project to suggest.	Suggest that he identify the historical conflicts in which he believes power was a motivating force. Hold a discussion of the relationship between power and technology in modern society.	Recommend that he use 2 different research designs to test his new solar collector and compare them. Analyze the data using more than one number system and compare the results.	Practice creative problem solving as a process for developing new products and technologies. Develop a pessimistic and an optimistic "picture" of this country and the world in 20 years. Explain what needs to be done now to increase the likelihood that the positive scenario will be true, and describe what needs to be done now to decrease the chances that the negative one will come true.
Jeannie	Encourage her to analyze literature and humor in	Have her develop "tough" questions about the classi-	Encourage her to do "dramatic readings" of	Stories and sketches could be made up by	Recommend that she interview her friends about	Introduce her to computers and calculators, allow-	Teach her to use a spelling correction program on

the different countries. Suggest that she create a humorous story about the country she is studying.

fication systems being studied, then see how many creative answers she can generate for each question. Classifying animals, social institutions, and types of literature in as many ways as possible would present a challenge and help in the learning of academic content.

poetry and other literature. Have an impromptu story-telling session, tape record it, and have each student listen to the tape and then retell the story in a way that is more interesting or effective.

Jeannie about different animals, their habitats, and their friends. An emphasis on using stories to illustrate concepts such as the usefulness of protective coloration for survival of animals, and the need to allow the natural food chain to operate without human disruption.

their significant past experiences, why these events were important, and which of their current characteristics resulted from each of these experiences. Analysis of the data from these interviews would be the next step, and could include use of a variety of methods such as classification of content into groups, analysis of percentages of answers in certain categories, and "path analysis" by developing visual diagrams of cause-effect chains. An extension would be to challenge her to design a new method of analysis.

ing her to use them after she has demonstrated understanding of arithmetical operations. Encourage her to choose from a variety of options related to the topic of number bases and number systems (e.g., word problems to solve using at least 2 number systems, investigation of new systems for computation, developing her own "shortcuts" to computation, playing simulation games or other games in which computation skills are necessary).

the word processor and develop skills in using other software. Identify a mentor who is interested in working with her to develop stories, plays, or poems.

Table 2-2. Continued

Student	Abstractness	Complexity	Variety	Organization	Economy	Comprehensiveness	Relevance for the Future
John	Have John develop an analogy explaining the interdependence of nations and cultures by relating them to parts of a machine. Suggest that John develop a mathematical model of the relationships between	Activities involving the grouping and labeling of various parts of old machines could help in vocabulary development while building on abilities. Examining the characteristics of classification systems in mathematics and how	Encourage development of two audio visual presentations on the same topic, but designed for different audiences. Encourage him to assist other students in developing multi-media presentations.	Suggesting that he examine the relationships of various animals near his home through photographs, videotapes, audiotapes, or observation might be a way to help him experience success and gain the respect of	Suggest that he interview tribe members and family about the significant conflicts in their tribe's history. An interview could also focus on identifying their perceptions of significant events in American history, and the	Recommend that he develop wiring diagrams for computers using different number systems or bases. Involve him in a small-group discussion of the differences in attitudes and values of artists and mechanics.	Design technology to meet future needs identified through projects of other students and class discussions (e.g., technology to improve long-range planning in underdeveloped and developed countries, develop

elements of individual cultures and the relationships between different cultures (an even more complex challenge would be to integrate the two models into one).

they have evolved might capture his interest.

other students in the class. Another possibility would be to study changes in the animal and plant population of certain areas on the reservation through interviews with older members of his tribe and extended family.

effect of these events on the tribe at the present time.

technology to facilitate achievement of the positive scenario and prevent the negative one). Help John to identify skills he may need to develop if he chooses either of the following alternatives: return to the reservation and live with his family, get a job off the reservation.

students can be used with many other youngsters as well. In Table 2-2, the students' names are listed on the side, and across the top are principles for selecting and presenting content described in this chapter. The intersection of principles and children contains suggestions for application of a particular principle to the education of a specific gifted student.

The vignettes presented in this section illustrate how the interests and strengths of individual students can be matched with a curriculum focus. Even though the students are of different ages, the same content focus was used in all illustrations of a given principle for all children. For instance, since the examples used to illustrate "abstractness" are from social studies, particularly involving study of various countries and related to underlying principles, the activities of each child involve a cross-cultural (or cross-national) analysis of important areas.

In addition, examples illustrate ways to combine a student's interest and strengths with the learning content from the basic curriculum. Small group, large group, and individual activities are included, and in many cases, extensions of group activities are suggested that build on the interests and strengths of the students.

Conclusion

The focus of this chapter has been on the development of curriculum content in a regular classroom setting that is qualitatively different from the basic curriculum in ways that are appropriate for gifted students. Gifted children are gifted 24 hours a day. Most provisions and programs for gifted children are part-time solutions for a full-time problem. Gifted children find themselves in regular classrooms most of the time. The time has come for us to face up to this situation and to provide special education for gifted children in regular classrooms.

REFERENCES

Bloom, B. S. (1956). *Taxonomy of educational objectives: The classification of educational goals. Handbook I: Cognitive domain.* New York: Longmans, Green & Co.

Bruner, J. S. (1960). *The process of education.* Cambridge, MA: Harvard University Press.

Gallagher, J. J. (1975). *Teaching the gifted child* (2nd ed.). Boston: Allyn & Bacon. Inc.

Grobman, H. (1962). Some comments on the evaluation program findings and their implications. *Biological Sciences Curriculum Study Newsletter, 19,* 25–29.

Guilford, J. P. (1967). *The nature of human intelligence.* New York: McGraw-Hill.

Institute for Staff Development (Eds.). (1971). Hilda Taba teaching strategies program: Unit 1. Miami, FL: Author.

Lowman, L. M. (1961). An experimental evaluation of two curriculum designs for teaching first year algebra in a ninth grade class. (Doctoral dissertation, University of Oklahoma). *Dissertation Abstracts International,* 22,502. (University Microfilms No. 61-2864)

Maker, C. J. (1987). *Curricula and teaching strategies for gifted students.* Monograph prepared for the Leadership Accessing program. Purdue, IN: Indiana Department of Education and Purdue University.

Maker, C. J. (1987). Gifted and talented. In Virginia Richardson-Koehler (Ed), *Educator's handbook: A research perspective* (pp. 420–456). New York: Longmans.

Naisbitt, J. (1984). *Megatrends: Ten new directions transforming our lives.* New York: Warner Books.

Task Force on Economic Growth. (1983). *Action for excellence: A comprehensive plan to improve our nation's schools.* A report of the Education Commission of the States.

Wallace, W. L. (1962). The BSCS 1961–62 evaluation program—A statistical report. *Biological Sciences Curriculum Study Newsletter, 19,* 22–24.

Chapter 3

INDIVIDUALIZING INSTRUCTION
FOR MAINSTREAMED GIFTED CHILDREN

Rita Dunn

Throughout the world a wide variety of administrative arrangements are currently being used to provide special education for gifted and talented children. These administrative arrangements are often referred to in the professional literature as delivery systems. It is important to distinguish between issues related to what is taught (curriculum materials), how the material is taught (the teaching-learning process), and issues relevant to where and in what time-frame special education is provided for gifted and talented children (delivery systems). There is no necessary connection between a specific approach to curriculum and instruction and a particular delivery system. In the current chapter, we will focus on how the regular classroom teacher can provide enrichment and/or acceleration for the gifted within the setting of the regular classroom. However, the teaching-learning process can be individualized within the framework of any full or part-time delivery system. For example, there is no reason why instruction cannot be individualized in the full-time special school for the gifted as well as in part-time afternoon, summer, vacation week programs.

Dunn and Dunn (1978), Dunn and Price (1980), Griggs and Dunn (1984), and Griggs and Price (1980) have concluded that effective individualization of instruction for gifted students should give major attention to learning style differences. In a recent comprehensive and authoritative review of the findings on learning style, Dunn (1987) summarized convincing empirical evidence that has accumulated over the years as a result of her research and that of her students and collaborators. The most impressive finding is the higher scholastic achievement and more positive attitudes toward school that resulted when the learning environment matched the individual student's learning style preference than in situations where such a match did not obtain.

In addition to the positive effects of matching learning style preferences and instructional environment, negative effects have been noted, particularly with gifted learners, when learning style is ignored. Some gifted learners remain unidentified because teachers misinterpreted and misunderstood their individual learning style that was in sharp contrast to conventional perceptions of requisite school behavior (Dunn, Dunn & Price, 1977). Many able learners became adolescent dropouts when they were required to learn in programs antithetical to their learning styles (Gadwa & Griggs, 1985; Griggs, 1986).

The current chapter is designed to help teachers and counselors who work with mainstreamed gifted children to understand and to use the concept of learning style. We will discuss how individual learning style preferences can be identified, on the one hand, and suggest ways to modify the environment to match individual learning styles, on the other. The chapter is divided into four sections, the first focuses on the definition of learning style, the second on its measurement, the third on learning styles of the gifted, and the fourth, on practical suggestions on how to modify instruction for gifted students in regular classrooms in terms of individual learning style preferences.

I. WHAT IS LEARNING STYLE?

Numerous definitions of learning style that differ somewhat from one another have been suggested in the literature (Dunn, Debello, Brennan & Murrain, 1981). In this chapter learning style is defined as the conditions under which each person begins to concentrate on, absorb, process, and retain new or difficult information and skills. Every person has a characteristic learning style regardless of intelligence or achievement level, or socioeconomic status. Psychobiologists have identified which elements of learning style are biologically imposed and which develop out of individual life experiences (Restak, 1979; Thies, 1979). Learning style is a reasonably stable characteristic. It can, however, change over time as a result of maturation. Strong learning style preferences change only over years and as a result of high motivation and strong personal effort. As stated above, learning style is of critical importance, because when learners are taught in ways that complement their learning styles, they achieve at higher levels and demonstrate more positive attitudes and behaviors than when they are not.

Dunn and Dunn (1972) developed a theoretical model of learning style. According to the model, each person's learning style is comprised of a unique combination of environmental, emotional, sociological, physical, and psychological elements that permit individuals to receive, store and then use their knowledge and skills (see Fig. 3-1).

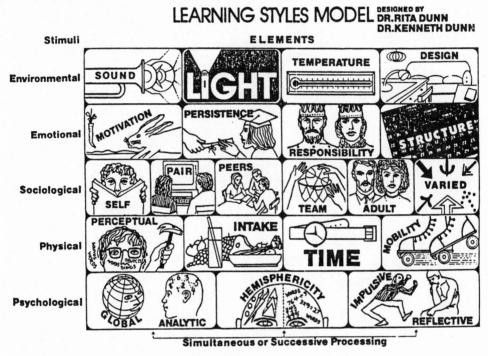

Figure 3-1.

Later Dunn, Dunn, and Price (1984) defined learning style in terms of individual student reactions to 23 elements of instructional environments: (a) immediate environment (noise level, temperature, light, design); (b) emotionality (general motivation, being motivated by the teacher, being motivated by a parent; persistence, responsibility, structure); (c) sociological preferences (learning alone, learning with peers, learning with adults present, learning in combined ways), (d) physical characteristics (auditory, visual, tactile/kinesthetic preferences, time of day, intake, mobility); and (e) psychological inclinations (global/analytic, hemispheric preference, impulsive/reflective).

Most people have between six and fourteen elements that affect them strongly; some have more. Of the more than one million persons we have tested, no one has evidenced fewer than four.

Many differences in learning style have been reported in children and adults: (a) among average, gifted and highly gifted students in grades five through twelve (Cody, 1983); (b) between gifted and nongifted elementary (Ricca, 1983) and secondary students (Vignia, 1983); (c) between low and high reading achievers in the seventh and eighth grades (Murray, 1980); (d) between learning disabled and gifted (Pedersen, 1984); and (e) among students high or low on divergent thinking and feeling variables (Wittig, 1985).

We will discuss differences between gifted and nongifted children in greater detail in a subsequent section of this chapter.

Husbands and wives tend to have many elements of style that are different from each other. Children do not necessarily reflect their parents' styles. And in the same family, siblings' styles appear to be more different from each other than similar. We cannot at the present time explain why differences in learning style occur, but they do.

II. HOW IS LEARNING STYLE IDENTIFIED AND MEASURED?

The Learning Style Inventory (LSI). Research has demonstrated that teachers are able to identify only a few elements of their students' learning style through observation: other elements appear to be identifiable through personal interviewing or administration of learning style tests (Dunn, Dunn & Price, 1977).

Based on the Dunn model five separate learning style instruments have been developed: (a) Learning Style Questionnaire (Dunn & Dunn, 1977), a 228-item survey appropriate for students in Grades 3 through 12; (b) Learning Style Inventory (Dunn, Dunn & Price, 1984), a 100-item instrument that provides individual and class profiles and subscale summaries of students in Grades 3 through 12; (c) Productivity Environmental Preference Survey (Dunn, Dunn & Price, 1981), a 100-item instrument that provides individual and group profiles and subscale summaries for post high school adults; (d) Learning Style Inventory: Primary Version (Perrin, 1982), an illustrated questionnaire appropriate for children in Kindergarten through Grade 2; and (e) Reading Style Inventory (Carbo, 1981), a survey appropriate for students in Grades 3 through 12.

In a recent study (Curry, 1987), the style conceptualizations and psychometric standards of 20 different instruments,—nine measuring individual learning style preference, eight concerned with information processing, and three focused on cognitive personality dimensions—were compared. The Dunn Learning Style Inventory (LSI) was the *only* one in the first category rated as having good or better reliability and validity. The LSI was one of only three instruments in the combined categories of learning style preference and instructional processing receiving a good or better rating on reliability and validity.

The Dunn Learning Style Inventory (LSI) is a test that is easy to administer and to interpret. Perhaps because of that, Keefe (1982) found that it "is the most widely used assessment instrument in elementary and secondary schools" (p. 52). The Dunn, Dunn, and Price Learning Style Inventory (LSI) (1984), in particular, is of potential value to teachers and counselors in their efforts to identify the learning style preferences of mainstreamed gifted and talented children and to customize the teaching-learning process for them accordingly. In the pages that follow, we will describe: (1) the 23 elements of learning style postulated by Dunn as they frequently appear in the classroom behavior of pupils, and (2) the instruments developed by Dunn, Dunn, and Price that can be used to measure the 23 elements at different age levels. Review of the elements of learning style as measured by the Learning Style Inventory (Dunn, Dunn & Price, 1975, 1978, 1979, 1981, 1984), the Learning Style Inventory: Primary Version (Perrin, 1982) and the Productivity Environmental Preference Survey (Dunn, Dunn, & Price, 1979, 1981) will provide teachers and counselors specific information concerning how individual gifted children should be taught in mainstreamed classes.

At our Center for the Study of Learning and Teaching Styles we experimented with different learning styles tests for various purposes. One that has consistently discriminated between extreme populations is the *Learning Style Inventory* (LSI) (Dunn, Dunn, & Price, 1975, 1978, 1979, 1981, 1984). Developed through content and factor analysis, the *Learning Style Inventory* (LSI) is a comprehensive approach to the identification of an individual's learning style. The instrument allows analysis of the conditions under which students in Grades 3 through 12 prefer to learn through an assessment of each of 23 elements of instructional environments previously listed. The LSI used dichotomous items (e.g., "I study best when it is quiet," and "I can ignore sound when I study") that are rated on a 5-point Likert scale and can be completed in approximately 30 to 40 minutes.

The LSI group learning style summaries are divided into two parts. The first summary is based on those individuals who have a standard score higher than 60 in any of the 23 areas, and the second summary is a list of those individuals having a standard score of 40 or lower in any of the areas. These summaries can be used to identify which individuals have similar preferences. The LSI subscale summary indicates the number and percentage of the total group that identified a particular area as important (standard score higher than 60) or not important (standard score lower than 40). These data can be used to determine which of the 23 areas are of major or minor importance to the group.

The LSI reports a Consistency Key to reveal the accuracy with which each respondent has answered its questions. Ohio State University's National Center for Research in Vocational Education published the results of its 2-year study of instruments that identify learning style and verified that the LSI has "established impressive reliability and face and construct validity" (Kirby, 1979, p. 72). Since examination by the National Center for Research, the LSI also has evidenced predictive validity (DeBello, 1985; Della Valle, 1984; Hodges, 1985; Krimsky, 1982; Kroon, 1985; Lynch, 1981; MacMurren, 1985; Martini, 1986; Miles, 1987; Murrain, 1983; Pizzo, 1981; Shea, 1983; Virostko, 1983; White, 1980).

The 23 Learning Style Elements. As stated above, Dunn, Dunn, and Price (1984) defined learning style in terms of individual reactions to 23 elements of instructional characteristics. The results of the investigation of Learning Style are presented in the form of an individual learning style profile. This report provides an excellent basis for discussions between learners and their teachers and counselors. Let us now examine each of the 23 elements in more detail.

Environmental Elements 1-4

1. Silence Versus Sound

Sound affects each individual differently. Some youngsters, including almost eight out of ten of the high IQ gifted, need absolute quiet when working on new or difficult tasks. Other learners work better with music or sounds of one type or another and many people can block out noise when they wish to do so. The results of a prize-winning experimental study of the effects of sound versus quiet on sixth graders with strong learning style preferences demonstrated quite clearly that increased achievement resulted when learners who reported a strong preference to study in a quiet environment were taught in a quiet room and those who reported a preference for noise in the environment were taught with noise. Moreover, decreased achievement resulted when learning style preference and learning environment were mismatched on the element of sound (Pizzo, 1981). Furthermore, a study by DeGregoris (1986) demonstrated that the *kind* of music played is important. Educators are cautioned to provide melodies without words, preferably baroque, to maintain concentration for those who work better with sound than in silence.

Teachers who wish to experiment with this phenomenon need only identify those students whose LSI printout indicates either below 30 or between 30 and 40. Those youngsters either always require quiet or, if their scores fall into the latter category, usually or often require quiet. For them, use carpeting squares below their desks to subdue distracting sounds. Use cardboard appliance boxes as dividers for the same purpose. Permit headsets *without music* to provide extreme quiet (see Fig. 3-2). One "Learning Disabled" teenager taught himself to read in merely four months after his teacher began permitting him to wear earmuffs while reading in school. He told his mother that it was the first time he could *think* in school.

For those who concentrate best with sound, permit earphones, headsets, or Walkman which cannot be heard by classmates. Establish firm rules:

- Students must pay attention whenever the teacher addresses the class or them;
- Their music must not interfere with anyone else's learning;
- They must achieve better on each subsequent test than they ever did before or, obviously, the experiment is not working and there is no need to continue.

2. Bright Versus Low Light

Some students, many among the gifted, need brightly illuminated environments whereas others learn more efficiently in dim light (Krimsky, 1982; Dunn, Krimsky, Murray & Quinn, 1985); those predispositions appear to be influenced to some extent by whether a person initiates processing with the right or left hemisphere (Dunn, Cavanaugh, Eberle & Zenhausern, 1982). By using available furniture and cardboard perpendicular to classroom walls, we establish areas of brighter or lower illumination. We also loosen a light bulb or two in a corner of a room and permit soft-light preferents to work there (see Fig. 3-3).

Figure 3-2. Some students achieve significantly higher test scores when permitted to listen to baroque music *while* studying; others require absolute quiet while concentrating. (Photograph courtesy of the Roosevelt Elementary School, Hutchinson, Kansas.)

3. Warm Versus Cool Temperatures

Few people can learn in either extreme of warmth or cold, but the cold affects more students negatively than heat does (Murrain, 1983). However, temperature is relative; few people react identically to the same thermometer readings. Making students aware of their temperature needs and encouraging them to carry sweaters or to wear lighter clothing than others is often enough to provide the physical comfort that they require in order to maintain concentration.

4. Formal Versus Informal Design

Some people do their best studying seated on the floor, lounging on a bed, a chair, or carpeting, or lying prone. Others can work only at a wooden chair and table, as in a conventional classroom or library. The need for an informal design increases with adolescence (Price, 1980). In one study, ninth graders demonstrated highly significant increments in

Figure 3-3. Notice that, despite the low illumination in this redesigned classroom corner, the young student is shading his eyes while trying to respond to questions on an assignment. Some students relax and concentrate better in soft, rather than in bright light, and the younger they are the less light children seem to require. (Photo courtesy of P.S. #220, Queens, New York.)

academic achievement when those who needed an informal design were matched correctly with that environment; they suffered drastically reduced achievement when mismatched (Shea, 1983). That study was replicated with junior high school underachievers in mathematics and yielded identical findings (Hodges, 1985).

Some teachers intuitively know that some students learned better out of their chairs than in them. Those educators have always "bent a little" to help certain youngsters who needed an extra bit of assistance to succeed. In their schools, parents donated couches, easy chairs and carpet squares. In others where those accountrements are not available, children are given the option of sitting wherever they wish in the room—as long as their grades reflect their improved learning. Many teachers, however, initially were concerned that if youngsters were permitted to sit on mats or on carpeting while learning, they would become disorderly or inattentive. Quite the opposite occurred. Those who *needed* an informal design paid more attention, behaved better and learned more when they were permitted to sit in class informally—but quietly (Hodges, 1982, 1983; Lemmon, 1985). Responding to students' environmental needs tends to produce increased achievement within a six-month period (Dunn, Dunn, & Freeley, 1984).

Although approximately eight of ten gifted youngsters prefer to learn in conventional seating, the remaining two or three often cannot tolerate sitting in a wooden, plastic, or steel chair for more than ten to twelve minutes. It may be important to note that when seated on such furniture, approximately 75 percent of the body weight is supported on only four square inches of bone. In addition, prolonged sitting without postural changes can cause decreased blood circulation which, in turn, causes aches, pains, cramps, and/or numbness (Shea, 1983). However, the more students squirm in their seats trying to find a comfortable position, the more likely it is that they will be accused of fidgeting and urged to sit still.

During a visit to exemplary learning styles secondary schools throughout the United States during Spring, 1987, Dunn and Griggs (1988) observed many middle school and high school classrooms that responded to adolescents' needs for varied designs by providing carpet sections, bean bags, a couch or easy chairs and/or backrests for those who apparently achieved and behaved better when permitted to work informally (see Figs. 3-4, 3-5 & 3-6). Not one teacher reported negative consequences related to their efforts to respond to this learning style characteristic.

The Emotional Elements 5–10

5. Motivation

Level of motivation interacts with learning style and seems to mediate its effects. Students of all ages who are highly motivated to achieve in school are better able to overcome the mismatch of learning style prefer-

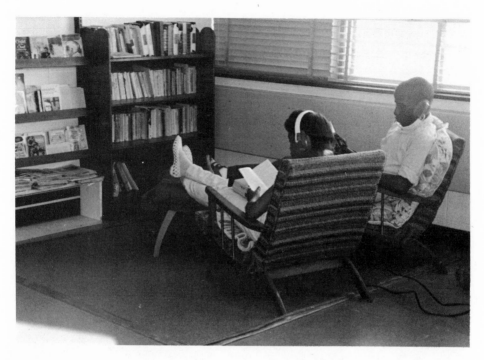

Figure 3-4. Because certain students concentrate best on difficult material when they are permitted to relax in an informal design, many schools provide easy chairs, carpeting, pillows, or bean bags for those who demonstrate increased achievement after studying that way. (Photo courtesy of Franklin Township Middle School, Franklin Township, Indiana.)

ence and instructional environment than those who are unmotivated. It has been well documented that especially poorly motivated youngsters require materials that they can master, learning tasks divided into small segments, positive feedback while learning, and frequent—if not constant—supervision. Consideration of learning style preference may now be added to the list of adjustments of the teaching-learning process that may result in higher academic achievement and more positive attitudes toward school in students with low levels of motivation.

Gifted students tend to be highly motivated to learn, but at least some report that they are bored in school. They cite the routines and requirements in the instructional environment as being unnecessarily authoritarian and restrictive (Dunn & Griggs, 1988). Selected elementary school gifted reported themselves as being irresponsible (Dunn & Price, 1980). When questioned on this point, they explained their "irresponsible" behavior as resulting from difficulty in performing responsibly in situations where they are required and directed to do exactly what has been

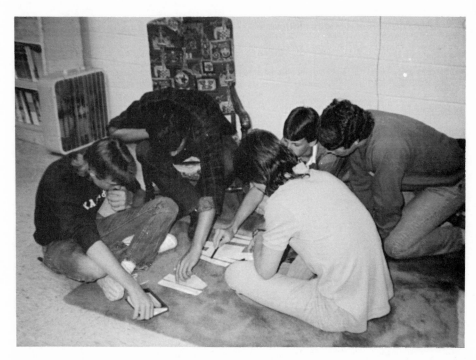

Figure 3-5. Informal areas permit more than merely a relaxed environment; they also provide opportunities for peer interaction and cooperative learning for peer-oriented students. (Photo courtesy of Corsicana High School, Corsicana, Texas.)

assigned and are not permitted to try alternatives. Hence, the strict routines of many school procedures and the comparative rigidity of some teachers' attitudes is often out of kilter with an individual child's learning style preference. Such mismatch results in decreased motivation among the gifted, as in other learners. For these reasons and other learning style-instructional environment mismatches, some gifted adolescents become dropouts. One alternative program in Edmonds, Washington brought them back to school by responding to their learning style preferences. Teachers reported that a better match of learning style and instructional environment increased motivation within weeks of their return (Gadwa & Griggs, 1985; Dunn & Griggs, in press).

Figure 3-6. Informal areas also permit teachers to work with youngsters in colleageal, rather than authoritative, ways. Mary Ellen Kasak-Saxler teaches her students French by involving them in new vocabulary through play-acting with real properties. (Photo courtesy of Blake Middle School, Hopkins, Minnesota.)

6. Being Motivated by a Teacher

7. Being Motivated by a Parent.

8. Persistence

It frequently was reported that persistence is an element of learning style that appears to be related to IQ (Dunn, 1986). That conclusion had been reached by 1980, because whenever highly achieving students with high IQs were tested, they also were identified as highly persistent (Dunn & Price, 1980; Price, Dunn, Dunn, & Griggs, 1981; White, 1980).

9. Responsibility

The learning style element of responsibility tends to correlate with conformity (White, 1980; White, Dunn, & Zenhausern, 1982). Hence, children with high scores on the responsibility element of learning styles, who are often highly conforming personalities, may be expected to do fairly well in the conventional school setting. The match of learning style and an instructional environment with few options presents no problem for them. For nonconformists, by contrast, who often learn better when permitted options, the traditional school environment may represent a mismatch of learning style and instructional environment. Nonconformists are frequently gifted and/or creative youngsters who feel stifled in traditional schools and may eventually rebel (Gadwa & Griggs, 1985). One group of nonconforming elementary school age children viewed themselves as being "not responsible," because they often had been reprimanded by teachers for not doing what they had been told (Dunn & Price, 1980, p. 34).

10. Structure

Some students, regardless of age or IQ level, cannot begin an assignment without specific directions concerning its exact focus or length, whether it should be written with pen or pencil, whether spelling "counts," and so on. Others need only general requirements before starting a task and establishing their own guidelines. One's need for externally-imposed structure appears to decrease with age and maturity (whichever comes first!) (Hunt, 1979; Price, 1980). Among elementary school age youth, Kaley (1977) found that one element of learning style is a stronger and more reliable predictor of reading achievement than IQ. The more field independent the learning style, the higher the child's reading level; the more field dependent, the lower the reading level.

Field independent persons tend to pursue active, participant approaches to learning which permit them to structure much of the task their way, whereas field dependent learners perform significantly better with a highly structured assignment (Tanenbaum, 1982). Each group achieves equally well when permitted to learn through instructional strategies that complement their needs and significantly less well when required to employ noncomplementary strategies (Douglas, 1979; Tanenbaum, 1982; Trautman, 1979).

The Sociological Elements 11-14

11. Learning Alone

12. Learning with Peers

13. Learning with Adults Present

14. Learning in Combined Ways

Some people do their best thinking alone; the presence of others distracts them. Others work better in pairs or in teams. Some like to learn with adults, whereas others need peers. A small percentage cannot concentrate with anyone present and may not have the independence skills to work alone; some of these work well with media-computers, language masters, videotapes, filmstrips, and so on. Some can learn well in any combination—alone, with others, or with media. The latter group is described as "learning in several ways" or varied (see Figs. 3-7 through 3-10).

In several studies that examined the sociological preferences of gifted youngsters, data revealed that the gifted preferred learning alone significantly more often than the nongifted. The only exception occurred when seven highly gifted youngsters were permitted to work with each other (Perrin, 1984, 1985). One especially thought-provoking finding was reported in an examination of first and second graders where the sociological preferences of all primary children had been identified. There was not a single gifted child in the entire school district who wanted to learn directly with the teacher (Perrin, 1984).

Perceptual Strengths 15-17

The senses through which each individual absorbs and retains new and difficult information have become known as perceptual strengths. Those usually develop in sequence with maturation, beginning with the tactile/kinesthetic among primary children, to the visual at approximately second grade and, finally, to the auditory at the end of elementary school (Price, 1980).

15. Auditory

An auditory learner can remember approximately 75 percent of what is discussed in a 40- to 50-minute lecture or discussion. When children

Figure 3-7. Although they appear to be seated close to each other, these two youngsters actually are working alone, each absorbed independently. Gifted students tend to prefer working by themselves—unless the task is difficult (for them!) (Photograph courtesy of Midwest High School, Midwest, Wyoming.)

enter kindergarten, very few can remember such a high percentage. Most do not become auditory before 5th or 6th grade and girls become auditory learners earlier than boys (Restak, 1979). Phonics is an excellent way to teach auditory youngsters (Carbo, 1980; Kroon, 1985; Martini, 1986; Weinberg, 1983; Wheeler, 1983; Urbschat, 1977) because it is a method of teaching children through emphasis on their ability to discriminate among sounds. Even secondary students achieve significantly higher test scores when their perceptual preferences are congruent, rather than incongruent, with the instructional strategy (Kroon, 1985; Martini, 1986).

Although most kindergarteners remember best the things they learn through manipulation and real-life activities, those who can remember easily 75 percent or more of what they hear or see tend to be gifted. When children are tactual/visual during the primary grades, they usually are/ become academically achieving in school. Apparently a relationship exists between the early development of perceptual skills and high IQ.

Figure 3-8. This pair is using a book, a tactual game, and a tape which the girls made to demonstrate the knowledge they acquired while using a Contract Activity Package in science. They often work together and report they find learning easier and more fun when they can master assigned objectives collaboratively, (Photograph courtesy of Sacred Heart Academy, Hempstead, New York.)

Phonics as a reading approach is more successful with auditory youngsters than with visual, tactual/kinesthetic children. Phonics is an analytic approach in which the sounds are analyzed one-by-one and put together to form a word. Global approaches to reading are more effective for young global learners (Carbo, Dunn, & Dunn, 1986). In addition to the perceptual strengths as elements of learning style, the global/analytic element, discussed later in this section, may be even more critical in the process of learning to read.

16. Visual

A visual learner can remember approximately 75 percent of what he or she has read or seen during a 40- to 50-minute session. More people are visual than auditory in style. Research evidenced that approximately 40 percent of the school-age population is visual; however, most children

Figure 3-9. These secondary students are working as a team to solve advanced algebra problems. Three elected to sit informally on a carpet in a corner of their classroom whereas a classmate who wished to be part of the group sits in a nearby chair. (Photograph courtesy of Corsicana High School, Corsicana, Texas.)

are not visual until third or fourth grade (Price, 1980). Some kindergarteners are visual, but in general, the older the child, the more likely he or she is to recall precisely what has been seen or read. At the stage where youngsters are strongly visual in style, a word recognition approach is an excellent way to teach them to read (Burton, 1980; Carbo, 1980; Urbschat, 1977; Wheeler, 1980, 1983). Again, even secondary students achieve significantly higher achievement scores when their perceptual preferences are congruent, rather than incongruent, with the instructional strategy (Kroon, 1985; Martini, 1986).

17. Tactile/Kinesthetic

Most kindergarteners are essentially tactile and kinesthetic in style; they find it easiest to learn by manipulating resources and actually experiencing through activities (Price, 1980; Keefe, 1979). Most previous investigations of how young children learned to read neglected both to test for tactile/kinesthetic abilities and to teach that way (Dunn & Carbo,

Figure 3-10. This section of the classroom contains two youngsters working together on the left and two others studying directly with their teacher (on the right). The part of the environment not seen contains other children engaged in varied activities—some by themselves, others in pairs, a few in teams, and some using various forms of media. (Photograph courtesy of Sacred Heart Academy, Hempstead, New York.)

1981); when they did either, kinesthetic activity was restricted to tracing over words (which is actually tactile) rather than the use of tactile/kinesthetic materials such as task cards, electroboards, learning circles and strips, body games, and "real life experiences" (Carbo, Dunn, & Dunn, 1986; Dunn & Dunn, 1978).

Montessori's methods were based on observations that young children learn and remember most easily through manipulative (tactile) and experiential (kinesthetic) activities. Price's study of 3,972 subjects in grades 3 through 7 verified that the younger the child, the more tactile/kinesthetic he or she was. Keefe also reported that "Perceptual preferences seem to evolve for most students from psychomotor (tactile/kinesthetic) to visual and aural as the learner matures" (1979, p. 127). In addition, Restak documented the auditory superiority of females over males and that boys tend to be more kinesthetic longer than girls (1979). However, in that regard, note that most studies test primary children for visual and/or auditory abilities and rarely include tactile or kinesthetic treatments. Our research has verified that when new information is introduced through the strongest perceptual strength, reinforced through the second, and used creatively, significant increases occur in academic achievement (Wheeler, 1980; Kroon, 1985). Furthermore, students should do their homework through their perceptual learning styles (Dunn, 1984, 1985) (see Figs. 3-11 through 3-16).

Figure 3-11. Both youngsters are learning new information visually through a Programmed Learning Sequence but one chose to hear the text being read to her by the accompanying tape and the other preferred to read it by herself. (Photograph courtesy of P. K. Yonge Laboratory School, University of Florida, Gainesville, Florida.)

18. Time of Day or Night Energy Levels

We all are aware of "early birds," "night owls," and people with either high or low energy levels at different times of the day or evening. Extensive research demonstrates that no matter when a class is in session, it is the wrong time of day for almost a third of the population (Price, 1980). In addition, those statistics apply to teachers as well as students (Freeley, 1984).

Figure 3-12. In one instructional area of the classroom four youngsters are using Team Learning to visually and verbally learn new material. Right behind them (to the right of the photograph, the teacher is explaining difficult material to a small group of six students who need to *hear* the explanation and have their questions answered by the authority. (Photograph courtesy of Sacred Heart Academy, Hempstead, New York.)

One study of chronic and initial high school-age truants verified that when their time-of-day preferences were matched correctly to their academic schedules, truancy was significantly reduced (Lynch, 1981). Another investigation demonstrated reduced behavior problems, increased motivation and a trend toward improved mathematics scores of junior high school students when they were matched with their preferred times of day (Carruthers & Young, 1980).

Finally, Virostko (1983) won the Kappa Delta Pi International Award with her experimental investigation of the time of day preferences of third through sixth graders who were assigned to one hour each of mathematics and reading every day. When matched for their learning style time preferences, children achieved significantly higher reading and math scores than when mismatched. The second year of that study, math and reading were reversed. Interestingly, although they were taught the OPPOSITE subject at the reverse time of day during the second year,

students again achieved significantly higher scores in whichever subject was taught at their preferred time of day. Patricia Lemmon (1985), Principal of the Roosevelt School in Hutchinson, Kansas, experimented with administering standardized achievement tests at students' best time of day and obtained statistically higher test scores than those same students had yielded in each of three previous years.

One interesting phenomenon is that high IQ children, in contrast with nongifted and underachieving populations, reflect early morning time preferences significantly more often than their classmates. It is a matter of conjecture whether students who happen to be chronologically alert in the morning perform better in school because reading and mathematics often are taught during that time of day or whether, indeed, morning

Figures 3-13 & 3-14. Both Figures 3-13 and 3-14 demonstrate the use of tactual resources to teach students new and difficult materials. The pair in 3-13 are using an electroboard to introduce new science information. The young boy in 3-14 is using a tactual game to learn how to write a news story. (Photographs courtesy of East Islip Junior High School, East Islip, New York and P.S. #220 Queens, New York respectively.)

people tend to become gifted. Bear in mind, however, that Virostko (1983) found that children achieved significantly higher scores on a standardized test whenever the teaching paralleled their learning style energy patters and significantly lower scores when taught at the "wrong" time of day (for them).

19. Intake

Intake is another element of learning style. Some people eat, drink, chew, or bite objects as they concentrate; others do not. MacMurren (1985) identified sixth graders' needs for intake during a testing situation and then placed them into complementary and dissonant conditions. Students whose learning style scores had revealed them as requiring intake while concentrating achieved significantly higher when permitted snacks during the test. Those who needed intake but were not afforded

Figure 3-15. Many students are kinesthetic learners, meaning that they concentrate best when their entire body is involved in actively learning. In this figure their teacher is supervising a science Body Game contest on The Human Heart; in Figure 5-16 a primary student is learning correct grammar with a Body Game made from a Twister canvas. (Photographs courtesy of East Islip Junior High School, East Islip, New York and the Lafayette Contemporary Academy, Cleveland Public Schools, Ohio.)

it, scored significantly lower. Those who did not require intake scored better without it.

20. Mobility Versus Passivity

Many children cannot sit still for long periods of time; others cannot sit even for short periods. We have found that when highly active youngsters are permitted mobility through scheduled periods in varied

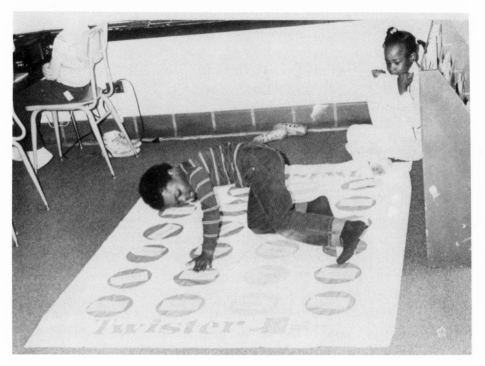

Figure 3-16.

instructional centers, they concentrate for longer periods of time, learn and recall more than when required to remain still.

In another study, Della Valle (1984) identified 217 seventh graders with a preference for mobility and 89 with a preference for passivity. Twenty youngsters at each end of the continuum were chosen to participate in this research. Word-pair recognition tasks were developed for both the passive and mobile environments, and all students were taught and tested in both conditions.

Students with either preference performed equally as well when matched, corroborating that both mobility and passivity are strengths when they are responded to positively. No differences were evidenced between the scores of students in the two extremely different environments, substantiating that no single environment—one that permits students to move or one that requires them to sit still—generates higher achievement. In addition, significant differences were yielded when students' environments were both matched and mismatched with their learning style preferences. Specifically, although actively and passively preferenced students performed well in the passive (conventional) room, those with a need for mobility obtained the highest scores of ALL groups when they were taught in the condition that permitted them to move while learning. Conversely, those who preferred a passive environment scored relatively poorly when required to engage in activity while learning. Those findings suggest that each school should provide at least two different environments if both types of students are to achieve as well as they are able.

The Psychological Elements 21–23

21. Global Versus Analytic

Global versus analytic processing is another dimension of learning style (Carbo, Dunn, & Dunn, 1986). Brennan (1982) described analytic learners as those who learn sequentially (step-by-step), are inductive (going from the parts to the whole), emphasize the importance of language and verbal ability and tend to be reflective in style (p. 212). On the other hand, global-style learners are described as holistic, deductive (going from the whole to the parts), emphasizing spatial relationships and emotions, and tending to be more impulsive than reflective.

Some youngsters learn sequentially, step by step, in a well-ordered continuum. Many school subjects such as biology and grammar are often taught just that way. Other learners cannot begin to focus on the content without an initial overall Gestalt of the meaning and use of what will be taught. Such students require a visual image of the topic and an illustrative anecdote to involve their thinking and motivation. The first type of learning is called analytic; the second, global. Regardless of the difference in learning style, global and analytic preferents are equally as able and achieve equally as well when taught through instuctional strategies that complement their characteristics. Thus, in both the Douglas (1979) and Trautman (1979) studies of secondary students, analytics taught with analytic materials and globals taught with global materials achieved significantly higher test scores when matched, and lower scores when mismatched.

The global-analytic dimension of learning style is positively related to the previously discussed element of persistence. Analytic learners are more persistent than global learners. Emotionally, they want to complete a task once they have begun it. Global learners appear to have limited attention spans and need frequent "breaks." Apparently, global students prefer involvement with several short tasks simultaneously, rather than the single, comparatively lengthy assignment characteristic of much classroom instruction. We have observed that when time-on-task becomes a problem, it generally is for global, rather than analytic youngsters. However, when the teacher divides the same assignment into small sections (perhaps three or four different parts), permits movement from one section of the environment to another during their completion, and encourages rather than berates youngsters, global learners tend to persist.

During the past few years research findings indicate that high IQ students tend to be characterized by an analytic learning style (Bruno, 1988). It may well be that IQ tests are satisfactory indicators of analytic but not global giftedness because the latter tends to be evidenced in spatial rather than verbal ability, holistic rather than sequential analyses, and generalizations based upon intuition rather than factual recall (Brennan, 1982). In addition, we must not overlook the finding reported by Cody (1983), that profoundly gifted learners (IQ 145 or higher) were, for the most part, characterized by a global learning style.

22. Hemispheric Preference

During the past few years we have learned that students who tend to use a left-processing style learn in very different conditions from those who are right preferenced (Dunn et al., 1982; Bruno, 1988). For example, right-preferenced students: (a) are less bothered by sound when studying; (b) prefer dim illumination; (c) require an informal design; (d) are less motivated (in school) than lefts; (e) are less persistent; (f) prefer learning with peers; and (g) prefer tactile to auditory or visual stimulation—even at the high school levels. Apparently, students who are right- and left-preferenced have different environmental and organizational needs within the classroom, as well as different motivational and personality characteristics.

Of interest is that in a survey of 2,000 teachers and administrators in the New York metropolitan area, less than 25 percent were aware of the relationships between learning style and brain behavior (Zenhausern et. al., 1984). The two, however, tend to go hand in hand. As indicated previously, there are similarities among analytic, inductive, left processors and among global, deductive, rights.

23. Impulsivity Versus Reflectivity

Impulsive students often call out in class or respond to questions on a written examination without considering various possibilities, while reflectives rarely volunteer information although they may know the answer. The latter group often "reads into" test questions, wondering what the major focus is and examining many alternative possibilities. Thus, verbal participation and timed test taking causes tension for some and is relatively easy for others. Everyone is both impulsive and reflective at times, but each person's dominant pattern determines how well he/she functions when required to think under pressure.

Rather than calling on individuals to provide answers in front of their peers, teachers might experiment with writing the exact number of seconds that students, divided into groups of four and five, will have to consider responses to a question that will be posed. Then, for example, the teacher might say, "You are divided into six groups of five. You have 12 seconds to develop as many answers as you can to the following question: Explain all the ways you can make your mother happy on Mother's Day without spending one penny. Take the 12 seconds. Go!"

Within each group, students can contribute as quickly as ideas develop. They can take notes if they prefer or draw possible reminders of their thoughts. At the end of 12 seconds the teacher can say, "Let's see how many ideas you've found!" Pointing to any single group, she can ask, "Who will volunteer *one* answer?" A volunteer from the group can respond and the answer should be recorded on the chalk board, a sheet of newsprint or an overhead transparency. Then, pointing to a second group, she can request another answer from one more volunteer. Indiscriminately moving among the groups and seeking volunteers only, gradually the many ideas discussed will be printed for all to see. No duplications should be accepted.

This technique permits both impulsives and reflectives to participate actively in the thinking process instead of merely the individual who would have been called on. The pressure is reduced and the activity becomes almost gamelike—which is one way that gifted children—and others—often like to learn. The technique is multisensory; children discuss their thoughts in the group, record some of them, call them out when volunteering, see them recorded by the teacher and cross them off their own lists to avoid duplication. It also makes learning cooperative instead of competitive.

III. LEARNING STYLES OF THE GIFTED

In this section we will summarize the findings on the learning style characteristics that are reported most frequently in gifted children.

Two Caveats. Before we proceed, two caveats are in order. First, when considering the remarks that follow, the reader should recall our earlier statement that every individual, including every gifted individual, has a unique personal learning style. Accordingly, the findings reported in this section on learning style of gifted learners, are valid for gifted learners as a group, but may not be interpreted as applying to any single gifted learner. Second, during the last few decades, a continuing expansion of our understanding of the phenomenon of giftedness has taken place. As Ricca (1984, p. 121) pointed out, "The gifted are no longer viewed as a single homogeneous group." Our view of giftedness has expanded beyond the simple high IQ definition to include focus on the demonstration of behaviors that reflect a variety of abilities and talents. In the current chapter, we have limited our discussion for the most part, to discussion of learning style in high-IQ-type gifted learners. It is, however, reasonable to expect that gifted children who differ in their abilities and talents will be characterized by different learning styles as well.

In the introduction to the current volume, Milgram described her 4×4 Structure of Giftedness model in which she conceptualizes gifted behavior in terms of four categories (overall intellectual ability, specific intellectual ability, overall original or creative thinking, and specific creative talents) interacting with four levels (profoundly, moderately, and mildly gifted, and nongifted. We are currently conducting an investigation of learning style as a function of the categories obtained through the 4×4 model (Milgram, Dunn, Griggs, Price, Wechsler, & Treffinger, in preparation) that will contribute to the clarification of the relationship between learning style, type, and level of giftedness. In the meantime, we now turn to a summary of the relatively large amount of data that has accumulated about the learning style of high IQ-type gifted children. These data can provide direction to teachers and counselors in regular school settings seeking ways to meet the needs of these children.

The Learning Styles of Gifted Learners. Some elements of learning style that are characteristic of gifted children were cited in the previous section in discussion of each of the 23 elements separately. In this section we first will summarize what is known about the learning style characteristics of gifted learners and compare their learning styles to that of nongifted pupils. We will next examine the effects of matched versus mismatched learning style/instructional environment on achievement and attitudes of gifted children and adolescents.

Children identified as gifted consistently report learning style characteristics that are significantly different from those of children not so identified (Griggs & Dunn, 1984). For example, they are persistent (Dunn & Price, 1980; Griggs & Price, 1980; Price, Dunn, Dunn, & Griggs, 1981; Ricca, 1983), highly motivated (Cody, 1983; Dunn & Price, 1980; Griggs & Price, 1980; Cross, 1982; Price, Dunn, Dunn, & Griggs, 1981); and perceptually strong (Dunn & Price, 1980; Griggs & Price, 1980; Kreitner, 1981; Ricca, 1983; Price, Dunn, Dunn, & Griggs, 1981). In addition, the gifted strongly prefer to learn by themselves rather than with others (Cross, 1982; Griggs & Price, 1980; Kreitner, 1981; Price, Dunn, Dunn, & Griggs, 1981; Ricca, 1983), unless those others are their similarly achieving peers (Perrin, 1984, 1985). They also consistently prefer learning in a formal, rather than in an informal, physically relaxed instructional environment when concentrating on new and/or difficult material (Price, Dunn, Dunn, & Griggs, 1981).

Many gifted children report that they require absolute quiet (Cody, 1983) and bright light (Griggs & Price, 1980), when working on new or difficult tasks. Moreover, high IQ-type gifted children seem to prefer to learn in the early morning. Gifted children as a group were especially strong in registering *lack of desire* to learn directly with the teacher. There does not appear to be any relationship between temperature preferences and either intelligence level or global/analytic hemispheric processing style (Dunn, Cavanaugh, Eberle & Zenhausern, 1982). See Figure 3-17 for a summary of the learning style elements found to characterize gifted learners.

The preference for high versus low structure is an element that consistently discriminates between the gifted and nongifted. Dunn and Price (1980) found that gifted children prefer low structure and flexibility when learning. Lyne (1979) studied adults and college students and found a relationship between cognitive development and structure. Adults at the lower stages of cognitive development preferred a highly structured format whereas those at the higher stages preferred more flexibility and diversity in learning. Indeed, youngsters with an IQ between 120–130 and in the 90th percentile or above in reading or mathematics tend to be extremely independent (Stewart, 1981; Wasson, 1980), internally controlled and desirous of providing their own structure (Cross, 1982; Dunn

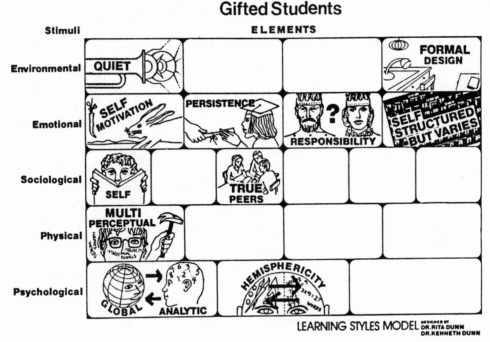

Figure 3-17.

& Price, 1980; Kreitner, 1981; Ricca, 1983; Stewart, 1981).

Findings on the perceptual modalities included in measures of learning style suggest that gifted children remember easily auditorially (by hearing), visually (by reading or observing), tactually (by note-taking or with manipulatives), and kinesthetically (through real-life experiences and activities). Different diagnostic instruments and extensive interviews document that high achievers actually dislike drill, recitation, lectures, and class discussions. Ricca (1983) and Wasson (1980) found that gifted learners much prefer games, projects, independent study, and programmed learning sequences (when additional structure is necessary). Peer teaching ranked fourth in Ricca's (1983) findings and was desirable among gifted first- and second-graders, but only, as cited above, when they were permitted to learn with their equally gifted classmates (Perrin, 1984).

Gifted children can be either analytic or global, but the higher the IQ, the more global they tend to be (Cody, 1983). When the 240 students in grades five through twelve were divided into three IQ ability groups-average (100–119), gifted (130–139), and highly gifted (145 and above) and compared for their learning style characteristics and hemisphericity, highly significant differences were evidenced among the groups.

1. Average students preferred studying in a warm, quiet environment, late in the day, and knowing exactly what was required of them, indicating a strong need for external structure. They were less motivated than the other two groups and evidenced more integrated and left (analytic) processing styles.
2. Gifted youngsters also preferred quiet, but studied better in a moderate temperature, in the morning, and with less structure. Several previous studies substantiated the consistent preferences of gifted students for being internally controlled and providing their own structure (Cross, 1982; Dunn & Price, 1980; Kreitner, 1981; Ricca, 1983; Stewart, 1981). The gifted were more integrated and tended to demonstrate a right (global) processing style.
3. Highly gifted students preferred sound (music) while learning, a cool environment, evening, and the least amount of structure imposed. They were the most motivated, the most integrated, and the strongest right processors.
4. The gifted and highly gifted demonstrated highly significant preferences for right hemisphere and integrated processing.
5. Left dominant students preferred the formal design of conventional classroom seating, more structure than rights, less intake, and tended to be visual, but less tactual/kinestic. Right-dominant youngsters *disliked* structure and rarely were adult-motivated; they tended to be self-motivated.

It is important to note that Bruno (in press), Cody (1983), Dunn, Cavanugh, Eberle, and Zenhausern (1982), and Jarsonbeck (1984) all found essentially similar learning style characteristics between analytics and left-preferred students and between global and right-preferred students when the differences that occur at various age levels were accounted for (Price, 1980). For example, the more analytic the students, the more they preferred learning in quiet, with structure, often in well-illuminated areas and in a formal design without much need for intake while studying. In contrast, highly global students often prefer sound while learning, afternoon or evening hours, soft lighting, an informal design, and intake when concentrating.

Thus, global, or right-dominant students, tend to be among the most gifted students (Cody, 1983) while, simultaneously, they constitute a majority of underachievers (Clay, 1984; Dean, 1982; Hodges, 1985, Johnson, 1984; Murray, 1984; Pederson, 1984; Sinatra, Primavera, & Waked, 1986). However, what differentiates between the gifted global student who achieves in school and both the gifted and average IQ underachiever are other elements of learning style, namely motivation and responsibility; however, it is necessary to remember that the LSI scale of Responsibility correlates significantly with the California Psychological Inventory scale of Conformity (White, 1980).

Thus, high IQ and talented students who drop out of school may be highly g fted youngsters who become unmotivated because conventional schooling does not complement their learning style characteristics of often requiring sound, soft illumination, an informal design, late morning, afternoon, or evening hours, and the option to work in their own way (self-structured) with many breaks while learning (Gadwa & Griggs, 1985; Dunn & Griggs, (1988). On the other hand, although nongifted underachievers may have the same characteristics, poorly achieving globals, *and* poorly achieving analytics appear to have another element of learning style in common; they both either tend to be tactual/kinesthetic learners with no auditory or visual strengths or often are tactual/auditory preferents with visual deficits. Sometimes, however, such youngsters also have no perceptual strengths. The gifted, in contrast, often have several perceptual strengths, although highly achieving students may have only one or two perceptual strengths; when that occurs, they invariably are either highly motivated or learn easily by either listening to the teacher or by reading.

Despite these differences, both the high school dropout and the poorly achieving elementary students begin to achieve well academically when they are permitted to learn through whatever happens to be their individual learning style strengths rather than through the teacher's preferred instructional style (Gadwa & Griggs, 1985; Dunn & Griggs, 1988).

Learning Style and Instructional Environment Match in Gifted Learners. The large amount of empirical data presented above provides convincing evidence that (1) the learning style of gifted and nongifted children are both distinct and empirically distinguishable, (2) that matching of individual learning style and instructional environment results in higher academic achievement and improved attitudes toward school in many groups of children who vary in age and intelligence level, and (3) that mismatching produces opposite, highly undesirable results. Is the matching of learning style and instructional environment equally important for gifted and nongifted children? Perhaps gifted children do not derive as much benefit from the matching or suffer similarly severe consequences of mismatching. When the styles of the gifted and nongifted were matched and mismatched, for learning alone and learning with peers (Perrin, 1984, 1985), each child in both the gifted and nongifted groups achieved at a significantly higher level. Debello (1985) reported that eighth graders assigned to classes based on their sociological preference for either Learning Alone, with Peers, or with the Teacher, demonstrated significantly higher achievement and attitudes scores when matched than when they were mismatched. And two years later, Miles (1987) reported identical results for career awareness achievement and career decision-making skills for fifth and sixth graders. On the basis of these data it is reasonable to conclude that both gifted and nongifted children benefit at least equally when permitted to learn with procedures that are congruent with, rather than dissonant from, their unique learning style characteristics.

INDIVIDUALIZING INSTRUCTION FOR MAINSTREAMED GIFTED CHILDREN: CONTRACT ACTIVITY PACKAGES (CAPS)

Teachers *want* to individualize instruction but often lack the knowledge and skills for effectively providing approaches that complement their students' diversified strengths. In the previous sections we have presented evidence designed to demonstrate that learning style is a critical determinant of academic achievement and attitude toward school. In this section we will suggest that individualized instruction, in general, and the use of Contract Activity Packages, in particular, is one of the most useful approaches and set of materials available today to help teachers meet the needs of mainstreamed gifted children.

Contract Activity Packages (CAPS) are self-contained units that teach a specific topic or theme (Carbo, Dunn & Dunn, 1986; Dunn, Bruno & Gardiner, 1984; Dunn & Dunn, 1987; Gardiner, 1982). A CAP generally consists of six component parts. Each part is designed to serve a specific purpose. We will first list the six parts and define each briefly. The list will be followed by a more detailed description of each of the six CAP components.

1. **Objectives** describe what must be learned.
2. **Resource Alternatives** provide different ways of learning the informa-

tion enumerated in the objectives. Students may choose from among books and pamphlets, films, filmstrips, records, tapes, tactual/kinesthetic resources, and/or student-developed resources.

3. **Small-Group Techniques** introduce and/or reinforce new and difficult information and permits the expansion of individuals' higher-level cognitive skills.

4. **Activity Alternatives** permit creative acquisition and application of the newly learned material; that usage causes retention.

5. **Reporting Alternatives** provide opportunities for instructional interaction and sharing among students.

6. **Pre- and Post-Assessments** permit students to bypass selected objectives by demonstrating prior knowledge; they also verify mastery.

Objectives

Each CAP includes specific objectives which can be mandated for students who perform better under structure while simultaneously providing options for those learners, and there are many among the gifted, who blossom when permitted choices and prefer to create their own structure rather than to conform to that imposed by others. Objectives should be written to the student and clearly specify what must be mastered.

SAMPLE OBJECTIVES[1]

- List the parts of the human digestive system.
- Explain the function of each part.
- List the principal digestive enzymes.
- Identify where each enzyme is produced, the kinds of foods they act on, and end products of the breakdown.

Students may be required to demonstrate mastery of each objective, but it is a good strategy to itemize more objectives than would be assigned normally and then to permit some choice. Thus, a twelve-objective CAP might include nine required, but two optional objectives; students would have the privilege of omitting one objective entirely.

Students may demonstrate mastery of their required and selected objectives by applying their newly gained knowledge through a creative activity that capitalizes on their individual perceptual strength or

---

[1]The Contract Activity Package and Programmed Learning Sequence samples in this chapter were extracted from one designed by Victor Spetalnick, Assistant Principal, Wingate High School, Brooklyn, New York.

preference. Thus, because gifted youngsters often have two or more perceptual strengths (which tend to include visual or auditory), each might choose the Activity Alternative of most personal interest. Making something original, which includes applying their knowledge, reinforces what students have been exposed to and contributes substantially to long-term retention.

Sample Activity Alternatives
1. Draw a diagram of the human digestive system and label each of its parts.
2. You have just eaten a hamburger with lettuce and lots of cheese. Trace the pathway of the food through your digestive system on either an overhead transparency or a papier mache or clay model.
3. Write a rhyming poem naming each of the parts of your digestive system.

Each Activity Alternative has a related Reporting Alternative through which students share, with between one and three classmates, the original Activity Alternative they developed. Although gifted students prefer to *learn* alone, that does not preclude their willingness to share creative products with others. That sharing provides an additional reinforcement of the information for both the youngster who made the finished product and the ones who examine it.

Sample Reporting Alternatives

1. Show your diagram to two classmates and have each initial it to verify its accuracy.

2. Project your transparency on the overhead projector and ask someone working on this same CAP to check your information and to initial the acetate if it is 100% correct. If there are errors, correct them before you share this with your teacher, but have another student initial it before the teacher sees it.

3. Read your poem to a friend, answer any questions that may arise, have it initialed to indicate accuracy of information, and then submit it to your teacher.

As positioning on this page indicates, the Activity Alternatives are typed/printed on the left side of the page in a column. The Reporting Alternatives appear on the right side of the page counter-balancing its related activity alternative. The objective is written at the top of each page across both columns. Thus, a CAP might look like this:

Sample CAP Page

Objective: List the parts of the human digestive system

Activity Alternatives	*Reporting Alternatives*
1. Draw a diagram of the human digestive system and list each of its parts.	1. Mount your diagram on the the bulletin board. Have a classmate initial it to indicate that it is correct.
2. You have just eaten a hamburger with lettuce and lots of cheese. Trace the pathway of the food through your digestive system on either an overhead transparency or a papier mache or clay model.	2. Display your transparency or model for at least two classmates and ask both to initial your work to show they believe it is accurate.
3. Write a rhyming poem naming each of the parts of your digestive system.	3. Mount your poem on the bulletin board. Have a friend check its accuracy and write a sentence commenting on the information.

The objectives tell the student what must be learned; the *Resource Alternatives* indicate how it may be learned. Thus, the Resource Alternatives provide a choice of multisensory sources of information through which the objectives can be mastered by youngsters working either alone, in pairs, or in a small group.

Sample Resource Alternatives[2]

Books

Asimov, Isaac. A Guide to Nutrition In Space. New York: Doubleday, 1985.
Shear and Lehman. Living A Better, Longer Life. San Jose, California, 1987.

---

[2]Actual CAP would have extended list.

Films

Your Body, Your Mind, Your Life. Metropolitan Health Series. Washington, D.C.:
    United States Institute of Science, 1987, Series 1, Part 7.
Digesting Your Way To Good Health. Metropolitan Health Series. Washington,
    D.C.: United States Institute of Science, 1985, Series 2, Part 4.

Filmstrips

Danny Digestions Does It Again!
Do You Understand Your Digestive System?

Pamphlets

Recordings and Tapes

Student-Developed Resources

Tactual/Kinesthetic Games: Flip Chute on The Digestive System;
Pick-A–Hole on The Digestive System; Electroboard on The Digestive
System; Learning Circle on The Digestive System. For a detailed description of each of the tactual/kinesthetic games that is cited above as a
possible student-developed resource, including explicit directions on
how each is prepared, see Chapter 7 in Carbo, Dunn, & Dunn (1986).
    Small Group Techniques. At least three small-group techniques are
included in each CAP. A Team Learning is used to introduce new
material; one or more Circles of Knowledge reinforce what the Team
Learning has introduced. Case Studies and Group Analysis provide
opportunities to engage in many higher-level cognitive skills. Brainstorming provides opportunities for impulsive youngsters to think off-
the-top-of-their-heads without being chastised and provides a group
situation for problem solving. Each of these instructional strategies is an
excellent alternative to lectures. For explicit descriptions of each small
group technique, see Dunn & Dunn (1978), Chapter 3, or the Teacher
In-service Package on Alternatives to Lecture from the Center for the
Study of Learning and Teaching Styles, St. John's University, New York.
That Center also publishes a Teacher In-service Package so that teachers
can learn how to create CAPS through *their* learning styles.

Pre and Posttest

As the name implies, this test assesses the student's knowledge of the
assigned or selected objectives both before they are prescribed and after
they have been studied.

We conclude this section with a final note about making Contract Activity Packages (CAPS) attractive to students. Children, especially those characterized by a predominantly global learning style, are drawn to illustrations, anecdotes, humor, symbols, and getting a general idea of a topic before needing to concentrate on the facts. Thus, add pictures and drawings to the CAP to capture students' attention. If you can think of puns or clever jokes related to the theme, insert them onto the pages in odd shapes, such as triangles, circles, or trapezpoids, and unusual forms, such as the center of a star, a car, a banana, or anything that will attract. Use color and thematic figures, like Pinnochio, or a famous sports star, to wave the objectives through the CAP. Victor Spetalnick, who designed this CAP on the digestive system, used many such eye-catchers. For example, his cover for the CAP, although busy, is certain to catch the attention of young people who often believe that the digestive system is "dry."

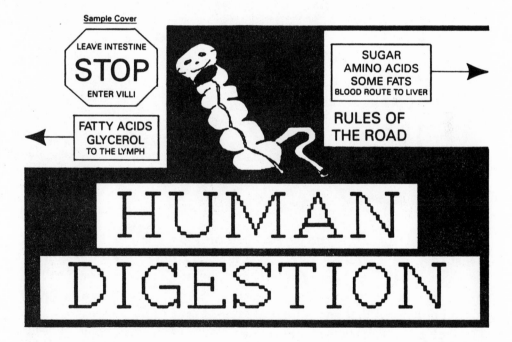

These "jokes" may not seem very funny to professional adults, but many students delight in them and quickly begin developing their own to add to the writing they do for the CAP Activity Alternatives. Youngsters share their cartoons and jokes and the added interest that results entices many global children into learning. Many analytics enjoy the related humor too, but global children *need* it to trigger their concentration and to help them memorize facts.

Mr. Spetalnick also used cartoon-like illustrations in the Small-Group techniques within his CAP. Thus, in the section of Team Learning which explained:

HYDROCHLORIC ACID MAINTAINS THE PROPER
pH (SOLUTION) FOR DIGESTION OF PROTEINS.

He also added the attached.

All students concentrate better when they are interested in and enjoy what they are learning, but gifted youngsters quickly develop skills for emulating their teachers' creativity and, before long, their own submitted assignments begin to sparkle with lively art, humor, and a special brand of delight that few youngsters reflect on a daily basis.

Finally, elementary-age gifted students should be encouraged to design some of their own Objectives, Activity, and Reporting Alternatives and Resource Alternatives. In particular, they should try to develop the tactual flip chutes, electroboards, task cards and Pick-A–Holes through which they will apply new information. If well done, those resources can be used to introduce tactual students to the same unit at a later date.

Older and more sophisticated gifted students can and should design entire CAPs as a motivational and instructional strategy for learning how to teach themselves.

Summary and Conclusions

Because they tend to be highly motivated, independent, persistent, internally controlled, capable of providing their own structure, perceptually strong, and enjoy learning by themselves or with other gifted peers, individualized instruction, in general, and Contract Activity Packages, in particular, correspond well to the learning styles of many gifted youngsters. Both global and analytic Activity and Reporting Alternatives should be offered and individuals should be encouraged to choose between them wisely based on their identified learning styles. Learners should be permitted to work away from class members to obtain the quiet they may need or to use earphones for music as they prefer. Seating in either well-illuminated or dimly-lit areas should be optional, as would be sitting at one's desk or in a less formal section of the environment. Certainly, sweaters or jackets should be permitted for those who require warmth and their opposites might wear lighter clothing.

This instructional approach will increase motivation, for it responds to the characteristics of gifted youngsters—it provides degrees of freedom, options, quickly-paced mastery for those who are able, sociological and environmental choices, and structure for those youngsters who require it. This method may be used at any time of the day, and students may move while they work or remain passive in the confines of the area each has selected.

Gifted children using this approach can achieve at their own pace in a mainstreamed classroom where some advance more or less rapidly than others. CAPs also permits each learner to select his/her own objectives, resources, and activities and move on to the next unit as soon as the previous unit's requirements have been mastered. The process of individualized learning increases involvement, reduces boredom, and leads to greater enthusiasm and better retention. The Reporting Alternatives and Small-Group techniques prevent total isolation, but teachers must remember that many of the gifted often need quiet and a lack of distraction, perhaps because of their strong task commitment or need to complete whatever they begin. In addition, contrary to popular misconception, the majority of these highly achieving students learn better by themselves than they do in either large- or small-group instruction (Price, Dunn, Dunn, & Griggs, 1981).

The advantages of a system in which gifted children are totally integrated with their peers not identified as gifted, on the one hand, and yet receive the special education required by their exceptional abilities, on the other, over systems in which gifted pupils are separated from their agemates for periods of time ranging from a few hours to the whole school week, are obvious. Nevertheless, unfortunately, it is probably the system least used to provide special education for the gifted throughout the world.

By responding to learning style differences as suggested in this chapter, and by experimenting with a CAP system for gifted youngsters, teachers will have made a breakthrough toward maximizing the potential and innate talents of individuals. Our superior learners no longer will be restricted to group pacing. Instead, they will advance as quickly as their interests, ability, and motivation permit. In addition, the CAP system is so organized and well-designed that the clarity of objectives, repetition through diversified means, and opportunities to learn in their own style in accordance with their individual strengths make this an effective instructional tool for use with the very special children in our classes, children whose minds are restricted only by the boundaries schools and society artificially create for them.

REFERENCES

Burton, E. (1980). An analysis of the interaction of field independence/field dependence and word type as they affect word recognition among kindergarteners. *Doctoral dissertation*, St. John's University, NY.

Brennan, P.K. (1982). Teaching to the whole brain. In *Student learning styles and brain behavior*. Reston, Virginia; National Association of Secondary School Principals, 212–213.

Bruno, J. (1988). An experimental investigation of the relationships between and among hemispheric processing, learning style preferences, instructional strategies, academic achievement, and attitudes of developmental mathematics students in an urban technical college. Doctoral dissertation, St. John's University, NY.

Carbo, M. (1981). *Reading Style Inventory*, Englewood Cliffs, NJ: Prentice-Hall.

Carbo, M., Dunn, R. and Dunn, K. (1986). *Teaching students to read through their individual learning styles*. Englewood Cliffs, NJ: Prentice-Hall.

Carruthers, S.A. & Young, L.A. (1980). Preference of condition concerning time in learning environments of rural versus city eighth grade students. *Learning Styles Network Newsletter*, 1(2), 1.

Center for the Study of Learning and Teaching Styles, St. John's University, Utopia Parkway, Jamaica, NY: 11439.

Clay, J.E. (1984). A correlational analysis of the learning characteristics of highly achieving and poorly achieving freshmen at A&M University as revealed through performance on standardized tests. Doctoral Dissertation Normal, Alabama: A&M University.

Cody, C. (1983). Learning styles, including hemispheric dominance: A comparative study of average, gifted and highly gifted students in grades five through twelve. Doctoral dissertation, Temple University. *Dissertation Abstracts International, 44,* 1631-6A.

Cross, Jr., J.A. (1982). Internal locus of control governs talented students (9–12). *Learning Styles Network Newsletter, 3*(3), 3.

Curry, L. (1987). *Integrating concepts of cognitive or learning styles: A review with attention to psychometric standards.* Ottowa, Ontario: Canadian College of Health Services Executives.

Dean, W.L. (1982). A comparison of the learning styles of educable mentally retarded students and learning disabled students. *Doctoral dissertation,* The University of Mississippi.

DeBello, T. (1985). A critical analysis of the achievement and attitude effects of administrative assignments to social studies writing instruction based on identified, eighth grade students' learning style preferences for learning alone, with peers, or with teachers. Doctoral dissertation, St. John's University, NY. *Dissertation Abstracts International, 47,* 68-01A.

DeGregoris, C.N. (1986). The effects on reading comprehension of the interaction of individual sound preferences and auditory distractions which vary in intensity and kind. Doctoral dissertation, Hofstra University.

DellaValle, J. (1984). An experimental investigation of the relationship(s) between preference for mobility and the word recognition scores of seventh grade students to provide supervisory and administrative guidelines for the organization of effective instructional environments. Doctoral dissertation, St. John's University, NY. *Dissertation Abstracts International, 45,* 359-02A. Recipient: Phi Delta Kappa National Award for Outstanding Doctoral Research 1984; National Association of Secondary School Principals' Middle School Research Finalist Citation 1984, and Association for Supervision and Curriculum Development Finalist for Best National Research (Supervision), 1984.

Douglas, D.B. (1979). Making biology easier to understand. *The American Biology Teacher, 41*(5), 277–299.

Dunn, R. (1984) How should students do their homework?: Research versus opinion. *Early Years, 15,* 43–45.

Dunn, R. (1985). A research-based plan for doing homework. *The Education Digest, L*(9), 40–41.

Dunn, R. (1986). Learning styles: Link between individual differences and effective instruction. *In Education For the Future: Towards Effectiveness and Beyond.* North Carolina: Association for Supervision and Curriculum Development, 2(2), 3–33.

Dunn, R. (1987). Research in instructional environments: Implications for student achievement and attitudes. *Professional School Psychology, 2,* 43–52.

Dunn, R., Bruno, A. and Gardiner, B. (1984). Put a CAP on your gifted program. *Gifted Child Quarterly, 28,* 70–72.

Dunn, R. & Carbo, M. (1981). Modalities: An open letter to Walter Barbe, Michael Milone and Raymond Swassing. *Educational Leadership, 38,* 381–382.

Dunn, R., Cavanaugh, D., Eberle, B. and Zenhausern, R. (1982). Hemispheric preference: The newest element of learning style. *The American Biology Teacher, 44,* 291–294.

Dunn, R., DeBello, T., Brennan, P. and Murrain, P. (1981). Learning style researchers define differences differently. *Educational Leadership, 38,* 372–375.

Dunn, R., and Dunn, K. (1972). *Practical approaches to individualizing instruction: Contracts and other effective teaching strategies.* Parker Publishing Co. Division of Prentice-Hall.

Dunn, R. & Dunn, K. (1977). *Learning Style Questionnaire,* Englewood Cliffs, NJ: Prentice-Hall.

Dunn, R. and Dunn, K. (1978). *Teaching students through their individual learning styles: A practical approach.* Reston, VA: Reston Publishing Co.

Dunn, R., Dunn, K. and Freeley, M.E. (1984). Practical applications of the research: Responding to students' learning styles—step one. *Illinois State Research and Development Journal,* 1–21.

Dunn, R. and Griggs, S.A. (1988). *Learning styles: The quiet revolution in American secondary schools.* Reston, Virginia: National Association of Secondary School Principals.

Dunn, R., Krimnsky, J., Murray, J. and Quinn, P. (1985). Light up their lives: A review of research on the effects of lighting on children's achievement. *The Reading Teacher,* 863–869.

Dunn, R., Dunn, K. and Price, G. *Learning style inventory.* Lawrence, KA: Price Systems, 1975, 1978, 1979, 1981, 1984. (Available, Box 3067, Lawrence, KA. 66044).

Dunn, R., Dunn, K. and Price, G.E. (1977). Diagnosing learning styles: A prescription for avoiding malpractice suits against school systems. *Phi Delta Kappa, 58,* 418–420.

Dunn, R., Dunn, K. and Price, G. *Productivity environmental preference survey.* Lawrence. KA: Price Systems. 1979, 1981. (Available. Box 3067, Lawrence, KA. 66044).

Dunn, R. and Price, G.E. (1980). The learning style characteristics of gifted children. *Gifted Child Quarterly. 24,* 33–36.

Freeley, M.E. (1984). An experimental investigation of the relationships among teachers' individual time preferences, inservice workshop schedules and instructional techniques and the subsequent implementation of learning style strategies in participants' classrooms. Doctoral dissertation, St. John's University, NY. *Dissertation Abstracts International, 46,* 403-021.

Gadwa, K. and Griggs, S.A. (1985). The school dropout: Implications for counselors. *The School Counselor, 33,* 9–17.

Gardiner, B. (1982). These thinking CAPs are for real. *Early Years, 12,* 39–40.

Griggs, S.A. (1985). *Counseling students through their individual learning styles.* Ann Arbor, Michigan: ERIC Counseling and Personnel Services Clearinghouse. Available through Center for the Study of Learning and Teaching Styles, St. John's University, NY.

Griggs, S.A. and Dunn, R. (1984). Selected case studies of the *Gifted Child Quarterly, 28,* 115–119.

Griggs, S.A. and Price, G.E. (1980). Learning styles of the gifted versus average junior high school students. *Kappan, 62,* 604.

Hodges, H. (1982). Madison prep. Alternatives through learning styles. In *Student Learning Styles and Brain Behavior.* Reston, VA: National Association of Secondary School Principals, 28–32.

Hodges, H. (1985). An analysis of the relationships among preferences for a formal/informal design, one element of learning style, academic achievement and attitudes of seventh and eighth grade students in remedial mathematics classes in a New York City junior high school. Doctoral dissertation, St. John's University, New York. *Dissertation Abstracts International, 45,* 2791A. Recipient: Phi Delta Kappa National Finalist for Outstanding Doctoral Research, 1986.

Hunt, D.E. (1979). Learning style and student needs: An introduction to conceptual level. In *Student Learning Styles and Brain Behavior.* Reston, VA: National Association of Secondary School Principals, 27–38.

Jarsonbeck, S. (1984). The effects of a right-brain and mathematics curriculum on low achieving, fourth grade students. Doctoral dissertation, University of South Florida. *Dissertation Abstracts International, 45* 2791A.

Johnson, C.D. (1984). Identifying potential school dropouts. Doctoral Dissertation, United States International University.

Kaley, S.B. (1977). Field dependence/independence and learning styles in sixth graders. Doctoral dissertation, Hofstra University, NY.

Kaufman, A. and Kaufman, N. (1983). *Mental Measurement Yearbook, 9,* Circle Pines, Minnesota: American Guidance Service Publishers' Building.

Keefe, J.W. (1979). Learning Style: An overview. In *Student Learning Styles: Diagnosing and prescribing programs.* Reston, VA: National Association of Secondary School Principals, 1–18.

Keefe, J.W. (1982). Assessing student learning styles: An overview. In *Student learning styles and brain behavior.* Reston, VA: National Association of Secondary School Principals, 42–53.

Kirby, P. (1979). *Cognitive style, learning style and transfer skill acquisition.* Columbus, Ohio: The Ohio State University's National Center for Research in Vocational Education.

Kreitner, K.R. (1981). Modality strengths and learning styles of musically talented high school students. Master's dissertation, Ohio State University.

Krimsky, J. (1982). A comparative analysis of the effects of matching and mismatching fourth grade students with their learning style preference for the environmental element of light and their subsequent reading speed and accuracy scores. Doctoral dissertation, St. John's University, NY. *Dissertation Abstracts International, 43,* 66-01A. Recipient: Association for Supervision and Curriculum Development,

First Alternate National Recognition For Best Doctoral Research (Curriculum), 1982.

Kroon, D. (1985). An experimental investigation of the effects on academic achievement and the resultant administrative implications of instruction congruent and incongruent with secondary, industrial arts students' learning style perceptual preferences. Doctoral dissertation, St. John's University, NY. *Dissertation Abstracts International, 46,* 3247A.

Lemmon, P. (1985). A school where learning styles make a difference. *Principal,* Reston, VA: National Elementary Principals' Association, *64,* 26–29.

Lynch, P.K. (1981). An analysis of the relationships among academic achievement, attendance and the learning style time preferences of eleventh and twelfth grade students identified as initial or chronic truants in a suburban New York school district. Doctoral dissertation, St. John's University, NY. *Dissertation Abstracts International, 42,* 1880A. Recipient: Association for Supervision & Curriculum Development. National Recognition for Best Doctoral Research (Supervision), 1981.

Lyne, N.A. (1979). The relationship between adult students' level of cognitive development and their preference for learning format. *Doctoral dissertation,* University of Maryland.

MacMurren, H. (1985). A comparative study of the effects of matching and mismatching sixth-grade students with their learning style preferences for the physical element of intake and their subsequent reading speed and accuracy scores and attitudes. Doctoral dissertation, St. John's University, NY. *Dissertation Abstracts International, 46,* 3247A.

Martini, M. (1986). An analysis of the relationships between and among computer-assisted instruction, learning style perceptual preferences, attitudes and the science achievement of seventh grade students in a suburban, New York school district. Doctoral dissertation, St. John's University, NY. *Dissertation Abstracts International, 47,* 877-03A.

Miles, B. (1987). An investigation of the relationships among the learning style sociological preferences of fifth and sixth grade students, selected interactive classroom patterns, and achievement in career awareness and career decision-making concepts. Doctoral dissertation, St. John's University, NY.

Morgan, H.L. (1981). Learning styles: The relation between need for structure and preferred mode of instruction for gifted elementary students. Doctoral dissertation, University of Pittsburgh.

Murrain, P.G. (1983). Administrative determinations concerning facilities utilization and instructional grouping: An analysis of the relationship(s) between selected thermal environments and preferences for temperature, an element of learning style, as they affect word recognition scores of secondary students. Doctoral dissertation, St. John's University, NY. 1749-06A.

Murray, C.A. (1980). The comparison of learning styles between low and high reading achievement subjects in the seventh and eigth grades in a public middle school. Doctoral dissertation, United States International University.

Pederson, J.K. (1984). The classification and comparison of learning style preferences of learning disabled students and gifted students. Doctoral dissertation, Texas Tech University, 1984. *Dissertation Abstracts International, 45,* DA 842799.

Perrin, J. (1982). *Learning style inventory: Primary version.* Obtainable through the Center for the Study of Learning and Teaching Styles, St. John's University, Grand Central and Utopia Parkway, Jamaica, New York 11439.

Perrin, J. (1984). An experimental investigation of the relationships among the learning style sociological preferences of gifted and non-gifted primary children, selected instructional strategies, attitudes and achievement in problem solving and rote memorization. Doctoral dissertation, St. John's University, NY. *Dissertation Abstracts International, 46,* 342-02A. Recipient: American Association of Administrators (AASA) National Research Finalist, 1984.

Perrin, J. (1985). Preferred learning styles make a difference. *The School Administrator, 42* 16.

Pizzo, J. .(1981). An investigation of the relationships between selected acoustic environments and sound, an element of learning style, as they affect sixth grade students' reading achievement and attitudes. Doctoral dissertation, St. John's University, NY. *Dissertation Abstracts International, 42,* 2475A. Recipient: Association for Supervision and Curriculum Development First Alternate National Recognition for Best Doctoral Research (Curriculum), 1981.

Price, G. (1980). Which learning style elements are stable and which tend to change? *Learning Styles Network Newsletter, 1(3),* 1.

Price, G.E., Dunn, K., Dunn, R. and Griggs, S.A. (1981). Studies in students' learning styles. *Roeper Review, 4* 223–226.

Restak, R. (1979). *The brain: The last frontier.* Garden City, NY: Doubleday.

Ricca, J. (1983). Curricular implications of learning style differences between gifted and non-gifted students. Doctoral dissertation, State University of New York at Buffalo.

Ricca, J. (1984). Learning styles and preferred instructional strategies of gifted students. *Gifted Child Quarterly, 28* 121–126.

Shea, T.C. (1983). An investigation of the relationship among preferences for the learning style element of design, selected instructional environments and reading achievement with ninth grade students to improve administrative determinations concerning effective educational facilities. Doctoral dissertation, St. John's University, NY. *Dissertation Abstracts International, 44,* 2004-07A Recipient: National Association of Secondary School Principals' Middle School Research Finalist Citation, 1984.

Sinatra, R., Primavera, L., and Waked, W. (1986). Learning style and intelligence of reading disabled students. *Perceptual and Motor Skills 63,* 1243–1250.

Stewart, E.D. (1981). Learning styles among gifted/talented students: Instructional technique preferences. *Exceptional Children, 48,* 113–138.

School dropouts: A study and final report (1983), Lynwood, Washington: Edmonds School District.

Tanenbaum, R. (1982). An investigation of the relationships between selected instructional techniques and identified field dependent and field independent cognitive styles as evidenced among high school students enrolled in studies of nutrition. Doctoral dissertation, St. John's University, NY. *Dissertation Abstracts International, 43,* 68-01A.

Tappenden, V.J. (1983). Analysis of the learning styles of vocational education and nonvocational education students in eleventh and twelfth grades from rural, urban and suburban locations in Ohio. Doctoral dissertation, Kent State University.

Teacher Inservice Package (TIP). On Contract Activity Packages (CAPs). Available from the Center for the Study of Learning and Teaching Styles, St. John's University, Utopia Parkway, Jamaica, New York 11439, $95.00. Sample CAPs at primary, elementary, intermediate and senior high school levels available in diversified subject matter disciplines. Send for free brochure.

Teacher Inservice Packages (TIP). On Alternatives to Lecture. Available from the Center for the Study of Learning and Teaching Styles, St. John's University Utopia Parkway, Jamaica, New York 11439 ($65.00).

Thies, A. (1979). A brain-behavior analysis of learning style. In *Student learning styles: Diagnosing and prescribing programs.* Reston VA: National Association of Secondary School Principals, 55061.

Trautman, P. (1979). An investigation of the relationship between selected industrial techniques and identified cognitive style. Doctoral dissertation, St. John's University, NY. *Dissertation Abstracts International, 40,* 1428A.

Urbschat, K. (1977). A study of preferred learning modes and their relationship to the amount of recall of CVC trigrams. Doctoral dissertation, Wayne State University. *Dissertation Abstracts International, 38,* 2536-5A.

Vignia, R.A. (1983). An investigation of learning styles of gifted and non-gifted high school students. Doctoral dissertation, University of Houston.

Virostko, J. (1983). An analysis of the relationships among academic achievement in mathematics and reading, assigned instructional schedules, and the learning style time preferences of third, fourth, fifth and sixth grade students. Doctoral dissertation, St. John's University, NY. *Dissertation Abstracts International, 44,* 1683-06A. Recipient: Kappa Delta Pi International Award for Best Doctoral Research, 1983.

Wasson, F. (1980). A comparative analysis of learning styles and personality characteristics of achieving and underachieving gifted elementary students. Doctoral dissertation, Florida State University.

Weinberg, F. (1983). An experimental investigation of the interaction between sensory modality preference and mode of presentation in the instruction of arithmetic concepts to third grade underachievers. Doctoral dissertation, St. John's University, NY. *Dissertation Abstracts International, 44,* 1740-06A.

Wheeler, R. (1980). An alternative to failure: Teaching reading according to students' perceptual strengths. *Kappa Delta Pi Record, 17,* 59–63.

Wheeler, R. (1983). An investigation of the degree of academic achievement evidenced when second grade, learning disabled students' perceptual preferences are matched and mismatched with complementary sensory approaches to beginning reading instruction. Doctoral dissertation, St. John's University, NY. *Dissertation Abstracts International, 44,* 2039-07A.

White, R. (1980). An investigation of the relationship between selected instructional methods and selected elements of emotional learning style upon student achievement in seventh grade social studies. Doctoral dissertation, St. John's University, NY. *Dissertation Abstracts International, 42,* 995-03A.

White, R.T., Dunn, R. and Zenhausern, R. (1982). An investigation of responsible vs. less responsible students. *Illinois School Research and Development Journal, 191,* 18–25.

Wittig, C. (1985). Learning style preferences among students high or low on divergent thinking and feeling variables. Masters dissertation, State University College of Buffalo, New York (Center for Studies in Creativity).

Zenhausern, R., Dunn, R., Barreto, A.R., Bacilious, Z., Gemake, J., Griggs, S.A., Saunders, W., Schwartz, V., Spiridakis, J. and Swanchak, J. (1984). How brainy are you about the brain? *Early Years, 15,* 46–48.

Chapter 4

TEACHING GIFTED CHILDREN
FOR CREATIVE GROWTH

GARY A. DAVIS AND MARGARET A. THOMAS

Most people—students, teachers, and many others—are not necessarily unable to think creatively, they simply are not oriented toward thinking creatively. They do not think about being creative, make no effort to think creatively, and are not creativity conscious. By contrast, people who are creatively productive are quite aware of their creative tendencies, and make deliberate efforts to think in creative and innovative ways: "Today, I'm going to think creatively and do some creative work!"

One of the most common questions about creativity is "Can creativity be taught, or are you born with it?" The answer is "yes" and "yes." Realistically, no amount of creativity training will transform an average person into a Michelangelo or Thomas Edison. A few gifted people seem to be born with a special combination of creative genius, extraordinary drive, and a sense of destiny that leads them to dream and implement those creations that make the world a better place. However, it is probably also true that everyone's personal creativeness can be increased above its present level. Your authors have seen children, adolescents, adults, and even elderly persons in retirement homes discover that with interest and effort, they can indeed think more creatively and, to their great enjoyment, they can do creative things.

In the classroom, efforts to teach creative thinking take many forms. We see students brainstorming improvements for bicycles, listing uses for old tires, doing blind walks in creative dramatics, listening to descriptions of the attitudes and lives of Albert Einstein and Marie Curie, writing poetry, solving puzzles, researching planets and lizards, writing skits and plays, creating classroom newspapers, and even thinking of ways to get a hippotamus out of a bathtub. The remainder of this article

113

will outline what to teach when we try to foster creative growth, with an emphasis on the why and how.

The following four guiding principles offer worthwhile substance and method for teaching for creative growth at both the elementary and secondary level.

1. Develop a creative classroom atmosphere.
2. Teach learners to understand the topic of creativity, in general, and the process of creative problem-solving, in particular.
3. Teach creative thinking techniques, the same ones used deliberately and successfully by creative adults.
4. Involve students in activities that require creative thinking.

Everything you ever wanted to know about teaching for creative development is right there in those four principles. We will look at them one by one.

Before discussing the four principles cited above, one caveat is in order. This chapter is not meant to stand alone. All learners will benefit to some degree from learning in a creative classroom atmosphere. Learners will not benefit, however, from "creativity training" that is merely the enhancement of ideational fluency ability. In order to be of value, teaching creative thinking and providing practice in the process of generating multiple solutions to problems must be clearly embedded in the real-world school context. The focus of the current volume is teaching gifted and talented learners in regular classrooms. In this context, teaching for creative growth means using the knowledge, strategies, and techniques suggested in the following pages as tools in differentiating and individualizing curriculum content and process for gifted children.

I. DEVELOPING A CREATIVE CLASSROOM ATMOSPHERE

The most important aspect of becoming more creative is acquiring creative attitudes and developing a creativity consciousness. Creative attitudes and predispositions develop in a creative atmosphere. A creative atmosphere is one in which creativity is encouraged and rewarded. The late Carl Rogers called it *psychological safety* and cited creative atmosphere as a prerequisite for creative thinking (1962). In brainstorming it is called *deferred judgment*, the noncritical, nonevaluative atmosphere where fresh and even wild ideas may be safely proposed. A creative atmosphere is essential for nurturing creative growth in children.

Fortunately, it is possible to teach creative attitudes and consciousness in the classroom. They will be a natural by-product of a creative classroom atmosphere. Such an atmosphere would be characterized by efforts to teach for creative thinking, with emphasis on valuing original ideas, increasing receptiveness to others' ideas, and improving students' understanding of creativity and creative thinking. Moreover, abundant opportunities to practice creative problem-solving will constitute an integral part of the teaching-learning process. In a creative atmosphere students will:

Become more aware of creativity in general
Value flexible and original thinking
Become more receptive to creative (even wild) ideas
Become willing to think in a creative fashion
Become aware of barriers to creativity—habits, traditions, conformity
    pressures
Become motivated to involve themselves in creative activities

More subtle creative attitudes enhanced in a creative atmosphere include problem sensitivity, constructive discontent, and risk-taking. Problem sensitivity, as the name suggests, is a heightened awareness of problems and opportunities. Constructive discontent refers to the attitude that almost anything can be improved for the better (Parnes, 1981). Risk-taking includes a willingness and expectation to sometimes fail. Logically, an innovative person must dare to differ, make changes, stand out, challenge traditions, make waves, and sometimes bend a few rules. Such activities can easily produce embarrassment, humiliation, criticism, and failure. Von Oech (1984) explained that some successful creative people deliberately increase their failure rate as a means of increasing their creative productivity. Quoting IBM president Thomas Watson, "The way to succeed is to double your failure rate!"

Encourage and Reinforce Personality Characteristics of Creative Learners

A number of personality characteristics are common and recurrent among creative people (e.g., Barron & Harrington, 1981; Davis & Bull, 1978), for example:

Independence and confidence
Curiosity and wide interests
Interests in art and other aesthetic areas
A good sense of humor

High energy level and enthusiasm
Adventurousness and risk-taking
Attraction to the mysterious, the complex, the abstract
Need for time alone

Independent of one's innate creative abilities, such affective traits orient one toward thinking and behaving in creative ways much the same as do creative attitudes and creativity consciousness. We do not ordinarily speak of "teaching personality traits." However, there is evidence that many personality characteristics are amenable to modfification based upon experience. Accordingly, we can encourage and reinforce those personality characteristics that we consider desirable in our overall efforts to teach for creative growth. Students can be encouraged to have confidence, try new activities, develop new interest areas, explore art, literature, and theatre, add humor to some projects, and not to worry about an occasional set-back or failure.

We would not, of course, encourage negative traits that are frequently found in creative people, such as stubbornness, resistance to domination, uncooperativeness, capriciousness, sloppiness and disorganization with unimportant matters, and being egocentric, temperamental, demanding, withdrawn, and forgetful (Smith, 1966; Torrance, 1962, 1981). However, do not be surprised if some creative students and acquaintances show such characteristics.

In summary, although it is possible to teach creative attitudes and awareness, it is by no means simple and will certainly not occur automatically. Having established the critical importance of a creative classroom atmosphere, we now examine teaching strategies likely to produce it.

II. TEACHING UNDERSTANDING OF THE TOPIC OF CREATIVITY AND THE PROCESS OF CREATIVE THINKING

In college and other adult creativity courses and workshops, we help people strengthen their creativity consciousness and their creative output by helping them to understand the topic of creativity itself. Research in elementary schools with a new Apple Computer disk, *Creative Thinking and Problem Solving* (Davis, 1985), indicates that children as young as second grade can benefit from instruction in the nature of creativity and creative thinking (Davis, 1985; Davis & Rudmanis, 1986). Some memorable elementary pupils' quotes were, "The disk really got me going about the subject," "I feel more comfortable with creativity," "It (creativity) made more sense," and "I think it broadened my creativity."

The following topics probably are teachable at any level and will help students, and perhaps you, "feel more comfortable" with this mysterious phenomena called creativity:

Characteristics of creative people
Definitions and theories of creativity
The nature of creative ideas (e.g., as idea modifications, idea combinations, metaphorical relationships)
The creative process (e.g., as idea transformations or "changes in perception"; or as stages in creative problem solving)
Techniques of creative thinking
Tests of creativity, including the rationale behind the tests

Personality characteristics that contribute to or detract from creativity may be discussed, along with the reasons such traits help or hinder creative thinking. The notion that creative ideas usually are made up of new combinations of old ideas may be illustrated with consumer products such as calender watches, clock radios, Reese's® Peanut Butter Cups (chocolate + peanut butter), or any of a never-ending stream of new yogurt, soup, ice cream, and chip-dip flavors.

One also may illustrate examples of creative idea combinations that are based in metaphorical thinking. For example, many political cartoons and cartoon strips borrow ideas from movies, children's stories, current events, or historical events. For example, a sketch of Rambo sporting Ronald Reagan's face was entitled "Ronbo"; a cartoon drawing of Russian leader Gorbechev, standing in front of hundreds of missiles, was entitled "Mr. Gorbechev's neighborhood"—"Hi there . . . Can you say friend? . . . I'm your friend . . . Won't you be my friend?" Gordon (1974b) illustrated the role of metaphor in science and invention with a number of examples: Eli Whitney developed his cotton gin after watching a cat trying to catch a chicken through a fence and coming up only with a pawful of feathers; selective breeding of cattle suggested natural selection to Darwin; the jangling lid of his mother's tea kettle inspired Watt's steam engine (see Davis, 1986, and Gordon, 1974b, for more examples of innovation based in metaphorical thinking).

As for the creative process, visual puzzles and optical illusions may be used to illustrate how creativity involves changes in perception and mental transformations. With continued viewing and effort one can perceive new meanings, relationships, combinations, and transformations that were not seen just a moment before. Regarding stages in creativity, the timeless Wallas (1926) stages of preparation, incubation, illumination, and verification help explain a scientific method approach to creative problem solving. However, the Osborn/Parnes creative problem solving (CPS) model, with the five steps of fact-finding, problem-finding (problem defining), idea-finding, solution-finding (idea evaluation), and acceptance-finding (idea implementation), teaches an extraordinarily effective strategy for solving personal, educational or professional problems (see Parnes, 1981; Treffinger, Isaksen, & Firestien, 1982). In their book, *CPS for kids,* Eberle and Stanish (1985) explain how the model can be taught to children.

The computer program cited above, developed by Davis (1985), can help teachers teach creative thinking and problem-solving. A sample of principles of creative thinking and problem-solving that can be taught using the Davis computer disk *Creative Thinking and Problem Solving* includes:

> Creativity is not just for artists, inventors, scientists and writers, it is for everyone. It is for you.
>
> Creativity is a way of thinking and a way of living. It will help you use your ability; it will help you to live a more interesting, successful and enjoyable life.
>
> Creative people are flexible in their thinking. They try to see things from different viewpoints. Rigid people can see only from their own narrow point of view.
>
> Creative people are willing to take a creative risk, make mistakes, and sometimes even fail. The more daring and creative an idea, the more likely it is to flop.
>
> Creative people are aware of conformity pressure, and they are not afraid to be a little different. How can we have creative ideas and inventions if people are afraid to try something new and different?
>
> Creative people define problems broadly in order to open up new solution possibilities. They ask "What is the 'real' problem?" We don't want to "build a better mouse trap," we want to "get rid of mice."
>
> Creative people play with ideas and think of "wild" solutions. Good ideas often begin as wild and crazy ones. ("What should we do today, Wilbur?" "Well, Orville, let's see if we can fly!")
>
> Creative people think of lots of ideas before settling on a problem solution. With more ideas to consider, there is a better chance of finding a good one.
>
> Creative people use techniques to help them find new idea combinations. Techniques can multiply our intuitive idea supply.

Creative people think metaphorically. They borrow and build upon ideas. Could you find ideas for a short story or a play by looking through a history book? Or ideas for creative architecture by considering buildings in ancient Greece, Mexico, the orient, Sweden?

Good problem solvers evaluate their ideas carefully by using criteria and by listing good and bad points of each idea.

Creative people use their talents and abilities, not waste them.

Other exercises on the Davis (1985) disk include thinking of "ideal" or perfect solutions, then working backward from this goal; or imagining how a problem might be solved in the future—25, 100 or 500 years from now.

Teach the Measurement of Creativity

Students are often interested in understanding how creative behavior is assessed. Tests of creativity fall mainly into two categories, divergent thinking tests and personality/biographical inventories. Divergent thinking tests, such as the *Torrance Tests of Creative Thinking* (Torrance, 1966), are fun to take and they can be used to teach students firsthand the meaning of fluency, flexibility, originality, and elaboration.

Personality/biographical inventories, such as the adult *How Do You Think?* (Davis, 1975), the elementary-level *GIFT* (Rimm, 1976), and the secondary *GIFFI* (Davis & Rimm, 1980; Rimm & Davis, 1979) can be used to further explain the relationship between personality and creativity.

III. TEACHING CREATIVE THINKING TECHNIQUES

It is necessary to strengthen underlying creative abilities and skills through practice and exercise. Students at all age levels can learn some creative thinking techniques that are used by creatively productive people.

Techniques and Exercises for Enhancing Creative Thinking

Consciously or unconsciously, all creative people use techniques for finding new ideas. For example, inventors, designers, cartoonists, movie-makers, music composers, architects, clothes designers, and novelists and playwrights use metaphorical thinking. They borrow ideas from work by others or from mythology, history, the Bible, current events, or from other places or times, incorporating the ideas into their own creations.

Virtually all of Shakespeare's plays were metaphorically based upon historical events, mythology, or the poems and plays of others. Aaron Copeland's magnificent *Appalachian Spring* was based upon the Quaker folk tune *Simple Gifts,* while the *Star Spangled Banner* was an English drinking song. Ideas from popular movies and TV shows such as *Rambo, Star Wars,* and *Star Trek* are repeatedly used in political cartoons and cartoon strips.

Some creative thinking techniques, which originally were used unconsciously by creatively productive people, have been made conscious and knowable—and teachable. For example:

> **Brainstorming,** based upon deferred judgment, produces a creative atmosphere, encourages fanciful thinking, teaches receptive attitudes, and teaches the principle of considering many alternatives.
>
> **Attribute listing** includes modifying attributes of a product or process, or else transferring an attribute from one situation to another. Fran Stryker created years of *Lone Ranger* episodes by modifying attributes of characters, goals, obstacles, and outcomes (Shallcross, 1981). Transferring attributes from one situation to another is basically metaphorical thinking.
>
> **Morphological synthesis** amounts to using a matrix to produce new idea combinations. Five potato dishes combine with five kinds of meat and five vegetables to produce 125 dinner combinations.
>
> **Idea checklists,** such as Osborn's (1963) "modify, magnify, minify, substitute, rearrange, reverse, etc." suggest (almost involuntarily) innovative new idea combinations.

There also are a group of *synectics* methods (Gordon, 1961; Gordon & Poze, 1980):

> **Direct analogy** is finding metaphorically related ideas, usually from nature. How can we design a creative parking lot? With a synectics approach we ask how bees, squirrels, sunflowers, etc., store things.
>
> **Personal analogy** is finding new viewpoints by becoming part of the problem. What would you be like if you were a truly exciting educational experience for children?
>
> **Fantasy analogy** is using one's wildest imagination to help stimulate creative solutions? How can we make a new community swimming pool build and pay for itself?

Two excellent sources for *metaphorical thinking* exercises are Gordon's (1974a) *Making it Strange* workbooks and Stanish's (1977) *Sunflowering.* As a few examples:

Why is a calendar like a mirror?

How is a jar of paste like a school bell?

What animal is like a bass fiddle? Why?

Which is heaviest, a boulder or a sad heart? Why?

If you were a pencil, how would it feel to get sharpened? To get chewed on? To get worn down to a stub?

In what ways can noise be seen?

What could have given a cave dweller the idea for a spear? What was the connection?

If a classroom were a lawn, what would the weeds be? How do the weeds affect the rest of the class?

There also are such forced combination procedures as the fish-bowl, dictionary, and Yellow Pages techniques, all of which can stimulate ideas and idea combinations for many kinds of problems. For example, free-associating to the word *shrink,* found by flipping through a dictionary, led a Colorado greeting card company to their *Wee Greetings,* a line of greeting cards the size of business cards. *Enlarge* led to cards containing balloons and confetti (Smith, 1985).

Strengthening Creative Abilities

Many creativity exercise books seek to strengthen creative abilities in the same way we strengthen other cognitive or psychomotor abilities—through practice and exercise. Some abilities that seem to make important contributions to creative thinking are:

Ideational Fluency	Problem sensitivity
Flexibility	Problem clarification
Originality	Metaphorical thinking
Elaboration	Transformation
Visualization/imagination	Resisting premature closure
Evaluation	Inductive reasoning
Analysis	Deductive reasoning
Synthesis	Ability to regress
Intuition	Ability to predict outcomes
Logical thinking	Planning

Space will not permit presentation of exercises in each of these categories. Readers interested in a more thorough discussion of these topics are referred to Davis (1986), Davis & Rimm (1989), or Treffinger (1983). As a few examples: Fluency, flexibility, originality, and elaboration may be strengthened with divergent thinking exercises such as "What would happen if . . . ?" problems, thinking of unusual uses for common objects (e.g., discarded tires, junk telephones, a sheet of paper), generating improvements for products (e.g., a bathtub), designing a machine or a system (e.g., a dog walker, airplane for animals, burglary prevention system), or any number of mind-prodding problems (e.g., "How can bike thefts be stopped?" "How can the lunch menu be improved?"). Some mental visualization exercises are designed to strengthen visualization and imagination abilities: "Put a light bulb in each hand . . . hold your arms straight out to the side . . . pretend your light bulbs are jet engines . . . run down the street for a take-off" (Eberle, 1971). We mentioned above Gordon's and Stanish's exercises for strengthening metaphorical thinking. Other exercises for strengthening evaluation, logic, inductive and deductive reasoning, problem finding, transformation, planning, and other relevant abilities may be found in the thinking skills literature (e.g., DeBono, 1983; Feuerstein, 1980; Lipman, Sharp, & Oscanyan, 1980).

IV. INVOLVING STUDENTS IN ACTIVITIES REQUIRING CREATIVE THINKING

An important focus of the teaching-learning process should be on activities that foster creative growth. In order to learn to think creatively, learners will require practice. They should become involved in activities that inherently require creative thinking. Theatre is especially good. There also are art, music, science, writing, handicraft, filmmaking, journalism, photography, and innumerable other possible projects that virtually demand creative thinking and problem solving. Classroom or school newspapers, for example, require creative writing, planning, integrating, designing, interviewing, photography, and humor. Research reports also stretch problem clarification, planning, researching, logic, reasoning, and other creative muscles, especially if the reporting mode is imaginative—a news report from ancient Greece or by visitors from outer space, a short dramatic production, a film, video, or slide show, a sand table construction, or other media.

Future Problem Solving and Olympics of the Mind

The Future Problem Solving (Crabbe, 1982) and Olympics of the Mind (Micklus, 1983) programs are two outstanding national programs that incorporate all of the major concepts and strategies presented in this chapter and more, into motivating and challenging creative activities. Both of these fast-growing programs intrinsically teach creative attitudes, reinforce creative traits, help students understand creative ideas and creative problem solving, strengthen creative problem-solving skills and abilities, and they certainly involve students in brain-stretching creative activities. Both programs also teach such principles and techniques as brainstorming, attribute listing, fact-finding and information gathering, synthesizing ideas, using idea checklists, and evaluation.

With many of the kinds of problems used in these programs, a basic groundwork of ideas must exist before the students can synthesize them into new and relevant solutions, then present the solutions in attractive and appropriate ways. How are students able to acquire the needed knowledge and skills? By teaching them such basics as reading, writing, and speaking skills, along with relevant concepts and skills in science, math, art and other areas, and by teaching them fact-finding and researching skills. In part because of the heavy emphasis on basic skills, factfinding, and evaluation, many educators strongly encourage the adoption of these programs into the general curricula of the schools.

Future Problem Solving. A typical exercise in the Future Problem Solving (FPS) program begins with a one-page scenario which is read by students. The problem is accompanied by about 20 recent magazine and newspaper articles pertaining to the issues presented. Most of the articles are specifically recommended in the FPS materials. For example, the CANUSA problem describes a city designed in 1987 for the "traditional" family (father, nonworking mother, and 2.5 children). Now, 30 years later, CANUSA is home for a variety of changed family structures. CANUSA is located 20 miles southeast of Vancouver on the border of Canada and the United States and has a population of 65,000, only 2 percent of whom are in traditional families. Using the reading materials provided plus others which they locate, students research problems of divorced families, single parent families, retired persons, families in which mother and father both work, and couples with and without children. The general goal, of course, is to redesign the city, its schools, parks, work arrangements, etc., to meet the needs of the entire community.

After the fact-finding, students generate at least twenty problems that may exist or arise in CANUSA. This phase helps students understand that a situation or a problem will look differently to different people according to the information they bring with them, yet all interpretations can be valid. From the list of 20 problems, students select what they agree is the best underlying problem, focus on it, and brainstorm possible solutions.

An evaluation matrix, with the most appropriate ideas listed vertically on the left side and criteria across the top, permits an objective evaluation of ideas. After the single best solution is identified it is rewritten in essay form—the solution is carefully presented, and the outcomes and consequences of the solution are elaborated and explained. Other future-oriented problems have dealt with underwater colonization, space exploration, garbage disposal, water shortages, and illiteracy.

There are regional FPS team competitions, and if the troops are good they will participate in a state competition and perhaps even the National Future Problem Solving Bowl. FPS Bowls include a solution selling competition in which teams develop a five-minute presentation to convince the audience that their solution is clearly superior. There also is a scenario writing competition in which students' essays are judged. You can bet they attend to grammar, spelling, and organization.

According to director Anne Crabbe (1982), some main objectives of FPS are to help children:

- Become more aware of the future in order to deal with it actively, with the attitude that they can effect changes.
- Become more creative; learning to go beyond the logical and obvious.
- Develop communication skills, including speaking and writing persuasively, clearly, and accurately.
- Develop teamwork skills, such as listening, respecting, understanding, and compromising.
- Develop research skills, learning how to gather information, where to go, and who to contact.

Odyssey of the Mind. Odyssey of the Mind (OM), formerly Olympics of the Mind, is another excellent vehicle for the teaching of creativity. Creative, hands-on, problem-solving skills are needed to solve a series of long-term problems that require months to plan and implement prior to a competition. For example, components of a play will be specified, but students will create the script, scenery, costumes, humor, and "style"; they might construct a weight-supporting tower out of specified amounts of balsa wood strips; they might construct a moustrap-powered mousemobile that must perform specified tasks; or given dollar and material limits they construct a machine that will move potted plants from here to there. In the OM competitions, each task must be performed within a certain time frame and within a certain set of restrictions.

Along with the long-term problems, students also solve short-term spontaneous problems both in practice and on the day of competition. For example, students might be asked to list unusual uses for a piece of cowhide, or improvise with a ping pong ball ("It's a clown's nose," "It's an egg from a plastic bird"). Spontaneous problems are scored according to fluency and flexibility, with points awarded for quantity and uniqueness of the responses.

OM creator Sam Micklus (1983) argues that these kinds of exercises strengthen students' self-confidence and self-image and therefore their mental health. In everyday life, highly unique ideas and problem solutions present the greatest threat of criticism, but in OM they earn the most points. Confidence is one of the most important traits of creative people, and OM activities provide plenty of opportunities for confidence and creative risk-taking to be rewarded.

CONCLUSIONS

There are large differences in the degree to which individuals are willing and able to change. Some people, after a good creativity course or inspiring workshop, experience something of a rebirth. They feel like a new person, with a better self-concept, improved confidence, and feelings of greater personal creativeness. A not uncommon reaction is, "Hey, I can do things I didn't know I could do!" They begin using creative abilities that have been lying around all along. However, others will exit from such training with little or no personal change—"Yes, that was interesting. Now let's do things the old comfortable way!"

In teaching for creative growth, teachers should emphasize the importance of creativity to personal development and to society. Becoming a more creative person will help us to be better thinkers and problem solvers, to more fully use our mental abilities, and to approach all aspects of our lives in a more flexible, enjoyable and successful way. As for society, without creative people and creative ideas we still would be living in caves, digging roots, and clubbing rodents for breakfast and with luck living to the senior citizen age of 25 or 30. The history of civilization is a history of creative innovations in every area.

Few educational goals are as important for long-term life quality and success as creative attitudes and skills, particularly if creativity is seen as a self-actualized, mentally healthy and forward-growing approach to all aspects of one's life (Maslow, 1954, 1968; Rogers, 1962). While genetics plays a role, virtually everyone's creative skills and abilities can be strengthened with practice and everyone can become more creativity conscious, more disposed to use the creative abilities they have. The recommendations for strengthening creative growth presented in this chapter should help make creativity training in schools more sensible, comprehensible, organized, and effective.

REFERENCES

Barron, F., & Harrington, D. M. (1981). Creativity, intelligence, and personality. *Annual Review of Psychology, 32,* 439–476.

Crabbe, A. (1982). Creating a brighter future: An update on the future problem solving program. *Journal for the Education of the Gifted, 5,* 2–9.

Davis, G. A. (1975). In frumious pursuit of the creative person. *Journal of Creative Behavior, 9,* 75–87.

Davis, G. A. (1985). *Creative thinking and problem solving. Apple Computer disk and manual.* Buffalo, NY: Bearly Limited.

Davis, G. A. (1986). *Creativity is forever.* Second edition. Dubuque, IA: Kendall/Hunt.

Davis, G. A., & Bull, K. S. (1978). Strengthening affective components of creativity in a college course. *Journal of Educational Psychology, 70,* 833–836.

Davis, G. A., & Rimm, S. (1980). *Group inventory for finding interests. II.* Watertown, WI: Educational Assessment Service.

Davis, G. A., & Rimm, S. B. (1989). *Education of the gifted and talented.* Second edition. Englewood Cliffs, NJ: Prentice-Hall.

Davis, G. A., & Rudmanis, I. (1986). *Teaching creativity with a computer.* Unpublished manuscript, University of Wisconsin, Madison.

DeBono, E. (1983). The direct teaching of thinking as a skill. *Phi Delta Kappan, 64,* 703–708.

Eberle, B. (1971). *Scamper.* East Aurora, NY: DOK Publishers.

Eberle, B., & Stanish, B. (1985). *CPS for kids.* East Aurora, NY: DOK Publishers.

Feuerstein, R. (1980). *Instrumental enrichment: An intervention program for cognitive modificability.* Baltimore, MD: University Park Press.

Gordon, W. J. J. (1961). *Synectics.* New York: Harper & Row.

Gordon, W. J. J. (1974a). *Making it strange. Books 1–4.* New York: Harper & Row.

Gordon, W. J. J. (1974b). Some source material in discovery by analogy. *Journal of Creative Behavior, 8,* 239–257.

Gordon, W. J. J., & Poze, T. (1980). *The new art of the possible.* Cambridge, MA: EES Associates.

Lipman, M., Sharp, A. M., & Oscanyan, F. S. (1980). *Philosophy in the classroom.* Second edition. Philadelphia: Temple University Press.

Maslow, A. H. (1954). *Motivation and personality.* New York: Harper & Row.

Maslow, A. H. (1968). *Toward a psychology of being.* Second edition. Princeton. NJ: Van Nostrand.

Micklus, S. (1983). *What is Olympics of the Mind?* Glassboro, NJ: Olympics of the Mind Association.

Osborn, A. F. (1963). *Applied imagination.* Third edition. New York: Scribners.

Parnes, S. J. (1981). *Magic of your mind.* Buffalo, NY: Bearly Limited.

Rimm, S. (1976). *GIFT: Group inventory for finding creative talent.* Watertown, WI: Educational Assessment Service.

Rimm, S., & Davis, G. A. (1979). *Group inventory for finding interests. I.* Watertown, WI: Educational Assessment Service.

Rogers, C. R. (1962). Toward a theory of creativity. In S. J. Parnes & H. F. Harding (Eds.), *Source book for creative thinking.* New York: Scribner's.

Shallcross, D. J. (1981). *Teaching creative behavior.* Englewood Cliffs, NJ: Prentice-Hall.

Smith, E. (1985). Are you creative? *Business Week, Sept. 30,* 80–84.

Smith, J. M. (1966). *Setting conditions for creative teaching in the elementary school.* Boston: Allyn & Bacon.

Stanish, B. (1977). *Sunflowering.* Carthage, IL: Good Apple.

Torrance, E. P. (1962). *Guiding creative talent.* Englewood Cliffs, NJ: Prentice-Hall.

Torrance, E. P. (1966). *Torrance tests of creative thinking.* Bensenville, IL: Scholastic Testing Service

Torrance, E. P. (1981). Non-test ways of identifying the creatively gifted. In J. C. Gowan, J. Khatena, & E. P. Torrance (Eds.), *Creativity: Its educational implications.* Dubuque, IA: Kendall/Hunt.

Treffinger, D. J., Isaksen, S. G., & Firestien, R. L. (1982). *Handbook of creative learning. Volume 1.* Williamsville, NY: Center for Creative Learning.

Treffinger, D.J. (1983). Appendix A. In A.J. Tannenbaum (Author). *Gifted children: Psychological and educational perspectives.* New York: MacMillan.

Von Oech, R. (1983). *A whack in the side of the head.* New York: Warner Books.

Wallas, G. (1926). *The art of thought.* New York: Harcourt, Brace & World.

Chapter 5

USING COMPUTER APPLICATION PROGRAMS WITH GIFTED LEARNERS

KEN BAREFORD

The role of computers in education has been evolving and broadening. When computers were first introduced into the schools, computer literacy was equated with acquiring understanding and ability in computer programming. Classroom teachers and their students were told that they needed to learn the computer languages, LOGO and BASIC. Every student had to master a computer language in order to become computer literate. Schools rushed to buy additional computers and taught students computer programming in LOGO or BASIC. It was widely believed that students who did not know programming would be unemployable in a few years. Many experienced teachers had serious reservations about this approach. Nevertheless, at the initial stages few people could suggest better uses for computers in educational settings.

Computer programming can be an excellent way for students to practice skills required for problem-solving and logical thinking. The computer vividly displays how closely thinking matches expectations. The problem is that *not everyone* can be or can enjoy being a programmer. Many teachers and students were not able to master the new technology. They considered themselves failures, on the one hand, and became frustrated and disillusioned with computers, on the other. The fact is that few people, students or adults, "need" LOGO or BASIC. Everyone, however, can become computer literate without knowing anything about computer languages.

Teachers have changed their view of the place of the computer in education. Currently, teachers search for and buy software programs designed to help students with the regular curriculum. Some excellent programs are currently available. Programs are considered excellent if they combine appropriate educational content with the computer's interactive qualities, as well as with its sound and graphics. These programs can offer simulations that might be impossible to reproduce in the classroom. They can present logic or problem-solving situations that might be extremely difficult for a teacher to re-create without the computer.

In any given year the regular classroom teacher will be faced with the challenge of providing for the needs of one or more gifted children. The aim of this chapter is to help teachers meet this challenge. Numerous authorities in gifted education have cited individualization of instruction as an especially useful method of meeting the needs of gifted children in regular classrooms. Unfortunately, cost effective ways of individualizing instruction have proved elusive. The variety of software available today makes it feasible for teachers to provide for each student on an individual basis. Personal computers can provide the method of translating the goal of individualization into reality.

Gifted and talented children may be as different from one another as they are from their nongifted peers. In her 4 × 4 Structure of Giftedness Model presented in Chapter 1, Milgram described the numerous combinations of type and level of abilities that obtain in gifted children. The computer is an ideal, exciting, and motivating tool for gifted students. This chapter is designed to provide information and guidance to regular classroom teachers on how personal computers can be used efficiently and profitably by each and every one of the wide variety of gifted learners that might appear in a regular classroom. Innovative uses of personal computers can help provide educational enrichment and/or acceleration to individual learners who are characterized by overall general intellectual ability or creativity as well as to those who demonstrate actual or potential giftedness in a wide variety of specific spheres ranging from mathematics and computer sciences to foreign languages or music.

The two main categories of computer programs that are especially useful in providing special education for gifted and talented children within the framework of the regular classroom are (1) computer-assisted instruction programs and (2) application programs. Computer-Assisted Instruction programs (CAI) can be used to permit gifted learners to advance at their own pace. Application software such as word processing, data base management, spreadsheet programs, graphics packages, and communication programs give students new tools with which to analyze, synthesize, and evaluate information.

It is not uncommon in today's classrooms to find abundant use of Computer-Assisted Instruction programs (CAI) in which the computer acts as a teacher. Unfortunately, the quality of CAI software is a problem. Many CAI programs are technically poor, dull drills of material that a teacher could have presented in a more appropriate and stimulating way. Other programs attempt to duplicate material that is best presented as a printed text or workbook. Fortunately, the quantity and quality of educational software is steadily increasing. It is reasonable to expect that in the years to come teachers will find it less and less difficult to find acceptable computer-assisted instructional programs for use with gifted as well as with nongifted learners.

The uses of CAI for individualizing instruction for gifted learners in regular classrooms are generally recognized. We will not, therefore, belabor that point. We will, instead, focus on computer literacy in a new form. The new computer literacy suggested here is based on learning to use application software. It does not depend on learning computer languages or on acquiring programming skills for the future but on having students use higher level thinking skills today. This chapter is divided into three sections. In the first section the main types of application programs are presented. In the second section the integration of application software and the curriculum is discussed. The third section deals with computer hardware, software, and the classroom space requirements.

I. TYPES OF APPLICATION PROGRAMS

Application programs are also referred to as productivity software. They include word processing, data base or file management, spreadsheets, graphing, text/graphics processing, and communication programs. When computers were relatively new in schools, teachers were, in general, far less familiar with their potential as educational tools than they are today. Some teachers objected to their students' use of computers. Just a few years ago teachers debated whether students should be allowed to use a word processor or not. The assumption was that the word processor and the "magical" computer were going to write, to create for the students, and that they would not acquire writing skills as before. Teachers soon realized that their concerns were unfounded. The word processor provided only technical assistance by facilitating the students' ability to analyze and evaluate their work by providing simple ways to reorder, locate, edit, and examine text. Until the student begins to think, i.e., to create, the program does nothing. The word processor does not write a story, poem, or text any more than a pencil creates. It does, however, create a learning environment more conducive to the use of higher level thinking processes.

By the same token, other application programs such as data bases, graphing software and spreadsheets give students an efficient way to develop, analyze, evaluate and present data. Data base programs include ways to sort and separate data for analysis. The computer does not decide what criterion is to be used to sort, it merely carries out the students' plans. Sorting and regrouping data that may previously have taken hours or days to do, can be done by the computer in seconds and minutes. The computer's speed encourages students to revise and think more extensively and creatively about their plans for analysis. The drudgery is gone. The student is given time to think. Graphing programs helps learners organize their material and present it to others in an efficient and understandable form. Numerical data can easily be manipulated by spreadsheet programs. As students devise and try various "what if" schemes, the computer can automatically change all other related data. Now students can spend their time thinking about what data to manipulate rather than tediously rewriting changed data.

Of all the computer software available, the application programs are the most appropriate programs for gifted and talented students. They remove the time-consuming and often dull task of rewriting information and give the student the time to think of new strategies to analyze data and to solve problems.

Word Processing

Word processing software turns the computer into a much improved typewriter. Using a keyboard, students enter text that is displayed on a monitor. In addition, all word processing programs allow the user to easily edit the text, print the text in a variety of formats, save the text on a disk, and retrieve the text at a later time. Anyone who has needed to make changes on a page he has just typed will understand at once the initial value of word processing programs. Other options usually available include an easy way to locate and change specific words or phrases, to move paragraphs, and to copy blocks of text to new locations. Newer programs often offer several fonts, size, and style of letters, that may be easily selected and mixed on the printed page.

Data Base Management

Data base management software turns the computer into an electronic file cabinet. Any information that is usually kept on file cards or in manila folders could be stored on a diskette using one of these programs. For example, an address book is a data base, a collection of similar information. The electronic advantage of the data base software is that the computer helps the students manage the information. In an address book data base, the information about one person would be that person's record. Each piece of information, for instance the telephone number, is one field. These programs include ways to quickly find all the records that meet specific criteria. The selected information can then be arranged in a variety of formats and displayed on the monitor or printed on paper. The address book data base could provide address labels, a telephone list, or a list of all the records with a common field, such as a geographic area. There are also ways to edit and update information in the file.

Spreadsheet Programs

Spreadsheet programs are used to manipulate numerical data. The spreadsheet software divides the monitor display into a matrix. Each box formed by the rows and columns is called a cell. Either a word, a number, or a mathematical formula is entered in a cell. Cells can also have formulas that are related to formulas or numbers in other cells. The power of the electronic spreadsheet becomes apparent when the number in one cell is modified and the related cells, almost instantly, change. These programs have many built in functions including commands to find sums and averages as well as trigonometric functions. Information in the cells can be edited, saved on a disk, retrieved from a disk, and printed.

Graphing

Graphing software allows the user to enter data in a variety of ways and then graph the results in one of several formats including line, bar, and pie graphs. The graph can be displayed on the monitor or printed on paper. Although data can be entered via the keyboard, it is more efficient to use a graphing program that automatically accepts data from a spreadsheet or data base program. The spreadsheet data can then be presented within the spreadsheet and on a graph.

Text and Graphics Processing

There is a new breed of software becoming more and more popular. Software companies appear to be unsure how these programs should be marketed. They have been classified as application software as well as art software. In any case, these programs are effective publishing software for schools. These programs vary in complexity but they all combine text and graphic images in some way. Some help the user create a poster, greeting card, or calendar with a few lines of text and a picture. Others combine text and graphics on the same screen. One program can be used to create a newspaper. All of these programs come with clip art pictures, graphics, from which the user can select. Each program provides the simple features of a word processor such as a way to edit, save, and print the text. Many also allow at least some modification of the graphic images.

Communication Programs

Communications software opens the computer user to the world. These programs are used with a modem, a device which connects the computer to the telephone line. The modem itself is usually a small external box or an interface card that is connected inside the computer. Once the computer is connected to the telephone lines, the user follows simple menu choices and instructions to "call" another computer. Information produced by any of the application programs can be sent via the telephone lines to others through the computer. One of the major advantages of this type of communications is that different computers can exchange information. An Apple can "talk" to an IBM or even a mainframe computer. There are several communication services that provide members a large choice of options. Members can call the service via their computer and request information such as news reports, airline schedules, and computer games. A member can leave messages for other members and even "chat" with any other willing member who also happens to be using the service.

Of special interest to teachers of gifted children is the international electronic communication network BITNET. People in universities around the world communicate by means of this system. Most schools would probably be able to establish a link by modem to a university willing to make its facilities available to a select number of gifted children. The possibilities of this kind of development for the benefit of gifted children around the world boggles the imagination.

II. INTEGRATING APPLICATION SOFTWARE AND THE CURRICULUM

Learners with specific abilities and interests in Computer Science have special needs. Individualizing instruction for such students in regular classrooms might involve learning computer languages and programming as well as many other topics that focus on the hardware aspects of computers. There are chapters in this book devoted to helping teachers provide special education for learners gifted in science, mathematics, language arts, social sciences, and foreign languages but, unfortunately, not in computer science. Providing acceleration/enrichment for learners with specific abilities and interests in Computer Science in regular classrooms remains a challenge to be met.

One goal of gifted education today is that all gifted and talented children become end-of-the-line users of computers as an ongoing part of their lives, regardless of the specific discipline or talent. In order to accomplish this goal, children must learn to use the computer as a tool, to view it as a means and not as an end in itself. The discussion that follows is guided by that goal. It focuses on the integration of computer application software and the regular curriculum.

Word Processing Projects

An efficient and effective way to begin to integrate application programs and the curriculum is to use word processing to help students complete work in a content area such as language arts, science, or social studies. For example, younger students can type creative writing projects on the word processor. Correcting and revising becomes less of a chore because of the ease of editing with a word processor. Many students will become prolific writers, because of the increased motivation that frequently results from the satisfaction derived from the editing features of word processing and the interactive nature of the computer. A word processor is an ideal way for older students to type, edit, and store research information, essay, or lab report. Any information that is usually written or typed could be done on the word processor. The advantage to students and teachers of the word processor is the ease with which modifications in any written text can be made and printed.

As students of all ages use and become familiar with the application software, it will inspire them to seek unique uses of the software. The students will use word processing for writing projects as well as to create new presentation methods. A class or grade booklet of elementary or middle school students' creative writing stories can combine language arts, computer, and higher level thinking skills in one project. The students can type, edit, plan the layout, and print the booklet. Their involvement in the total project enhances their sense of accomplishment, and motivates the students to produce meaningful products of high quality. Older students could be entirely responsible for individual booklets.

Data Base Management Projects

As word processing is related to writing, data base management is related to storing and sorting relatively brief bits of information. Students can use data base management programs to create their own data bases of information or data base information may be purchased already stored on disks. If the goal is to have students research and record information, the data base should be developed by the students. For example, students could be asked to find specific facts about five people involved in the development of the computer. After several students have entered their data the students can compare and contrast facts about the individuals. For example, if recent computer-related people were compared it would be learned that most of them were under 30 years old when they made a major contribution to the development of microcomputers. Social studies students might compare presidents, other leaders, or a group of people who are associated with a particular time period or event. Of course, the data base is not limited to people. Economic conditions in various states or countries, philosophical ideas of different cultures, or geographical information could be entered for analysis.

A second approach would be to purchase the data base information. The students miss an opportunity to research the content but they gain more time to devise ways to analyze the data. If the goal is to analyze well known information that is available on a commercial disk, it would be foolish to have students type the same information. If the information is not available on disk, have the students enter it in a data base. Once the data base is typed for the first time it can be used later by other students. Whatever the content, data base management software can give students opportunities to uncover the unique relationships of the information.

Spreadsheets

Spreadsheets are intended to keep track of financial information, as well as other numerical data and mathematical formulas. In a classic example, a proposed budget could be analyzed to predict what would happen as several "what if" questions are asked. How much more profit could be made if an expense could be reduced? A more meaningful application to students might be to set up a spreadsheet to analyze students grades. The impact on their average could be demonstrated with a few "what if" grades. Students involved in school organizations can use spreadsheets to keep track of the organizations' budgets. A student council involved in raising funds and planning activities can forecast how changes in one area may affect other areas. Another use of spreadsheets might be in a school store. Both financial records and inventory records could be maintained on the computer. The spreadsheet could be set up to display items purchased, number sold, cost, price, gross sales, and profit in separate cells. Simply by changing the number sold, all other related categories would change.

Spreadsheets can also be used to demonstrate mathematical concepts. It may be easy to explain the Pythagorean theorem to middle grade student using a triangle with legs of 3 and 4 units and a hypotenuse of 5 units. It becomes very difficult to substitute other numbers for the legs and expect the students to calculate the hypotenuse. Using a spreadsheet, one cell could contain leg A, a second cell leg B, and a third cell the square root of A squared plus B squared. As various numbers are entered for legs A and B, the hypotenuse would be calculated. The spreadsheet offers many concrete examples for the students.

Teachers and students can use the spreadsheet to demonstrate any ideas that can be expressed mathematically. Although the spreadsheet programs have built in functions, spreadsheets do not think for the students any more than a word processor writes for students. In fact, because students may have to convert the usual mathematics formula to a format that can be entered into a spreadsheet, students may have to have an excellent understanding of the formula.

Text and Graphic Processing Projects

The text and graphics processing programs were developed for a specific purpose; therefore, the software's design often dictates the format of the final product. Nevertheless, students can use these programs to create sophisticated, intriguing, and creative projects. The best and most popular programs include Print Shop, Print Shop Companion, and The Newsroom.

The Print Shop and Print Shop Companion are easy to use programs. Students can combine a few lines of text and pictures for a sign, greeting card, or calendar. Although these programs are often used to produce very ordinary signs and cards, the program's potential is only limited by the creativity of the user. Perhaps birthdays of famous people could be entered on a monthly calendar. The program has an option that allows students to mark special days and to enter a note next to the date. The list of famous people could be limited to one particular group, such as famous scientists, mathematicians, poets, or political leaders. The sign option can produce masters for plastic overhead projector visuals. Students can use the visuals to vary their presentation methods. As students create their visuals they are forced to think about the information they are going to present.

The Newsroom program, developed to produce a newspaper, is one of the most exciting text and graphics processor programs. Although the program is complex, it has been used successfully with students as young as 8 years old. Giving any group of students an opportunity to create a class, grade, or school newspaper is a valuable experience. The project successfully integrates many language arts, computer, and higher level thinking skills. To vary the project, give the newspaper a specific focus, such as a science, mathematics, or language newspaper. The same program could be used to produce a literary magazine. A social studies newspaper project might focus on a specific time period. Students would have to assume the identity of a reporter from the selected period and report the events of the day. These activities may be intrinsically exciting to students, but the effect of actually producing a quality finished product using the computer cannot be overestimated.

Although word processing programs lend themselves to language arts activities, projects based on other content areas can be adapted to take advantage of the word processor. Once the word processor is seen as a powerful writing and graphics tool, the activities are only limited by the imagination of the students.

Communication Projects

Although using the computer to communicate with others is growing rapidly in business, schools have been slow to adopt this new technology.

Part of the problem is the need for extra equipment, the access to telephone lines, the additional knowledge to operate the system, and the expense. Unlike other facets of computing, telecommunications require an on-going financial commitment. One project that can be used with students of all ages is to have students contact other students who also have a modem connected to their computer. By typing on the keyboard the students can "talk" directly to the other students. It is also possible to send text that has been saved on disks using a word processor. School systems could also have students in two diverse schools or districts become more aware of each other using this kind of an electronic pen pal project. School districts that are widely separated geographically could work on joint projects. Ideally, each school could contribute unique information to the project. Students could also use the computer to contact experts who may be too far away to meet. Questions and answers could be typed on the keyboard or sent from a word processing file.

Although rather expensive, there are telecomputing services that provide large data bases of information including newspaper data bases. Students can search national newspapers for information about a research topic. For current, readable, material the newspaper is often the best resource. Information that is important for student research can be sent, downloaded, to the student through the computer. Although communications projects are worthwhile and exciting activities for students, they continue to be too expensive for most school systems.

Using Application Programs in Classroom Projects

A School Newspaper. *The Roaring Jaguar,* created by the students at the Jefferson Elementary School in Summit, New Jersey has been commended by The Columbia Press Association. This outstanding school newspaper project is an example of the benefits students can derive from using computers in regular classrooms. *The Roaring Jaguar* is published four times a year by about 20 fourth, fifth, and sixth graders using the computer program the newsroom. Using traditional identification methods only a few of these students would have been identified as gifted. The paper does have two or three students who are excellent writers and gifted in the conventional sense. In addition, one gifted student is in charge of the newspaper's layout. This task demands an exceptional understanding of the software, The Newsroom, as well as the ability to use higher level thinking skills. Among the participants in the newspaper project are students who need and receive academic help outside of the regular classroom. In the newspaper project and others like it, gifted children get a chance to interact in a most positive manner with their less gifted peers.

Graphing Survey Data. In another school, eight second grade students, as a culminating math activity, were shown how to use the graphing software, PFS: Graph. Each student had an opportunity to graph the survey data they had collected. One boy became so excited about using PFS: Graph, that he began conducting numerous surveys. He made it clear to the teachers that he needed the software, time on the computer, and a printer so that he could finish the project. With all of his needs met, the boy diligently graphed all the data. After deciding if a line, bar, or pie graph (a pizza graph to second graders) was more appropriate, he took his disks to a computer in another room to print out the finished graphs. As an expert, he was able to help other students and the teachers use the program. Although PFS: Graph is marketed as a productivity tool for adults, this boy demonstrated that motivated young students can also use this program.

The gifted behavior evidenced by the children in the projects cited above are examples of how computer projects can be used to provide opportunities for students to demonstrate abilities not usually tapped in other school projects. These experiences are not isolated incidents. Computer applications have the potential to help teachers create an educational environment that encourages students to use all of their abilities. Application programs turn the computer into a powerful tool. Teachers can use computer technology to provide learners with unequaled learning opportunities.

III. COMPUTER HARDWARE, SOFTWARE, AND CLASSROOM SPACE REQUIREMENTS

Classroom Space Requirements

The environment for computing is important. A good environment will help promote and facilitate student learning. A poor environment can be obtrusive and counterproductive. An environment conducive to using the computer will increase the students productivity. Computers are usually placed on desks, tables or rolling carts. In any case, the students' comfort must be considered. Commercial carts and work stations need to be adjustable if they are intended for students in grades

K–12. Often monitors are placed on a high shelf over the computer. This forces students to assume an inefficient, awkward typing position. Students also need an uncrowded work area. It is difficult to concentrate while shuffling disks, papers, books, and manuals in a cramped work space.

It is also important to consider the location of the work space. Most teachers choose a back corner of the classroom. This gives the students a feeling of privacy, and avoids distracting other students who may be working at their desks.

Teachers also contribute to the environment. Teachers of the gifted and talented are often told to think of themselves as guides. This is especially true for teachers who are working with students and computers. For whatever reason, computers make some adults and teachers tense. Students tend to feel exhilarated by the same machine. Teachers need to treat computer application projects as they would any other gifted project. Once the students know what is expected of them, teachers do not need to hover near the computer. A well-meaning but tense teacher can be unnerving to a student. The student needs the freedom to make his own mistakes, and learn how to use the computer to accomplish the goals of the project. Many teachers, have students who encounter a problem check with the class expert first. This procedure also gives the teacher more uninterrupted teaching time.

Software

There are catalogues filled with many pages describing application software. The price of software varies according to the computer for which it is intended. For example, software for the Commodore is usually the least expensive and for the Apple and IBM the most expensive. Computer software is almost always sold at less than list price. Since software is constantly being revised it is always a good idea to use the most recent catalogues available. In the current chapter, a number of general principles that will be useful to teachers in comparing and purchasing software will be presented.

Current computer periodicals such as *Electronic Learning* (R. Burroughs, Ed., New York, NY) and *Classroom Computer Learning* (H. Brady, Ed., Dayton, OH) evaluate and compare new and established software for most popular computers. For a list of software available, see The Educational Software Selector from the EPIE Institute (1986). In addition, numerous periodicals such as the following frequently review new software:

RUN (C-64, C-128), D. Brisson, Peterborough, NH.
PC World (IBM/MS–DOS), H. Miller, San Francisco, CA.
80 Micro (Tandy), E. Maloney, Peterbourough, NH.
A+ (Apple), M. Canon, New York, NY.
InCider (Apple), D. De Peyster, Peterborough, NH.

There are a few considerations that teachers should consider when deciding which programs are best for their students. First, it is absolutely essential that teachers know with exactly which computer the software will be used. The fact that software written for an IBM will not work on an Apple may be obvious, but there are other differences. For example, software written for one IBM may not run on another IBM. Software written for an older model Apple or IBM may not run on a newer model. Many IBM-compatible computers are not *fully* IBM compatible and will not run all IBM software. In addition, some software is written to support most but not all printers. It is relatively easy for software programs to print text to almost any printer; however, the software must contain the specific code necessary to print graphics to each printer.

There is wide disagreement among computer users about the relative merits of Apple and IBM software. Many are of the opinion that since most Apple software is less sophisticated and less expensive it is more appropriate for use in school settings. Others, just as fervently, extoll the virtues of IBM products. Some claim, that for gifted children who are able to handle the complexities involved, IBM software is a better bet. Since the field of computer software is in constant development, it would be unwise to take a stand on the Apple-IBM controversy in this chapter.

Good adult application software is powerful and usually just as easy for students to use as so-called "student" application software. Probably the best advice that one could give to teachers about purchasing software is to select popular application software. Popular software, like popular computers, offers several advantages. Newsletters and columns in computer magazines will be devoted to the more popular software. Other students, teachers and adults are probably using the software at school and at home. The programs are updated on a regular basis and other programs are written to add desirable options to the original software. It is always beneficial to have this kind of support for generating ideas as well as solving problems.

Learning Application Software Programs for the First Time

When given a new software program many teachers read the manual and attempt to understand the whole program all at once and before trying it on the computer. This is often an impossible and frustrating task. When given the same program, students tend to try it out, seldom giving the manual even a glance. They are not concerned about the "details." Teachers need to adopt a little of this cavalier attitude toward computer software. Adults, like children, do not need to know everything before they begin. Most people seldom use all of the features of a program, and even experienced users need to consult the manual from time to time.

Successful teachers who work with many different kinds of software don't have time to carefully read every page in each manual. They have devised quick ways to begin using application programs. First, they read only enough of the manual to be able to begin using the program. A few minutes on the computer often makes the written explanation clear. Second, these teachers ask the students if they know how to use the program, or they ask a student who enjoys computers to help them with the program. One word processor has a great deal in common with other word processors. Explanations that are unclear to a new user may be explicit to a more experienced computer user. Third, they begin teaching the students the program as soon as possible. It is difficult to learn a computer solely by reading about it. The student expert can help demonstrate the program. The demonstration only includes the basics, the necessary commands that will enable the students to begin their project. Although the initial goal of the session may be to learn the program, it is important to select a simple yet meaningful project. *The Teacher's Computer Book* by Shillingburg, Bareford, Pacigia, and Townsend (1987) presents specific lessons with step-by-step directions for using many popular Apple and IBM application programs. *The Apple Computer Clubs' Activities Handbook* by Miller and Caley (1984) describes tested student projects that can be used with many different brands of computers.

Meaningful projects help motivate students to learn the more advanced features of programs when needed. For example, every word processing program allows the students to enter, edit, save, retrieve, and print text. By learning those five tasks students can begin word processing. The word processor probably has a way to move and copy paragraphs. These are useful but not essential features that must be mastered before a word processor can be used. The day students want to move a few long paragraphs, rather than retype them, is the day students will be motivated to experiment with moving paragraphs.

Hardware

Students and teachers usually have access to a computer lab or at least one computer that can be wheeled into their classroom. The computer system for the classroom should include the computer unit, a monitor, at least one disk drive, and a printer. Apple computers are widely used in many schools. Some claim that the Apple has earned its popularity because of the abundant software programs of high quality that are available for use with it. Other people express equal devotion to IBM computers and others as well. Some computers appear to be fantastic bargains; however, a "bargain" computer is only a bargain if it fulfills the needs of the students and teacher. Technically, computers are all about the same. The price of the computer is determined by other factors, usually software availability, service, and demand. There are many brands of computers, and new models are constantly being introduced. Accordingly, it is impossible to recommend with any degree of certainty one computer over another.

The computer revolution is upon us. Early exaggerated expectations that the introduction of computers to classrooms would solve all teaching-learning problems was followed by sobering disappointment. Unbridled enthusiasm and a race to acquire hardware with the newest features and more sophisticated software has been replaced by an understanding that we have much to learn about how to use computers effectively in schools. Discussion in many schools is still frequently focused on the relative merits of different hardware and software products. Nevertheless, most educators are coming to view the computer as a tool, a technologically advanced tool, in the hands of the teacher. Computers are like other aids available to teachers, such as chalk, film projectors, tape recorders, and transparencies in that they are only as good as the teachers who use them.

REFERENCES

EPIE Institute (1986). *The educational software selector* (3rd ed.). Water Mill, NY: Teachers College Press.

Miller, S. & Caley, M. (1984). *The apple computer clubs' activities handbook.* Englewood Cliffs, NJ: Prentice-Hall.

Shillenburg, P.M., Bareford, K. C., Pacigia, J. A., & Townsend, J. L. (1987). *The teacher's computer book.* New York: Teachers College Press.

Chapter 6

THE SEEK (SUMMIT EDUCATIONAL ENRICHMENT FOR KIDS) PULL-OUT PROGRAM: A BOON AND NOT A BANE TO TEACHING GIFTED CHILDREN IN REGULAR CLASSROOMS

NANCY CHEZAR MILGRAM

Since 1979, I have been a teacher of gifted and talented programs in several suburban, northern New Jersey school systems all using variations of the pull-out program model. Pull-out programs refer to an administrative arrangement whereby gifted students receive most of their instruction in heterogeneous classrooms and are "pulled-out" to study with other gifted children in a special class for a portion of the school day or week. The children may meet with the special education teacher in resource rooms in their own school building where they are provided with individual and/or small group instruction. Sometimes the gifted learners travel by bus to a pull-out class held in a central location. Children may spend from one hour to a full day each week in the pull-out class.

Part-time, special "pull-out" classes, whether for an hour, a few hours, or a full day a week are the most frequently used format for gifted/talented education in New Jersey elementary schools and in the rest of the United States as well (Cox, Daniel, & Boston, 1985). Many innovative, educationally sound, group and individual activities were developed and implemented with and for gifted and talented students. Some were based on the specific interests of the students, district, or teacher involved. Others were county, state, or nationwide programs, such as the Olympics of the Mind (Gourley, 1981; Micklus & Gourley, 1982; Olympics of the Mind Association, 1983), Convocation Model (Gourley & Burr, 1978), and Teen Arts Festival (1987). In addition, independent projects such as those sponsored by the Weekly Reader National Invention Contest (1985) allowed students to pursue individual interests under the guidance of the G/T (gifted/talented) program teacher.

Problems With Pull-Out Programs

In an earlier chapter of this book, R. Milgram cited the numerous problems presented by pull-out programs when compared with the other delivery systems used to provide special education for gifted and talented learners. In addition, the serious limitations of the pull-out program model have been well documented in the prestigious and authoritative Richardson Report (Cox, Daniel, & Boston, 1985). Nevertheless, in our school system, as in most others that use the pull-out program model, the G/T students and their parents were, in general, quite satisfied with the program. Unfortunately, despite the overall success of the program based upon this criterion, a number of problems consistantly appeared in all the districts in which I taught.

The first and most important problem has to do with identification. Students for the G/T (gifted/talented) programs were identified by a formula that relied on a combination of standardized achievement and IQ test scores. In addition, teacher and/or parent ratings of various characteristics of the students that experts have defined as common to the gifted such as task commitment, creativity, and motivation were considered. To some teachers and parents the identification system seemed flawed. Teachers often pointed to students, not identified as gifted, whose classroom work was superior to some of the identified G/T students. Parents, as well, were often able to point to the excellent report cards and test scores of their children who, despite this evidence, were not identified as gifted and not offered special education. The administration often found itself defending a hairsplitting "objective" point system with a somewhat arbitrary cutoff point. If a child was dropped from the program due to poor performance in the gifted and/or regular classroom, it was difficult to explain to parents how a child labeled "gifted" one year was no longer in the program a few years later. In an earlier chapter of the current volume, R. Milgram described the problems inherent in the definition and identification of gifted and talented children. Readers interested in a more detailed discussion of the assumptions of stability of giftedness and the validity of its measurement are referred to this chapter.

A second problem often cited by classroom teachers was that the G/T pull-out program combined with other mandated pull-outs (speech, ESL: English as a second language, resource room, and basic skills), and individual music lessons that some G/T students take on school time, left little time for teaching the curriculum for which they were held accountable to the whole class at the same time. Having the same students out for the same time all year often meant reteaching the material that they missed. Ideally, it would make sense to pull out the students at the least disruptive time. However, in practice this cannot always be achieved. The G/T teacher usually services more than one school in a district and it is impossible to schedule around the "special subjects" (physical education, art, music, and library) in each school.

A third problem, obviously related to but not overlapping with the second cited above, is the involvement of the regular classroom teacher with the special enrichment education that her pupil is receiving on a pull-out basis. Most classroom teachers appreciate what the G/T program accomplishes for their students and enjoy the presentations these students make to their classes. However, they sometimes feel removed from the substance and process of the program. The responses of regular classroom teachers to the pull-out programs of their students have been known to range from mild criticism to outright hostility. It is critical for the child's sake that we realize the importance of the regular classroom teacher in any part-time model of special G/T education. It is the classroom teacher who is ultimately responsible and held accountable for the gifted child's education.

This chapter is devoted to a discussion of the innovative and relatively unusual effort of one New Jersey school system to provide truly special, special education for its gifted and talented learners. It is divided into three sections. In the first section, the objectives and guiding principles of SEEK: Summit Educational Enrichment for Kids are described and in the second, a number of examples of "units that work" used within this system are presented in detail. In the third section, conclusions based upon the program presented in this chapter are summarized and the implications of these findings are cited.

I. THE SUMMIT PLAN:
A COOPERATIVE PERFORMANCE-BASED APPROACH

In 1985, after five years of experience in conducting a traditional pull-out program for gifted children, the School Board of Summit, New Jersey decided to restructure its program in order to alleviate the problems of the pull-out approach cited above. A G/T Steering Committee was appointed to study the problem and to make recommendations to the School Board. The committee was chaired by Dr. Bethene LeMahieu, Supervisor of Instruction, and the members included two principals, Dr. Diane Grannon, Washington School, and Ms. Grace Kingsbury, Franklin School, and two G/T teachers, Mr. Ken Bareford and Ms. Nancy C. Milgram. The program described in this chapter is the direct result of the Summit School Board's decision to implement the recommendations of the committee.

The dominant view of teachers and administrators in the Summit, New Jersey school system is that elementary school is a time for exploring ideas and interests. Programs of education for gifted and talented children that are based upon a rigid system of identification that results in hard and fast labeling and categorizing of children is at odds with this view. Accordingly, Summit developed a policy and program of G/T education that dispensed with a formal identification system. Test scores and classroom teachers are consulted when necessary, but student interest and motivation are the main criteria for initial participation and student performance the main criterion for continued participation, in enrichment programs designed for able learners.

The *overall objectives* of the Summit Program are:

1. To develop a more cooperative and integrated approach between the G/T program and the general curriculum and classroom teachers.
2. To broaden the definition of giftedness and to include as many students as possible.

The *specific guiding principles* are as follows:

1. The G/T program is designed to serve the changing needs of the students, classroom teachers, and individual schools.
2. The G/T program consists of discrete component units. Students may participate in one or more of these specific component units.
3. Student participants can be self-nominated or nominated by classroom teachers, the G/T teacher, the principal, and/or other school personnel (nurse, psychologist, reading specialist, etc.) for specific units.
4. Classroom teachers are encouraged to initiate G/T units, thus maximizing their awareness and appreciation of the G/T program, on the one hand, and increasing the degree to which the program serves to complement each child's overall educational experience, on the other.

These principles are reflected in *programming* with the following *characteristics:*

1. All children have an opportunity to participate in some G/T program units.
2. G/T teachers teach whole class lessons in every grade. These lessons lead to pull-out groups in noncurricula or extended curricula areas.
3. Pull-out units to enrich and accelerate the basic curriculum areas of reading, math, and language arts are formed when needed.

In day-to-day terms the Summit approach provides for the special needs of individual gifted and talented children by enriching and accelerating the basic curriculum, on the one hand, and/or by providing noncurriculum or extended curriculum experiences, on the other. Let us look at each of these dimensions.

Enriching and Accelerating the Basic Curriculum. Classroom teachers make the initial nomination of children for advanced or enriched work in curricula subjects based on the student's classroom work. Standardized test scores may be checked for corroborating evidence and to make sure that other advanced students are not overlooked. Often the G/T teacher is asked to teach the top reading and/or math group, especially in the primary grades, for a specified number of weeks or months. When possible, the students are taken out during their usual time for these subjects once or twice a week and the advanced work is in lieu of class assignments. The G/T teacher provides appropriate enrichment work to be done in class until the next G/T meeting. Some teachers request minimum time out of class, but maximum independent activities for the children to do in class. Other teachers prefer maximum activities during the pull-out sessions and fewer independent assignments in class. The G/T teacher assigns, corrects and monitors the enrichment work both in the regular classroom and in the pull-out setting.

Occasionally, with certain students, usually the profoundly gifted, the G/T teacher is responsible for a complete curricula area. The students meet with her at least two hours a week, preferably during the time scheduled for that subject, and then the student has differentiated assignments for the balance of the week. The G/T teacher administers tests as needed and decides on a joint report card grade with the teacher. Teachers welcome the arrangement because they are relieved of the responsibility to provide for the unique needs of one or two children and can, therefore, concentrate on the needs of the other students.

Noncurricula and Extended Curricula Performance Based Format. One format that has proven very successful has been for the G/T teacher to teach an introductory unit consisting of several enrichment lessons on a curricular or noncurricular topic to the whole class. Required and optional activities are developed. Students are told that one way to indicate their interest in pursuing the topic in a small enrichment group, is to complete the optional activities. An outline of activities and time commitment for the enrichment group is explained so that students can make an informed decision on whether to apply for continued participation or not. Students are chosen for the small pull-out group based on their performance in required and/or optional assignments on a given topic, their motivation, and teacher recommendation. Some students are sometimes actively encouraged to be in the enrichment group. Generally, most students who complete the required assignments and indicate a desire to participate in the small enrichment group on a given topic are accepted. Occasionally, a student may not be allowed to participate even if he/she has expressed interest, because, in the opinion of the classroom teacher, he/she cannot afford the time out of the classroom due to weakness in basic skills.

If time permits, two or three groups are formed, some intensive/long-term and some less intensive/short-term. The exciting part of this approach is that many students emerge as "gifted" based on their performance in the program who would never have been identified as gifted if conventional methods of identification had been employed. Classroom teachers report that success in the type of gifted program being described here can boost students' confidence and positively influence their overall school performance.

II. UNITS THAT WORK

The possibilities for programming using the Summit approach are limited only by the creativity of the students and teachers involved. In the current section I will present several examples of programs that have stimulated achievement and interest. The description and discussion of each unit is followed by presentation of the formal teacher's outline for the unit developed by the author.

Invention Unit

One impressive example of how the Summit model works is the story of a girl who became the national third grade winner of the 1987 Weekly Reader National Invention Contest (1985). Two years earlier, a pilot invention unit was instituted for the fourth grade in conjunction with the New Jersey Mini Invention/Innovation Team (MIIT) Contest (Peck, 1987). Based on its success, it was decided to implement a whole class invention unit for grades one through five as an excellent vehicle to stimulate creative thinking. In the primary grades, after several inventive thinking exercises, each student prepared a final drawing and written explanation of his/her best invention idea. Beginning in December, 1985, the *Weekly Reader* elementary school newspaper (1985) has conducted an invention contest based on the principles of New Jersey's and other areas' invention programs. A drawing and explanation of one invention per class may be submitted. Usually, there are a few qualified invention ideas and instead of the teachers making the final decision, the opinions of the other students are solicited. All the drawings are displayed on a bulletin board. The G/T teacher chooses the three or four best ideas and the inventors explain their ideas to the whole class. The children then vote on the class inventor by secret ballot. That is how our winning girl was selected. She was a transfer child to our system and had been receiving remedial help in basic skills the previous year. Her classroom teacher said this would be a great boost to her self-image as she had been a rather shy child. The child proved to be a creative and committed youngster who took her celebrity status in stride. After winning the national award, she diligently built two models for display at national expositions.

In Summit's fourth and fifth grades, students with the best ideas are invited to participate in small enrichment groups that develop working or nonworking models of their inventions. Following the rules of the MIIT (Peck, 1987) contest, students keep a log of all aspects of the invention process including research, sketches, and explanations of problems they encountered and solutions found. Schoolwide and districtwide contests are held to determine the two inventions per division that will represent Summit in the regional contest. This year our award-winning third grade inventor plans to join such a group to refine and perfect her idea. Her parents are even investigating the feasibility of patenting her invention.

The following is the formal teacher's outline for the SEEK Invention Unit for Grades 1–4.

Key Topics: Problem Solving/Critical Thinking/Research

    I. Goal: To provide environment, opportunities, and strategies for students to think creatively and develop an original invention.

    II. Objectives: The student will:
        A. Prepare a drawing/diagram of the invention.
        B. Design and build a working or nonworking model of the invention.
        C. Keep an accurate log of all research and activities related to the invention including preliminary drawings and list of parts.
        D. Write a one page explanation of the invention.
        E. Prepare a five-minute oral presentation of the invention.
        F. Participate in state sponsored Mini Invention/Innovation Team Contest.

    III. Identification Procedure:
        A. SEEK teacher evaluation of final diagram/drawing and written explanation of invention idea.
        B. SEEK teacher evaluation of optional activity (IV, B-1, 4).
        C. Teacher recommendation based on task commitment, creativity and ability.

    IV. Activities—Whole Class:
        A. Core activities
            1. Discussion and definition of terms:
                "Invention" = a new creation that meets a need.
                "Innovation" = an improvement or modification of existing item.
            2. Help students generate invention ideas with some of the following or other appropriate inventive thinking exercises adjusted to grade level:
                a. List and describe various types of spoons, brushes, or other common object. Then draw and describe innovative and/or improved spoons/brushes or new way of doing "spoon or brush jobs."
                b. Activity #12 from Stanish's "The Unconventional Invention Book" (see Resources–VII. below).
                c. Brainstorm ideas for improving safety. Then design products that promote safety.

        d. Combine random nouns and verbs to inspire invention ideas—Bug Crunchers, p. 53 Stanish (see Resources–VII. below).

        e. Discuss concept, "Necessity is the mother of invention." Brainstorm needs and invent inventions to meet these needs.

        f. Design, draw, and explain in writing and orally new games/toys/sports.

    3. Explain and demonstrate how the following strategies aid the invention process:

        a. Divide into smaller parts and list ideas for each part.

        b. Simplify.

        c. Elaborate.

        d. Add, subtract.

        e. Combine.

        f. Substitute.

        g. Reverse.

        h. Magnify, minimize.

        i. Redesign (change some or all).

    4. Prepare final sketch and explanation of invention idea.

  B. Optional activities

    1. Students will read about an invention/inventor, make a poster advertising the invention and explain it.

    2. Visit the Edison Lab.

    3. Film, "To Communicate is the Beginning."

    4. Student may elect to prepare identification project.

V. Activities—SEEK Class:

  A. Core activities

    1. Share, discuss, and critique each other's invention ideas.

    2. Students to decide whether to work individually or in teams.

    3. Discuss and demonstrate how to keep a log of all aspects of the invention process (research, materials, and skills needed, sketches, problems, and solutions).

    4. Introduce and explain the five required parts of MIIT contest: Log, model, drawing, written and oral reports.

    5. Students to refine their invention concepts and develop a final drawing and model.

    6. Display and presentation of inventions to grade.

  B. Optional activity: Participate in the Invention Process workshop at the Edison Laboratory.

VI. Evaluation:
   A. SEEK teacher evaluation form for each invention.
   B. In-school evaluation by students and teachers for inclusion in district contest.
   C. District contest according to rules of Mini-Invention Innovation Team (MIIT) Contest—primarily grade 4 and others as needed.

VII. Resources:
   A. "The Unconventional Invention Book," Bob Stanish, Good Apple Inc., Box 299, Carthage, IL 62321.
   B. Mini Invention Innovation Team Contest, 200 Old Matawan Rd., Old Bridge, NJ 08857, Tel: (201) 390-1191.
   C. Books on inventors and inventions.
   D. Edison National Historic Site, Main St. and Lakeside Ave, West Orange, NJ 07052, Tel: (201) 736-0550.
   E. Film, "To Communicate is the Beginning," New Jersey Bell, Tel: (201) 649-3674, Resources for Educators.
   F. "The Book of Firsts," Patrick Robertson, C.N. Potter, Crown Publishers), 1974, available from Resources for the Gifted, 3419 North 44th Street, Phoenix, AZ 85018.

Third Grade Space Unit

In the previous year, two highly gifted second graders worked with the G/T teacher on long-term, independent research projects. This year the teachers involved were hoping to expand the research group. After consultation between the two third-grade teachers and the G/T teacher, it was decided to develop a unit on space. The multimedia introductory lessons were well received and many children were motivated to do several optional assignments. Books and other pertinent materials were set up in a corner of the room so the children could use them when they had free time. After evaluation of the assignments, eight students were selected for the first enrichment group. We promised the children that all who wanted to do a special space project would eventually get time with the enrichment teacher and perhaps we would have a total class space presentation at the end of the unit.

The first group of students were similar in their cognitive abilities to those who are generally selected for gifted education programs by using standardized measures of intelligence and achievement. However, the second and third groups included some students who were very interested and knowledgable about space, but who had mediocre reading and writing skills. These children were so highly motivated, that they produced projects of very high quality. Eighteen out of thirty-one students prepared reports/projects on aspects of space and presented their work to the entire third grade. At that point, all the children, the two classroom teachers and the enrichment teacher decided to develop an assembly program on space for the fourth, fifth, and sixth grades. Thirteen other students volunteered to have speaking parts and the music teacher taught the whole class a "space song" to conclude the presentation. It was a year-long, cooperative educational experience with each child contributing at his/her level of interest and skill.

The following is the formal teacher's outline for the SEEK Unit on Our Place in Space for Grade 3.

Key Topics: Science, Problem Solving/Critical Thinking/Research

   I. Goals:
      A. Broaden students' awareness and appreciation of the complexity of space and man's activities in space.
      B. Provide opportunity for use of research, critical and creative thinking skills.
  II. Objectives: Students will:
      A. Research various celestial bodies and their relation to each other.
      B. Research and evaluate man's past, present, and proposed activities in space.
 III. Identification procedure:
      A. SEEK teacher evaluation of required and optional activities and students' proposals for space-related research topics.
      B. Teacher recommendation based on task commitment, aptitude and interest in science, research, and math.
 IV. Whole Class Lessons:
    Lesson 1
      A. Objectives:
         1. Students will recognize names of planets and differences in sizes and distances from the sun.
         2. Students will be able to write their "space address": Planet Earth, Solar System, Milky Way Galaxy, The Universe.
      B. Activities:
         1. Using scale models of the planets, students will compare

each planet to the size of the Earth and will place in proper order on a "sky map."

2. Students will role model as planets and line up in proper order from the sun and practice rotating on their axes and revolving around the sun.

3. Students will write the names of the planets in proper order on the worksheet.

Lesson 2

A. Objectives:

1. Students will be able to verbalize the relationship between asteroids, meteors, and meteorites.

2. Students will be able to identify at least one special characteristic of each planet.

B. Activities:

1. View filmstrip, "The Solar System" (National Geographic, 1978).

2. Explain orally and in writing how planets are the same and different from one another.

C. Optional Activity: Students will complete fact sheet on one or more planets.

Lesson 3

A. Objectives:

1. Students will be able to distinguish and identify stars, galaxies, and nebuli.

2. Students will be able to draw top and side view diagrams of the Milky Way Galaxy and locate our Solar System's position therein.

B. Activities:

1. View the filmstrip, "You and the Universe" (Harper and Row Singer SVE).

2. Using black construction paper and chalk, students will draw a top and side view of our galaxy to be displayed on hall bulletin board.

Lesson 4

A. Objectives:

1. Students will design and draw an original, peaceful spacecraft, label its parts and describe its mission.

2. Students will be able to define satellite, spacecraft, shuttle, space station.

B. Activities:
  1. Read pages 5–12 in "Visitor from Outer Space" (Radio Shack).
  2. Draw spaceship design to be displayed on hall bulletin board.
  C. Optional activity: Complete one or more fact sheets on an actual space mission.
V. SEEK Activities:
  A. Core:
    1. Each student will prepare a report on a planet, other celestial body, or another approved aspect of space.
    2. Group will prepare a presentation for an appropriate school audience.
  B. Optional activities:
    1. Slide/tape program.
    2. Learning center.
    3. Bulletin Board, time line.
    4. Models.
    5. Prepare position papers on advantages and disadvantages of various space activities and communicate ideas to appropriate sources (NASA, government officials).
    6. Visit a planetarium.
VI. Evaluation by SEEK teacher and students:
VII. Resources:
  A. NASA, Washington, DC 20546.
  B. Odyssey–A magazine of space exploration and astronomy for young people. Robert A. Maas, Publisher. Astromedia Division of Kalmback Publishing Co. 1027 N. 7th St., Milwaukee, WI 53233.
  C. Current periodicals and newspapers (Tuesday edition of *The New York Times*).
  D. N.J. Bell Resources for Education, Tel: (201) 649-3674.
  E. Maps, models, and pictures of the universe.
  F. Local and state planetaria.

Sixth Grade Convocation (Milgram, 1986)

A two-day convocation on Solid Waste Management was planned to provide sixth graders with an opportunity to participate in a series of goal-directed group problem-solving sessions dealing with a real-life issue. This project was supported in part by a grant from the Summit Board of Education.

The first day was devoted to developing an in-depth understanding of the problem. This is accomplished by obtaining information from experts in various workshops and then sharing it with the team. The second day was devoted to developing a possible solution for the problem that is the topic of the convocation and to designing, preparing, and then presenting the team's solution to the rest of the convocation participants. The presentations were frequently multimedia in that they used graphics, drama, and music as well as the more conventional verbal means of presentation.

From its inception, this convocation on Solid Waste Management was viewed as the centerpiece of a long-term unit for the entire sixth grade and the enrichment teachers worked closely with the sixth grade teachers in planning the events. A teacher workshop was conducted at the convocation site, an environmental center situated between New Jersey's largest landfill and a salt water marsh. Half of the classroom teachers were released to attend the convocation as facilitators.

The eighty students (40% of the class) who would actually attend the convocation were viewed as representatives of the total class. A minimum of four total class lessons were prepared on the topic of solid waste management with required and optional activities following each. It was explained to the students that in order to qualify as a representative to the convocation, they had to satisfactorily complete at least three of the optional assignments. The number of qualified applicants ranged from 5 percent to 85 percent of any one of the 9 sixth-grade classes. Some applicants were completely unexpected by the teachers, yet were very successful participants.

The entire sixth grade came to the team presentations on the second afternoon of the convocation. They took notes on the various ideas and solutions presented since they knew that each class had to plan and implement a program/product that would promote citizen education and compliance with the town's upcoming mandatory recycling law. Following the convocation, new committees were organized to plan and to implement each class project. Some of the convocation participants stepped down at this point and many new students joined some of the original convocation participants. Student leadership and communication skills emerged and developed. Skits, slogans, banners, posters, flyers, and news articles were prepared for the schools and community at large generating much interest and response. Again, a very successful cooperative approach with children participating at their particular level of interest and skill.

Other Units

Other units using the basic format described above are, for example, in the areas of archaeology, advertising, creative writing, and current events. In each unit, students are chosen for a more intense enrichment group based on their performance on required and optional activities assigned during the introductory lessons to the whole class. Presentations of final products are always made to the home class and other appropriate audiences and can take various forms such as slide lectures, bulletin board displays, information booklets, dramatic presentations, hands-on demonstrations, and original video tapes.

The SEEK approach can be profitably used to develop knowledge and appreciation of topics of critical importance. The following unit on responsible citizenship and the U.S. Constitution illustrates this point.

The following is the formal teacher's outline for the SEEK Constitution/ Citizenship Unit for Grades 4–6.

Key Topics: Research/Critical Thinking

I. Goal: To broaden and deepen students' understanding and appreciation of the US Constitution and its amendments and how they have helped mold our modern system of government especially with reference to who is eligible to vote and how we elect the legislative and executive officers.

II. Curriculum Objectives: Students will . . . :

A. Identify and describe how several constitutional amendments increased the number of eligible voters.

Article XV (1870): Extended the vote to people of all races regardless of their former status as slaves.

Article XIX (1920): Extended the vote to women.

Article XXIII (1961): Allowed citizens of Washington, DC to vote for president and vice president in the same manner as other U.S. citizens.

Article XXIV (1964): Allowed citizens to vote in federal elections without paying a poll tax.

Article XXVI (1971): Extended the vote to citizens age 18 or older.

   B. Compare and contrast the Electoral College system of electing
      the president and vice president with the popular vote system
      of electing the Congress.
   C. Discuss the pros and cons of the Electoral College system, exam-
      ine alternative proposals for electing the President and Vice
      President, and formulate possible constitutional amendments
      changing the way we vote for President and Vice President.
III. Identification procedure:
   A. SEEK and classroom teacher evaluation of required and optional
      class activities of this unit.
   B. Student self-nomination based on interest and motivation.
   C. Teacher recommendation based on task commitment, creativ-
      ity and ability.
IV. Activities—Whole class:
   A. Core activities:
      1. Discussion of why we vote and who is eligible to vote.
      2. Discussion of how and when suffrage was extended
         over the past 200 years. Refer to relevant Constitutional
         amendments.
      3. Discussion and participation in popular vote (i.e., choose
         one ice cream flavor for class) where majority rules.
      4. Simulation of Electoral College system. Students to decide
         on what basis to divide the class into several unequal
         groups and vote on the same issue.
      5. Comparison and evaluation of different forms of voting
   B. Optional activities:
      1. Speaker from League of Women Voters to explain elec-
         toral system.
      2. Constructing charts and maps to indicate the number of
         electors each state has.
      3. Prepare a time line of the relevant constitutional amend-
         ments.
V. SEEK Activities:
   A. Core activities:
      1. Students to plan and implement simulated Electoral Col-
         lege election.
      2. Students to research and evaluate alternative proposals of
         electing the president and vice-president.
      3. Students to formulate possible constitutional amendments

regarding the election of the president, the vice-president, and present to the whole class to vote upon.
  B. Optional activities:
     1. Prepare a time-line of the relevant constitution amendments.
     2. Solicit opinions on the issue from presidential candidates and other interested parties.
     3. Invite another fifth grade to participate in a simulated "Constitution Convention."
VI. Evaluation:
  A. Pre and post test of student knowledge of relevant facts.
  B. Teacher and student evaluation questionnaire.
VII. Resources:
  A. U.S. Constitution.
  B. Murray, J. (1987). *Summit Constitution Activity Packet.* Franklin School, Blackburn Road, Summit, NJ 07901.
  C. Milgram, N. *Celebrate the Constitution.* Washington School, 507 Morris Avenue, Summit, NJ 07901.
  D. League of Women Voters of the United States (1969). *Who Should Elect the President.* 1730 M Street, NW, Washington, DC 20036: Author. Publication #345.
  E. King, D. C. (1984). *Electing the President—1984.* A Weekly Reader Skills Book. 245 Long Hill Road, Middletown, CT 06457.
  F. Klein, E. (Ed.), Emerson, K. (Issue Ed.), (September 13, 1987) *The Great Voyage: Two Hundred Years of the Constitution.* New York Times Sunday Magazine, Special Issue, Section 6.
  G. Ryan, P. (Managing Ed.). (Fall, 1987). *The Constitution.* Life, Special Issue. Time & Life Building, Rockefeller Center, New York, NY 10020-1393: Time, Inc.
  H. Marienhoff, I. (1971). *Electing the President—1972. Election Reform* (filmstrip/record). Library of Congress Card No. 74-739260. New York: Educational Division of the New York Times Company. Frames 54–80 deal with the Electoral College System and possible alternatives.

Ultimate Challenge

Ultimate Challenge is a good example of the SEEK approach in which the emphasis is on giving all of the children the opportunity to express their special gifts and talents. Ultimate Challenge is an annual, end-of-the-year creative problem solving event open to all students in the school on an optional basis. It may be competitive or noncompetitive (usually grades 1 and 2) depending on the specific grade and school. Most often, the challenge problem is solved at home by individuals or small groups of children. In some cases, class time is devoted to this project or participating students meet with the G/T teacher for short periods. This is particularly true when it is a team problem and/or practice is needed on a special field. The emphasis in Ultimate Challenge is on originality and innovation. The children appreciate the variety of solutions to a given problem such as designing a model of a piece of playground equipment incorporating a straw, a moving part, and not to exceed a foot in height, width, or depth.

III. CONCLUSIONS

The Summit performance-based, cooperative approach to gifted education has many advantages over the traditional pull-out method. The G/T teacher teaches in all the classrooms at some time during the fall semester thus becoming aware of special talents and interests of students and teachers that can be pursued in the spring or the following year. Many students who might be overlooked by conventional identification procedures, have a chance to develop their special gifts. Students in many instances are self-nominated and come to the enrichment groups highly motivated to participate with enthusiasm and to produce high quality work. Nonparticipating children are stimulated by their classmates' projects to offer their candidacy for future enrichment units.

The classroom teachers are intimately involved with the selection of students and topics and are therefore more comfortable and satisfied with the G/T program. Classroom teachers have a deeper understanding and respect for the G/T program and teacher as a result of the whole class lessons and often choose to be present during these lessons. The classroom and G/T teachers learn from each other and integrate the new ideas into their respective lessons. The G/T teachers provide more structured units in the form of extensions and additions to the curriculum, some at the teacher's request and some at their own or the students' initiative. Although there is still a pull-out dimension to the G/T program, it is with different students at different times and for shorter durations.

The teachers, parents, and students are especially pleased with the fact that in the Summit model all students have an opportunity to develop their special abilities and interests in both large and small group settings. Students have a degree of control over their learning and can decide whether or not to apply to the special G/T pull-out groups. Students learn to appreciate each other's special areas of giftedness.

The major problems with the new approach are administrative in nature. In the conventional pull-out model, the population of the G/T classes was the same throughout the year and fairly stable from year to year. The G/T teacher was able to build on past experiences and interpersonal relationships with the students. In the new model, because of the larger number of students being serviced by the G/T teacher, a longer time is needed to recognize the strengths, weaknesses and particular learning style of each child. In addition, group morale is slower in developing.

The constant change of grades and students taught demands frequent changes of schedule, for the classroom teacher and especially for the G/T teacher. Even when the new group of students comes from the same grade, the schedule may have to be changed because these particular students have some preexisting commitments. Another difficulty stems from the annual adjustments of units to meet the current needs of each class. Under these circumstances, it is often difficult to accurately predict the time requirements for each unit. Some projects may take more time than expected thus shortchanging another group.

In theory, the Summit approach described in this chapter has many advantages. Unfortunately, many of these advantages are only partially realized. In order to realize the full potential of the new system and to derive maximum benefit from it, the number of G/T teachers must be increased. If the number of G/T teachers is not increased, then you are simply spreading the service thinner so that many children are being serviced, but the program is necessarily diluted. Highly gifted students are the most likely to be shortchanged in the new system. The reason for the lack of concern about this situation is probably because of the widespread view that profoundly gifted children will realize their potential without society making special efforts on their behalf. Unfortunately, this view is erroneous. Recognized authorities in the field, cite the failure of many gifted children to realize their potential abilities as a major problem (Tannenbaum, 1983).

In summary, the Summit model represents an innovative advance in gifted education. One would hope that the positive response of the entire school community to this model will be reflected in increased budgets that will enable the program to fulfill its promise.

REFERENCES

Cox, J., Daniel, N. & Boston, B.O. (1985). *Educating able learners: Programs and promising practices.* Austin, TX: University of Texas Press.

Gourley, T.J. (1981) Adapting the varsity sports model to nonpsychomotor gifted students. *Gifted Child Quarterly, 24,* 147–151.

Gourley, T. & Burr, S. (1978). *Convocation Model.* National Network for Talent Identification and Development. Educational Information and Resource Center, RD 4, Box 209, Sewell, NJ 08080.

Micklus, S., & Gourley, T.J. (1982). *Problems, problems, problems.* Glassboro, NJ: Creative Competitions.

Milgram, N.C. (1986). *Convocation booklet on Solid Waste Management.* May be obtained upon request from Nancy Milgram, 1 Timber Lane, Randoloph, NJ 07869.

New Jersey State Teen Arts Festival. (1987). 841 Georges Rd., North Brunswick, NJ 08902. Tel: (201) 745-3898.

Olympics of the Mind Association (1983). *What is Olympics of the Mind?* Glassboro, NJ: OM Association.

Peck, E. (1987). *Investing in children: A guide to the Mini-Invention/Innovation Team Contest Program.* Rutgers The State University, Aberdeen, NJ: New Jersey Vocational Education Resources Center.

Tannenbaum, A.J. (1983). *Gifted children: Psychological and educational perspectives.* New York: MacMillan.

Weekly Reader. (1985). *National Invention Contest.* 245 Long Hill Road. Middletown, CT 06457.

PART II
CUSTOMIZING CURRICULUM CONTENT
FOR GIFTED AND TALENTED LEARNERS
IN REGULAR CLASSROOMS

INTRODUCTION

ROBERTA M. MILGRAM

The most difficult problem facing teachers who would like to offer the gifted students in their class something other than the regular curriculum is lack of familiarity with suitable materials in the specific disciplines and lack of experience with domain-specific teaching strategies. Much of the material designed for individualized instruction is not appropriate for gifted children and very little curriculum material produced specifically for gifted children is in a format that lends itself to individualization.

In this section, recognized authorities present the framework for understanding giftedness in five specific subject matter areas. They discuss the pedagogical framework for instructing gifted children in each of the following areas: language arts, mathematics, science, social studies, and foreign languages. Each expert provides classroom examples and offers practical advice on how to differentiate the curriculum and individualize instruction in the specific area. In addition, each lists the names and sources of books, articles, and other teaching materials that will help the teacher implement the suggestions.

The section opens with two chapters on teaching language arts to gifted learners. The language arts skills of listening, reading, speaking, and writing are the basic competencies of literacy and play a central role in learning all other subject matter areas. In the first chapter in this section, Kaplan summarizes general concepts designed to guide teachers in their efforts to help learners who are gifted in a wide variety of disciplines acquire the essential general language arts skills as well as the more specific skills related to each field. In the second chapter, Anderson focuses specifically on reading and discusses the policy issues that must be discussed and resolved in schools before initiating programs designed to provide for gifted children with special needs in reading and library skills. She details the assessment procedures and curriculum modifications that help teachers customize the reading curriculum.

Teaching science and math to gifted learners would appear to present no problem because the subject matter is well defined and structured and the relative abilities of students simple to assess. The authors dealing with these topics indicate that such is not the case. Tirosh draws on her experience as a researcher and a classroom teacher to distinguish between mathematical giftedness and computational superiority and suggests ways to deal with each kind of learner. Yager defines giftedness in science and draws our attention to the difference in many schools between demonstrating science giftedness and achieving high grades in science courses. He describes the progress being made in teaching science in the United States and provides several examples of the teaching of science in an exemplary manner.

Shermis argues that social studies is not simply the content of social science disciplines, such as history, political science, sociology, and geography simplified for children. In addition to appropriate subject matter, he recommends that reflective inquiry and citizenship transmission be stressed. He views reflective inquiry as especially relevant to teaching social science to gifted learners. Shermis provides abundant theoretical background for the position, and provides many classroom examples of how to customize the topics.

Modern technology has already made worldwide communication instantaneous. Individuals who play leadership roles in politics, business, or academia are more effective if they can communicate with their counterparts in their own language. Shrum presents an authoritative picture of the long-neglected topic of teaching foreign languages to gifted learners. She traces the theoretical developments that provide the base of understanding required to differentiate and individualize foreign language acquisition in gifted and talented learners.

Chapter 7

LANGUAGE ARTS FOR GIFTED LEARNERS

SANDRA N. KAPLAN

anguage Arts has been defined as the understandings and skills of receptive and expressive language. The abilities to decode and encode are fundamental to the study of language arts. The subjects included in a language arts curriculum are listening, reading, speaking, and writing. These skills are the basic competencies of literacy and an important means by which understandings in all other subject areas are acquired.

Even in communities that provide extensive alternative educational opportunities for the gifted, most gifted children spend most of their school time in regular classrooms. Unfortunately, when limited to the regular classroom curriculum, learners who are gifted in language arts cannot realize their full potential. For them equal opportunity means special education. This chapter is designed to provide guidance to classroom teachers in meeting the needs of gifted learners. The chapter is divided into four sections. In the first section, five basic guiding principles for differentiating the language arts curriculum for the gifted learner in the regular classroom are presented. In the second section, classroom management challenges are described and a number of solutions discussed. In the third section, the components of three dimensions of language arts that require differentiation are presented and in the fourth section, teaching strategies found useful by many teachers in meeting the needs of gifted learners are recommended.

I. DIFFERENTIATING LANGUAGE ARTS: GUIDING PRINCIPLES

Generally, a language arts curriculum designated as differentiated for the gifted should reflect the following principles:

1. *The curriculum should be responsive to the needs of the gifted student as both a member of the gifted population that requires specific differentiated learnings and as a member of the general population that requires the societally-defined learnings all individuals are expected to master.* Ignorance of the gifted student's dual membership in a curriculum as gifted and as a basic learner, can result in gaps in learning and faulty expectations. These learning gaps may appear as deficiencies in rudimentary or fundamental skills. Faulty expectations may cause the deferment of more complex learnings because of a perceived lack of readiness which many educators believe is dependent on the mastery of basic skills of literacy.

2. *The differentiated curriculum should include or subsume aspects of the regular curriculum.* It should be recognized that the differentiated curriculum must not exonerate the gifted student from opportunities to gain understandings and skills contained in the regular curricula.

3. *The curriculum should provide gifted students with opportunities to exhibit those characteristics that were instrumental in their identification as gifted individuals.* In other words, the differentiated curriculum should reinforce the display of the traits that demonstrate the giftedness of each learner. The curriculum then becomes a practice opportunity for the gifted to exercise further their recognized abilities of giftedness.

4. *The curriculum for gifted students within the regular classroom should not academically or socially isolate these students from their peers.* In some instances, gifted students who are involved in a differentiated curriculum feel that those differences which distinguish them as gifted individuals also cause them to learn differently and apart from their nongifted peers. Regardless of the nature and scope of the differentiated curriculum, there should always be opportunities for the gifted and the nongifted students to share similar teaching/learning experiences.

5. *The differentiated curriculum should not be used as either reward or punishment for gifted students.* It is the right of all students to be able to learn in accordance with their abilities, needs, and interests. Gifted students should not be led to believe that their involvement in curriculum that is differentiated for them within the regular classroom is a benevolent gesture of the teacher or school.

II. CLASSROOM MANAGEMENT

Two major challenges confront regular classroom teachers in their efforts to provide gifted learners with a comprehensive and articulated language arts curriculum. They are:

1. *How to select* the content areas, processes, or skills and products which match the needs, interests, and abilities of the gifted.

2. *How to organize* the classroom in a way that provides the time, space, and resources to implement the special educational opportunities for the gifted.

Selection is the process whereby the classroom teacher assesses formally and informally, quantitatively and qualitatively, and/or subojectively and objectively, the learner's progress in and thus need for the content and skill learnings of the existing language arts curriculum. The selection process is utilized to determine which elements should be eliminated from the curriculum because mastery has already occurred. Selection also determines which elements to retain in the curriculum because additional practice is needed. It also enables the teacher to decide which learnings to elaborate because the student's level of readiness requires more extensive and complex understandings of the content or skill.

Organization refers to the options for scheduling time and the classroom management techniques necessary to attend to the gifted within the regular classroom. Time can be arranged to accommodate the gifted in the context of the regular classroom by borrowing it from the regular curriculum. This can be accomplished in two ways, by replacing or by condensing the time assigned for the regular curriculum. The most appropriate approach to obtaining time to facilitate the needs of the gifted in the regular classroom is to be guided by the concept of replacing time. The regular curriculum is replaced by the differentiated curriculum. This approach assumes that the teacher views the teaching/learning of the differentiated curriculum as of more immediate value to the gifted student than the regular curriculum. This is especially desirable when the regular curriculum is repetitive or redundant to gifted students because they have confronted and mastered it previously. Time also can be provided by condensing the regular curriculum to fit a shorter time frame. This leaves enough time for a more elaborate and sophisticated language arts curriculum that matches the gifted students' needs.

There is not one best way to allocate time and organize the regular classroom for the gifted. However, the necessity to find a method to schedule the differentiated curriculum in an orderly and consistent manner is paramount to both the teacher and gifted students. The issue is not whether or not to facilitate the gifted students' needs in the regular classroom. The issue is for the teacher to decide on the most appropriate method of finding time and organizing that time productively.

III. DIFFERENTIATING THE
THREE DIMENSIONS OF LANGUAGE ARTS

A language arts curriculum for gifted students in a regular classroom should include the following three dimensions:

1. Acquisition of basic competencies
2. Appreciation of language
3. Specialization of language usage

Acquisition of Basic Concepts

Fundamental to the teaching/learning of the basic competencies are the gifted students' needs to be released from the lock-step presentation and acquisition of basic language arts understandings and skills. While a language arts scope and sequence has been developed to outline which skills and understandings should be taught and mastered at designated age/grade intervals, gifted students cannot be bound to or regulated by learnings that are aligned with developmental levels. The intellectual maturity and the advanced verbal abilities of gifted students demand a self-paced rather than an institutionally directed set of language arts opportunities. For these students, their acquisition of basic competencies should parallel their abilities for more complex and abstract learnings in language arts as well as other subject areas.

As gifted students learn the mechanical operations necessary to communicate, they also need to comprehend why people communicate. "Reading in context" is one example of language arts experiences that introduces gifted students to the how as well as the why of communication. For example, an essay assumes different and greater technical and personal meaning when it is read in context or interpreted in relationship to the economic, political, psychological, and social dimensions of the time when the author wrote the essay.

The eagerness of the gifted student to read and experience a spectrum of reading material often results in the exposure to or coverage of such material without commensurate in-depth understanding of that material. *Reading in context* is a process that demands savoring the reading material rather than presuming that to read is to simply complete the printed material. The goal of reading in context is to provide gifted students with a frame of reference or backdrop for the material they are reading. Two instructional strategies enhance this goal:

1. **Perspective Reading.** This refers to reading *collections* of rather than a single copy of material related to topics, themes, questions, etc. Given an aggregate of related materials, gifted students are engaged in perceiving simultaneously the breadth and depth of the topic, theme, question, etc., from varied perspectives.

2. **Reading Beyond the Page.** This refers to the idea that to "really know" is to search beyond what is read on the page to determine the variables that affected the author's production of the communication. The intent is to facilitate the gifted students' ability to read the author's message and to read *about* the factors affecting and/or motivating the author's development or creation of the communication. "Why" becomes the common denominator to comprehend what is read; for example, why did the characterization of the girl in *Something New* reflect the author's personality?

Appreciation of Languages

The purpose of developing the gifted students' appreciation of language is to extend their sense of wonder regarding the power and impact of words in spoken and written forms. Included within this aspect of differentiated curriculum for the gifted is learning about the existence and usage of languages for different purposes. Each of the languages to be discussed in this section has a specialized vocabulary, so to speak, and particular syntax which convey meaning with respect to the underlying intention of that language. Gifted students should be assisted to become aware of the origin and evolution of these languages and the factors in a society which promote or retard their use.

Language of Learning. This is the language of scholars and the language that precipitates scholarliness. It includes the language of questioning, challenging, and verifying information. Examples of this language include:

- "The accumulated evidence indicates that _____"
- "Another point of view might be _____"
- "The assumption proposed appears to be that _____"
- "The issue germane or central to the point seems to be _____"

Understanding when and how to use the language of learning appropriately is a necessary component of this element of a differentiated curriculum for the gifted.

Language of Decision-Making. This refers to the nomenclature used to process the variables which aid decision-making. These language patterns can be gleaned from the dialogues of fictional characters in decision-making situations. They also can be acquired from an analysis of the lives of famous people expressed in autobiographies and biographies. Importantly, the language of decision-making is also to be noted in the essays and other deliberations of individuals in crisis or conflict. This language includes phrases such as:

- weighing the consequences
- prioritizing data
- assigning value to
- assessing the alternatives
- pondering

Language of Leadership. This refers to the selection of words and style of syntax that distinguish individuals from one another as well as serves to influence others. Inherent in the development of this type of language is an understanding of intellectual as well as social leadership behaviors and skills. Listening to and reading from the speeches and debates of historic and contemporary leaders can be the bases for the acquisition of this type of language. In addition, gifted students need many and varied chances to use this language in written and spoken forms. The power of language to lead cannot be omitted from an appropriately developed curriculum for the gifted.

The appreciation of language also can be derived from the gifted students' encounters with printed materials. The concept of "sample reading" encourages students to develop a "bookstore mentality" or the opportunity to browse through books without being forced to commit oneself to the reading of the entire selection. Too often, the student's interest in handling a book is perceived as the student's interest in pursuing the book as reading matter. Such instances often deter rather than facilitate an appreciation for books.

An appreciation for language is taught directly by studying the psychology and philosophy of private as well as public expression. Gifted students can understand readily that reading, writing, speaking, and listening provide avenues for self-knowledge, retreats from the world and releases for self-expression. A differentiated language arts curriculum for the gifted must parallel the studies of psychology and philosophy so that it can be defined both personally and socially. Within this study of language arts multiple points of view and controversies regarding the changing value and importance of languages are anticipated.

Specialization of Language Usage

Unless the language arts program can be personalized for the gifted student, it may not be assimilated and internalized by the individual. Personalization of a language arts program for the gifted is based on the belief that language arts is a tool to be used to attain individual power. Gifted students should be aided in developing a personal language profile. Such a profile enables the individual to stylize language patterns which reflect personal values, interests, and abilities. What and when we read, what we say, and how we say it defines the individual and expresses one's sense of individuality. Effective writers, speakers, leaders, and listeners recognize the roles of preference, style, and personalization in becoming proficient in language usage.

A specialist in language distinguishes between the appropriate use of technical and creative language usage. While creative or expressive language is valued and taught continually to gifted students, the teaching of technical language is sometimes omitted from their curriculum. Technical language usage includes the types of vocabulary and syntax professionals require. Writing a proposal to present an idea or request for funds or support, writing the directions to accompany a model or inventions, writing a pamphlet, brochure or guide, are some of the language experiences which demand the skills of technical vocabulary and structures. Within this category of differentiated curriculum is the need to acquire the specialized language understandings and skills related to the student's particular interest and special aptitude.

For example, Irene, who is twelve, wants to be a musician. The fulfillment of that professional choice also necessitates specialized language usage: acquisition of related vocabulary describing music, musicians, etc.; development of a critique of a performance or artist, construction of a business letter requesting equipment and needs in order to perform, listing of rehearsal and performance schedules and bulletins, development of copy for advanced publicity.

Gary is studying psychology independently. His specialized language arts needs include writing a case study, presenting orally a point of view or evidence to substantiate a statement of opinion, developing an abstract, writing a journal article. Specialized language usage emanates from either the gifted student's professional or independent study choices. In either case, specialized language usage is associated with the specialized interests and abilities of gifted students.

IV. TEACHING STRATEGIES IN DIFFERENTIATING CURRICULUM

Language arts in the regular classroom can be differentiated for the gifted either within the subject itself or tangential to any other subject or discipline. Each approach has both positive and negative consequences and might be suited best to a particular teaching style.

Differentiating Curriculum Within the Language Arts Subject Area

Differentiation can occur through a unit study approach. Using "Style" as an organizing element, the skills (processes), understandings (content), and oral, written forms of communication (products) can be taught and learned in an integrated manner. Examples of these integrated activities follow:

• Identify the key words that define the elements which represent the style of characters and plot used to portray conflict in fairytales and fables. Prepare a speech to defend the use of conflict as a vehicle for creative expression.

• Identify the main idea which proves that style is a consequence of preferences and values. Read a collection of works by a selected author to gather evidence to prove the above statement. Present the findings in an essay.

Each of these activities is a composite of the interaction of processes or skills and content or subject matter plus products or communication forms. They are selected to meet the needs of the gifted and organized to provide an integrated approach to a differentiated language arts curriculum. It should be noted that with this approach, other subject areas or disciplines provide the support necessary for comprehension or mastery of these activities. In other words, the understanding of style is facilitated by understandings in the areas of psychology, art, etc.

The Tangential Language Arts Approach

Gold (1965) summarized the importance of language arts and their unique contribution to the education of gifted learners by saying "they represent both a means to achieve in other areas and an area for accomplishment in themselves." In the tangential approach the processes (skills), content (understandings), and products (oral and written forms of communication) are ancillary to other subject areas being taught. Examples of this approach follow:

• In the study of the Industrial Revolution (Social Studies), gifted children define new words and phrases coined during this era to describe technology and categorize who emerged in fiction according to their level of support for technological advances. They write a pamphlet or brochure to describe the uses and misuses of a new technological advancement in real and imaginary circumstances.

These activities are related to the central task of a discipline and are intended to extend the task into the language arts area.

Enrichment or Acceleration

Modifications of language arts curricula usually take the form of enrichment or acceleration. Traditionally, enrichment refers to the breadth or range of experiences which provides the learner with increasingly elaborative opportunities related to a content area or skill within a subject. Acceleration is the intellectual advancement of the learner beyond the specified age or grade-related content or skill learnings in a subject. While there have been many discussions about the advantages and/or disadvantages of enrichment versus acceleration for the gifted, many educators agree that one type of modification cannot take place without affecting the other.

For example, acceleration cannot be effective unless it is accomplished by some opportunities for enrichment; the thoroughness of understanding of content or skill must occur before the learner is ready for the next more advanced or difficult content or skill. Conversely, enrichment cannot be effective without some measure of acceleration, because there is a point wherein the next most appropriate complex learning opportunity necessitates an advancement in the content or skill. Thus, enrichment and acceleration are related symbiotically. An appropriate differentiated language arts curriculum for the gifted attempts both to enrich and accelerate the curriculum.

It is of little importance to determine if curriculum modification and differentiation of the content, process, or product aspects of the language arts cited above are characterized mainly by techniques of acceleration or enrichment. Depending on the grade level and the state and/or district standards, the three aspects can be differentiated by both accelerated and/or enriched curriculum.

CONCLUSION

Educators frequently express dissatisfaction with the language arts learning experiences provided for gifted learners. They criticize these efforts as superficial, fragmented, and "gimmicky." Kaplan (1979) and others have recommended that special education for the gifted take the form of developmental learning activities. Such activities would be guided by clearly stated objectives and understanding of the cognitive and personal-social characteristics of gifted learners. Moreover, they would be integrated with curriculum content, processes, and products and continuously reinforced in the teaching-learning process (Kaplan, 1979). This chapter is intended to help teachers implement these recommendations.

REFERENCES

Kaplan, S.N. (1979). Language arts and social studies curriculum in the elementary school. In Passow, A.H. (Ed.). *The gifted and the talented: Their education and development.* Chicago: The University of Chicago Press.

Gold, M.J. (1965). *Education of the intellectually gifted.* Columbus, OH: Charles E. Merrill.

Chapter 8

ASSESSING AND PROVIDING FOR GIFTED CHILDREN WITH SPECIAL NEEDS IN READING AND LIBRARY SKILLS

MARGARET A. ANDERSON

The literature on gifted and talented children often reports that they are both advanced in their reading development and are voracious readers of a wide variety of reading materials. The small amount of time and the limited experiences afforded gifted children in the usual enrichment program does not represent an adequate response to the reading interests and abilities of these children. Most gifted and talented children are in regular classrooms most of the time. Accordingly, the attitudes of regular classroom teachers towards gifted learners and their willingness to make efforts to modify curriculum content and process for them is a critical aspect of an appropriate *overall* response to educational planning for gifted and talented children.

A major portion of every school day involves reading activities of one kind or another (Cassiday, 1979). The place of reading in the school makes curriculum modifications in reading critical, not only to the development of higher reading skills, but also to providing greater depth and breadth in other curriculum areas as well. The purpose of this chapter is to suggest ways that teachers in regular classrooms can meet the needs of gifted and talented children with advanced reading abilities and interests. The chapter is divided into three sections in which policy issues, assessment procedures, and curriculum modifications are discussed.

I. POLICY ISSUES

Response to the educational needs of gifted and talented children begins with the establishment of administrative policies that both encourage and assist teachers in the utilization of the techniques and materials needed to enhance the reading programs of such children. Lack of response to the reading abilities of gifted and talented children is, in effect, a clear policy statement. This policy is reflected in inadequate or inappropriate educational programming that fails to facilitate the intellectual and creative growth of gifted and talented children. In such situations the fact that these children have developed skills beyond their current grade level is frequently ignored by either or both administrative and instructional staff.

For the child who has already mastered reading skills prior to entering school, the regular classroom reading curriculum can be repetitious, boring, sterile, and lacking in challenge. It has even been suggested that, all too often, the regular school reading curriculum retards the development of reading abilities in gifted and talented learners (Malone, 1974; Switzer & Nourse, 1979) and may adversely effect the child's attitude toward reading as he/she matures (Anderson, Tollefson, & Gilbert, 1985).

It is often appropriate for a gifted child to use material beyond the current grade level placement. Many school reading programs, however, are not flexible enough to respond to the need. Often there exists a written or "unwritten" school policy that prohibits access to materials above grade level. Such policy results from a concern, unsupported by the literature on good instructional practice, as to "what will this child read next year." This educational philosophy fails to recognize individual differences, emphasizes conformity to an average standard, and prevents instructional staff from utilizing materials that may be more appropriate for advanced readers.

Administrative recognition of the need for educational programming that provides for differentiation of curriculum and individualized instruction throughout the school for *all* children is highly desirable. The advantages of such an approach have been cited by many authors in the current volume. Gifted and talented learners with special abilities in reading will benefit greatly from a differentiated and individualized curriculum. Unfortunately, these approaches are still the exception rather than the rule in most schools.

Published reading programs for individualized instruction are more efficient in terms of preparation time required than teacher-made units. The problem of the additional time required from teachers for preparation is a real one. It creates resistance to change and unwillingness on the part of teachers to design qualitatively differentiated reading programs. Additional reasons for lack of instructional response to the reading needs of gifted and talented children are that teachers frequently lack knowledge about such children and skill in utilizing appropriate teaching techniques and materials with them. Moreover, they are often unfamiliar with published materials, especially those designed for individualized instruction with gifted and talented children. It is not ethical or professionally sound to let such considerations prevent the development of appropriate educational programming for gifted and talented children.

Administrative staff can assist instructional staff in the development of curricula that are more individualized within a class or school by providing support and encouragement in learning new instructional practices. Further support can be provided by modeling growth-directed attitudes. Assistance can be provided through direct administrative support, team teaching experiences, and *on-going* teacher development opportunities. An overt and clear administrative commitment provides teachers with a safe environment in which to explore new ideas, grow beyond inadequacies, and become more effective diagnostic-prescriptive professionals. These professional opportunities must be available on a schoolwide basis and involve all teachers working with gifted and talented children.

II. ASSESSMENT PROCEDURES

Gifted children often read before beginning school (Terman, 1925). Some estimate that approximately 50 percent of children, classified as gifted by intelligence tests, were already reading in kindergarten and nearly all were reading as they entered the first grade (Burns, Roe, & Ross, 1984). On the other hand, many gifted and talented children are not gifted readers (Swassing, 1985) and may score poorly on tests generally used in assessing children's reading abilities. By the same token, many children who score high on standardized reading measures may not be gifted. Accordingly, it cannot be assumed that identification of a specific child as gifted indicates an advanced level of reading development requiring an accelerated program. Standardized measures simply do not provide sufficient data for comprehensive awareness of the reading profiles of gifted and talented children.

Fundamental to developing good reading programs for gifted and talented students is an understanding of diagnostic-prescriptive concepts. In essence, this means teachers must be adept at recognizing which children would best benefit from an advanced or accelerated reading curriculum and which need remedial assistance or the traditional reading program.

Related to good diagnostic-prescriptive expertise is an awareness of reading components, processes, and stages of development. A knowledge and perception of reading as a continuum of development assists the instructional designer in recognizing individual levels of reading growth among and between gifted and talented children.

Chall (1983) proposed a stage theory that encompasses the development of reading from its "primitive beginnings to its most mature and highly skilled forms." Her reading stages provide understanding of the reading process and its application in reading instruction. Ages and grades are approximations.

Stages of the Development of Reading (Chall, 1983)

STAGE 0: Prereading

Characteristics
- covers a greater period of time than any other stage
- covers a greater series of changes than any other stage
- fund of knowledge developed about letters, words, books
- control gained over aspects of language (syntax/words)
- insight gained into the nature of words: sounds, word parts
- tends to be an "inside out" process (from the reader more than from the author)

Implications for Instruction

- discriminate and name most of the letters of the alphabet
- write own names and some letters
- write various approximations to writing
- recognition of road signs, brand names, commercials, words in favorite books
- demonstrate "concepts" of reading:

  holding a book right-side-up
  pointing at words while "saying" the words
  turning pages one-at-a-time

STAGE 1: Initial Reading, or Decoding

  Ages 6–7, Grades 1–2
Characteristics

- learn the arbitrary set of letters and associate these with words:
  - *bug* is different than *bun*
- insight gained about the spelling system of language
- awareness that words are made up of a finite number of sounds
- tends to be more "glued" to print process (outside-in)

Implications for Instruction

- decoding exercises
- awareness of vowels, consonants, combinations
- structural awareness
- medium to meaning

STAGE 2: Confirmation, Fluency, Ungluing from Print

Ages 7–8 Grades 2–3
Characteristics

- consolidates what was learned in Stage 1
- confirms what is already known to the reader
- uses decoding knowledge for message in medium

Implications for Instruction

- read many "familiar" books—"familiar" because stories, subjects, structure are familiar
- more attention to comprehension

STAGE 3: Reading for Learning the New

Ages 9–13 Grades 4–8
Characteristics

- uses reading to "Learn the new":
  - information
  - knowledge
  - thoughts
  - experiences
  - structures
- learns processes:
  - how to find information in a paragraph, chapter, book
- more abstract words, longer and complex sentences

Implications for Instruction

- chooses materials that contain one viewpoint, limited in technical complexity
- learn study skills
- learn content reading skills

STAGE 4: Multiple/Greater Viewpoints

Ages 14–18 High School

Characteristics
- involves dealing with more than one point of view
- involves layers of facts and concepts

Implications for Instruction
- use textbooks containing depth and greater variety of points of view
- use original sources and reference works
- explore mature fiction

STAGE 5: Construction and Reconstruction

Age 18 and Above

Characteristics
- development of the conception of knowledge as the qualitative assessment of contextual observations and relationships

Implications for Instruction
- focus on critical reading
- use of many sources

STAGE 6: College and Adult

Characteristics
- reader knows what to read *as well as* what not to read
- from reading, reader constructs knowledge for himself/herself (analysis, synthesis, judgement)

Implications for Instruction
- broad knowledge of content

It can be expected that the gifted and talented child, who is also a precocious reader, will move through the stages at a pace faster than more average children. Therefore, the precocious reader may enter school already reading on a Stage 1 or 2 level, or may already be reading expository prose for information, a Stage 3 skill, at age six (Bissex, 1980). It is essential that teachers not underestimate the reading abilities of these children and keep them in materials or programs below their already developed reading stage. The specific instructional needs of such children are those reading tasks that challenge and motivate their reading development.

It is equally essential for gifted and talented children who are not precocious readers, to receive materials and instruction that match their achievement as well as possible. The essence of diagnostic/prescriptive teaching and true individualized instruction is matching individual ability with appropriate materials and instruction.

Evaluation

In order to provide challenging reading instruction for gifted and talented children, from a diagnostic-prescriptive base, it is essential that evaluation go beyond the usual standardized assessment procedures and utilize more personal and individual assessment instruments and techniques. Evaluation serves four purposes essential to good instructional practices (Cushenberry & Howell, 1974):

1. Determines students' exact instructional needs.
2. Helps group students appropriately.
3. Provides information for selecting and using appropriate instructional materials.
4. Helps in the study of students' levels of reading competency.

If used correctly, the more information and data, the better the program of instruction.

Criterion referenced instruments can provide data on a profile of reading skills and are more useful than those instruments that only provide a single percentage or grade equivalent score. Instruments that reveal an individual child's strengths and weaknesses are far more useful to the instructional designer than ones that compare a child to some national standard. Two such instruments appropriate for use with gifted and talented children are the *Barbe Reading Skill Checklist* (Barbe, 1975) and the recording system developed by Mindell and Stracher (1980).

Most useful for assessment of individual reading ability is the Informal Reading Inventory (IRI). IRI's provide a structured observation or interview designed to measure an individual's performance of oral/ or silent reading of selections of increasing difficulty. Information can be gained as to the functional reading levels (independent, instruction, and frustration) of the reader, identification of any persistent reading difficulties, and awareness of a reader's reaction or attitude in a reading situation.

Teachers may prepare their own informal reading inventories (IRI's) or utilize published reading inventories that already have verified readability levels on selections with a balance of both literal and inferential comprehension questions. Some suggested published IRI's are:

1. Silvaroe, N.J. (1985). *Classroom Reading Inventory.* Dubuque, Iowa: William C. Brown.

2. Sucher-Allred (1983). *Reading Placement Inventory.* Oklahoma City, Oklahoma: Economy Publishing Company.

3. Burns, P. & Roe, B. (1985). *Informal Reading Inventory.* Boston, Massachusetts: Houghton-Mifflin Publishing Company.

The advantages of an IRI over other instruments lie in the direct implication for instruction related to the reader's performance, the flexibility of gathering general or specific information, and the insight gained by the reader as he/she notes changes in performance from level to level.

Reading Interests

Assessment of children's interest is also critical to designing reading programs for gifted and talented children. An example of an interest inventory is as follows:

INTEREST INVENTORY
Written or oral form

1. How much do you like to read?

   very much _____
   quite a lot _____
   not very much _____
   not at all _____

2. What are the titles of several books which you really enjoyed?
3. What are the titles of some of the books in your home?
4. Do you have a library card?
5. How many books have you checked out from the library during the last month?
6. What part of the newspaper do you like to read the best?

   comic section _____
   sport section _____
   news section _____
   society section _____

editorials _____
letters to the editor _____

7. What magazines do you read regularly?
8. What type of comic books do you enjoy reading?
9. What are the names of your three favorite television programs?
10. What sports do you like to watch on television?
11. What do you usually do after school?
12. Of all the things which you do after school, what one thing do you like to do best?
13. What do you often do on Saturday?
14. Of all the things you do on Saturday, what one thing do you like to do best?
15. What kind of hobbies do you have?
16. Do you have any collections? If you do, what do you collect?
17. What do you want to be when you grow up?
18. Where do you usually go on vacation with your family?
19. Have you ever gone to camp in the summer? If you have, what did you enjoy the most about camp?
20. What other states have you visited?

Interest inventories can be designed by teachers easily and structured to gain data, not only on interest areas, but also on attitudes toward reading and reading behaviors. Other aspects of reading, such as motivation, are difficult to assess, but can be observed and addressed if needed. Self statements, autobiographical accounts, and teacher-pupil involvement provide important data in understanding individual children and in making decisions regarding their readiness for new experiences or challenges.

It must be remembered that diagnostic material can result in an erratic skill profile. An irregular sequence of skill acquisition may indicate an underlying learning problem or be the result of the idiosyncratic way gifted and talented children acquire skills. In such instances there is no substitute for the experienced judgments of a well-prepared and knowledgeable teacher.

Since the validity of all evaluation depends upon the competence of the examiner, it is critical that classroom teachers become expert in the use of evaluation instruments and techniques and in the analysis of resulting data. Analysis and application of results are critical to the development of reading programs that benefit not only gifted and talented children, but all other children as well.

The results of diagnostic work will reveal whether a child needs a remedial, regular, or advanced reading program or combination thereof.

What is to be avoided is placement of a gifted and talented child in a reading situation far below his/her reading capabilities and interest or in a reading situation beyond the child's capacity to perform.

To sum up, for gifted and talented children who are average readers, the regular reading program may represent the best approach. The use of a basal reader with accompanying workbook may be appropriate *if* used in a diagnostic/prescriptive manner. On the other hand, for those gifted and talented children who are advanced in reading development as well, a qualitative differentiated curriculum is required. The instructional modifications in reading required as these children advance through elementary and secondary schools depends on particular stages of development in reading, learning characteristics, and interests related to these personal considerations. A detailed discussion of the content and process of a differentiated reading curriculum is the focus of the remainder of the chapter.

III. CURRICULUM MODIFICATIONS

How do schools respond to the reading needs of gifted and talented learners? On the basis of a survey, Oliver (1983) concluded that very few specific programs for gifted readers exist, and that literature extension and Junior Great Books seem to be the usual way of attempting to meet the needs of these readers.

Barbe (1961) suggested the following three goals for reading skill development leading to effective reading, appreciation of good books, and a lifelong appreciation of reading. The essential questions to be addressed when developing a reading program for gifted and talented children designed to reach these goals are as follows:

1. What should be taught?
2. When should it be taught?
3. How will it be taught?
4. How will learning be evaluated?

Answers to these questions provide structure as the reading curriculum is planned and implemented. They also assure that instruction will not be haphazard and/or based upon undocumented assumptions.

For those gifted and talented children with easily remediated reading problems, assistance for the teacher may be found in books written for remediation of reading problems. Suggested resources are Adams (1976),

Burns and Roe (1976), Harris and Sipay (1975), Ruddell (1974), and Schell and Burns (1972). If the reading problem is severe, assistance may be gained from the remedial reading or learning disability specialist. Daniels (in press) provides guidance on dealing with the problems of learning-disabled gifted children.

How to expand the reading instruction of gifted and talented children has been an ongoing controversy for some time. Issues related to the two major approaches—enrichment or acceleration—are a source of dialogue and disagreement among educational planners in the field of gifted and talented education. Advocates of reading enrichment generally support the idea of providing instruction at the *norm* ability level with supplementary reading experiences for the gifted reader. Acceleration advocates support instruction at the reader's level of achievement— even if that means several levels above the current grade level.

According to Chall (1983), both enrichment and acceleration are essential for the reading diet of the gifted and talented reader. If only an enrichment approach is used, the fast developer may experience reading challenges far too easy or familiar. Using only an enrichment philosophy too often results in teachers giving gifted readers *extra* activities rather than those that would move them ahead (Gaug, 1984). This results in curriculum which is quantitatively rather than qualitatively different. Acceleration is needed as well to maintain early reading momentum and to push the student into areas of new learning and challenge. A combination of both enrichment and acceleration provides both a greater depth and scope to the reading diet of the advanced reader.

In developing a reading program for the advanced reader the reading teacher must modify content, process, product, and learning environment (Gallagher, 1975; Maker, 1982; Renzulli, 1977). These modifications create a classroom where there is an escalation of expectations, use of a variety of quality resources, teacher utilization of open teaching strategies, and a learning environment that is exploratory in its dimensions.

Escalated expectations in *content modifications* will focus on development of advanced reading skills and greater abstraction both in ideas and concepts explored and in areas of study selected for study. The focus will shift from one of finding the "correct answer" to one of exploring questions, problems, unknowns, "could be's," and utopias. By extending the content into new and unusual areas of focus, the reader adds depth and flavor to the reading experience and creates opportunity for greater reading development.

In addition to challenging content, a commitment to *process strategies* which deepen the readers thinking is essential. Such reading experiences go beyond the literal reading experience and provide the reader with opportunities to interpret, evaluate, and extrapolate ideas from a reading selection.

Facilitating the critical and creative thinking processes of gifted readers engages these advanced readers in reading experiences that demand active participation. *Critical reading processes* present challenges in the analyzing of content, elements, trends, and patterns. These processes focus the reader on unique relationships, principles, use of propaganda, and author bias. Opportunities are created that develop vocabulary these gifted readers need in the connotative power of words, the use of figurative language, and the study of etymology. Both the inductive and deductive reasoning capabilities of these children are engaged in the use of such process strategies.

Employing creativity processes escalates and expands thinking by stimulating the fluency, flexibility, and associative thinking in readers. These techniques encourage risk-taking and the engendering of ideas. Fantasy and imagery lend originality and elaboration to the reading experience and enrich the learning of the reader. Creativity modifications can be applied to reading selections that result in new story combinations unique to the reader. Adaptations of material are manifested through magnification, minification, substitution, rearrangement or reversal of characters or events.

Instructional process models can be applied to reading selections and used in part or whole depending on the purpose set for reading. Examples of such applications developed by Bloom (1956) and Williams (1970) follow:

Reading Comprehension According to Bloom's Taxonomy (1956)

I. Knowledge—recall of given information

    a. Recall details
    b. Recall sequence of events
    c. Setting (if directly stated)
    d. Names of characters
    e. Characters' traits (as stated)

II. Comprehension—understanding

a. Elements of characterization (physical and emotional)
b. Identifying main characters
c. Main idea
d. Relevant details
e. Setting (if not directly stated)
f. Mood of story
g. Visualizing story elements
h. Paraphrasing
i. Fantasy vs. realism

III. Application—use of comprehension

a. Construction of a time line
b. Depiction of visualized story elements through art
c. Dramatization
d. Formulation of questions about the material read

IV. Analysis—take apart, compare and contrast

a. Draw analogies
b. Fact vs. opinion
c. Nonliteral language (figures of speech, similes, metaphors, etc.)
d. Cause and effect
e. Predicting outcomes
f. Drawing conclusions
g. Effect of setting
h. Theme—compare and contrast with other materials read
i. Symbolic meaning
j. Exploring different perspectives
k. Author's use of such things as irony, satire, personification, propaganda, etc.
l. Compare different illustrations, versions, etc., in different editions of the same tale
m. Predict future events

V. Synthesis—invent, produce, put things together in a way that is new and unique to the child:

a. Write original verse
b. Rewrite story into a screenplay

c. Change an aspect of the story and rewrite (change the setting, an event, a character, the ending, etc.)
d. Create a parallel story
e. Create a sequel to the story
f. Construct a bibliography of books with parallel or similar plots, themes, etc.
g. Make a diorama, display, model, etc.
h. Retell the story (from a different perspective, giving a different solution to the problem, etc.)
i. Place the character in hypothetical situations
j. Public speaking (discussion, debate, etc.)

VI. Evaluation:

a. Evaluate author's biases
b. Judge author's credibility
c. Evaluate validity of material (consult original and other sources)
d. Judge the worth, desirability and acceptability of the material
e. Evaluate statements based on own biases and beliefs
f. Critique the ways the characters and events relate to our lives
g. Predict future events
h. Evaluate the consistency of analysis and synthesis

Applications Developed By Williams (1970)

I. Teach about paradoxes:

a. Situation opposed to common sense
b. Self-contradictory statement or observation
c. Discrepancy in belief but true in fact
   Examples:
   In reading a selection portraying problems of poverty, let the reader consider old proverbs such as, "Hard work will solve any problem." Or, ask readers to prove or discuss some other old wives' tales, such as "touching a toad will cause warts." This strategy sensitizes pupils to evaluate between true fact and popular notion.

II. Ask pupils to look at attributes:

a. Inherent properties
b. Conventional symbols or identities
c. Ascribing qualities

Examples:

In a poem or paragraph have the child analyze the use of a word in a sentence (noun, verb, etc.) or the letters in the spelling of a word. Have them analyze the properties of a reading selection considered artistically pleasing or a work of a noted author. Ask children to consider the various individual parts of a story and think of the purpose for each part.

III. Use analogies

  a. Situations or likeness
  b. Similarities between things
  c. Corresponding circumstances
    Examples:

Allow pupils to discover how concepts or characters are adapted from some similar feature in nature. Have readers compare the way characters live and solve their problems of existence, survival, and protection to that of another character.

IV. Point out discrepancies:

  a. Gaps in knowledge
  b. Missing links in information
  c. Unknown elements
    Examples:

Ask children to think about and list things that the story leaves unsaid. Let children explore the differences between the way people of a certain race, religion, or country really act and the way they act in a given story.

V. Ask provocative questions

  a. Inquiry to bring forth meaning
  b. Inquiry to encourage knowledge exploration
  c. Summons to discover new knowledge
    Examples:

In reading, have children consider the differences between factual inquiries about what was read (what, who, when) and in-depth comprehension. (How would you? Why? How else? What does it really mean to you? How does it make you feel?)

VI. Cite examples of change

   a. Demonstrate the dynamics of things
   b. Provide opportunities for making alterations, modifications, or substitutions
   Examples:
   Have small groups of children react to change as they read various stories and compare changes in their social systems to those of human groups represented in a story.

VII. Use examples of habit

   a. Discuss the effects of habit-bound thinking
   b. Increase sensitivity to rigidity in ideas and functional fixation of things
   Examples:
   In a study of related stories show examples of how the lives and functions of man and society have been held back by habit-bound thinking or refusal to change old ways of doing things. Show how some principals remain stagnant due to human resistance to change.

VIII. Allow for an organized random search

   a. Use a familiar structure to lead randomly to another structure
   b. Set ground rules and allow pupils freedom to explore other ways within the ground rules
   Examples:
   After a poetry study, ask children to write their own poetry by using the rules of cinquains. Ask children to name all of the characters with similar characteristics or stories with similar themes.

IX. Teach the skills of search

   a. Consider ways something has been done before (historical search)
   b. Use trial and error search on various methods and describe results (descriptive search)
   c. Control experimental conditions and report subsequent results (experimental research)
   Examples:
   Study how men have searched for ways to seek truths by considering how they were received in the past (historical search); comparing and contrasting proven or disproved theories now accepted

(descriptive search); or how a law or theory was deduced through controlled observations (experimental research).

X. Build a tolerance for ambiguity

    a. Provide encounters which puzzle, intrigue, or challenge thinking
    b. Pose open-ended situations which do not force closure
       Examples:
       Show a portion of a film or filmstrip on any story and, after turning it off at some crucial or intriguing point, ask pupils to solve the problem or finish the story in their own way. Then, at a later time, have them verify or compare their ending to that in the film.

XI. Allow for intuitive expression

    a. Feeling about things through all the senses
    b. Skills of expressing emotion
    c. Inward hunches about knowledge
       Examples:
       Ask children to write, tell, or dramatize their real feelings about a story that was read in class. Point out examples of success where intuitive characters have been influenced by their hunches. Provide opportunities for children to express their feelings across all of the senses.

XII. Teach not for adjustment but for development

    a. Examine how failures or accident have paid off
    b. Learn how to learn from mistakes
    c. Use examples of process of developing from rather than adjusting to something
       Examples:
       Among great historians or contemporary political leaders, examine how sometimes they learn from their own mistakes, failures, or accidents. Read about famous people and how they overcame failure or learned from early mistakes.

XIII. Encourage pupils to study creative people and processes

    a. Analyze traits of eminently creative people
    b. Study the processes which have led to creation
       Examples:

Have children discover how personal, physical, or social malad-
justments of some people fostered their creative endeavors. Read
about how the scientific process was utilized by great minds and
the necessity for incubation and illumination of an idea before a
discovery came into being.

XIV. Require pupils to evaluate situations

a. Deciding upon solutions in terms of their consequences and
implications
b. Extrapolate from the results of ideas and actions
Examples:
In any story have pupils learn to apply the principle of cause and
effect by asking them to explore their answers or solutions in
terms of their implications and consequences. Always pose the
question, "If this were to happen, what would the result be?"

XV. Develop a creative reading skill

a. Develop a utilitarian mind-set for information
b. Learn the skill of idea generation by reading
c. Read not what it says, but where it takes you
Examples:
In any story allow many opportunities for children to produce
their own ideas from their reading, rather than merely asking
them to recall what they read. Ask children to scan a book or page
and have them rearrange its information in terms of new ideas
they had while scanning.

XVI. Develop a creative listening skill

a. Learn the skill of idea generation by listening
b. Listen for information which allows one thing to lead to another
Examples:
Have children listen to a record and create a story about what they
think they hear. As a story is read in class, tell pupils to list ideas
they have as they listen.

XVII. Develop a creative writing skill

a. Learn skills of self-expression through writing
b. Develop the ability to write one's ideas clearly
Examples:

Give the class a list of ten words and have them write a short story using each word in the order it appears in the list by adding other words they want included. Ask children to state an idea they have in written form but in a way that no one else ever thought of.

XVIII. Develop pupils' visualization skills

a. Practice describing views from unaccustomed vantage points
b. Express ideas in three-dimensional form
c. Look at things in an unusual or different perspective
   Examples:
   Draw children's attention to shapes, color, rhythm, textures, sounds, and odors present in a story, and have them perceive or visualize themselves in their context. Teach pupils to look at things in different perspectives or to draw something from a different position.

The use of such strategies by classroom reading teachers enhances the integration of rational thinking, feeling, sensing, and intuitive thinking and optimizes reading experiences.

The selection of both content and process strategies relates directly to materials selected for the reading program. Fortunately, there is no dirth of materials available for reading and lack of materials can never be an excuse for failure to respond to the reading needs of these children. Besides the many structured reading programs available, there is the entire body of written works (both children and adult) available as potential instructional materials for gifted and talented readers. The quantity of materials makes the issue for the teacher one of which materials to select in relations to the instructional goal.

The selection of materials at professional levels, the use of original resources, and the introduction of materials outside the school parameters are additional ways to expand the reading diet of gifted and talented children. Books should not be the only source of reading materials available. Current magazines and newspapers can be brought from home. Magazines can be subscribed to and collected, and maps, atlases, and globes can be placed in the reading area. Higher level readers may be interested in opera, musical scores, signs, advertising matter, catalogues, dictionaries, encyclopedias, or phone books.

The success or failure of utilizing process skills and materials that force the reader beyond literal levels into more ambivalent open-ended experiences lies in the creation of an environment where risk taking in both encouraged and supported. A "safe" learning environment is the result of learning environments where children are encouraged to initiate their own learning, conduct their own inquiry into deeper meanings, and where unusual associations and solutions are rewarded, not discouraged or dismissed.

The encouragement of self-directed learning in relationship to reading demands that the teacher be assured that the children develop skills needed to be successful in this challenge. Assumptions cannot be made that skills exist to the degree needed for effective use of such skills by the child.

Library Research Skills

Dole and Adams (1983) report that leaders in the field of gifted education believe that special emphasis should be given to independent research projects and development of library/research skills. These library and research skills support self-directed learning and are major components of a reading program for gifted and talented children. A learning continuum useful in developing library and related skills needed is as follows:

RESEARCH CONTINUUM

I. Exploring topics for investigation:

    a. Choose from given topics

    b. Given broad topic with several narrow topics, select a narrow topic for research

    c. Narrow a topic from a given broad topic

II. Planning the research design:

    a. State the purpose of research

    b. Formulate questions for inquiry

    c. Develop hypothesis

    d. Select research mode

        1. Descriptive

        2. Historical

        3. Experimental

    e. Formulate needed definitions

    f. Identify steps needed to complete research

III. Locating and collecting data:

a. Gathering information
   1. Conduct preliminary survey for sources
   2. Write subtopic questions
   3. Gather specific information according to questions
   4. Outline reading selection through subtopic
   5. Oral recall of main points and supporting details
   6. Take notes using direct quote
   7. Take notes summarizing information
   8. Take notes using note card formats
   9. Write a bibliography
   10. Take notes paraphrasing information
   11. Verify sources of information

b. Locating information
   1. Card Catalog
      Locate by subject card
      Retrieve by author and title card
      Retrieve nonprint material
      Locate through cross reference
      Locate biography
   2. Dewey Decimal System
      Retrieve material from fiction and nonfiction section
      Using call number, locate books from shelves
      Categorize broad subjects according to Dewey Decimal System
   3. Reference Books
      Dictionary—locate word
      Jr. Thesaurus—write synonyms
      Use index in book
      Advance Thesaurus—write synonyms and antonyms
      Encyclopedia—locate information by subject
         locate information by using key words
         use encyclopedia index
         locate through cross-reference
      Special encyclopedia—locate information
      Atlas—locate types of maps
      Geographical dictionary—locate information
      Biographical dictionary—locate information
      Use Media catalog to locate nonprint materials
      Almanac—locate information

Vertical file—locate picture and article
Use quotation book to locate information
Use anthology to locate information
Use history/chronicle to locate information
Use manual/handbook to locate information
Use diary/journal to locate information
Guide to children's magazine—locate article
Abridged reader's guide—list articles on a subject
Unabridged reader's guide—locate articles

4. Project Access—request through inter-library loan
5. Nonlibrary sources
Use telephone—state name and purpose of call
Phone directory—locate number and address (white pages)
Locate number and address of business (yellow pages)
Locate address and number of government agency
Use cross reference in yellow pages
Use newspapers to gather information
Collect data through observation
Follow an experiment procedure
Collect data from graphs
Collect data from tables
Write a letter requesting information
Conduct an interview
Develop questions for a group interview
Develop and conduct an individual interview
Use an opinion poll
Develop and interpret an opinion poll
Use a survey to collect information
Develop and interpret a survey
Design and conduct an experiment
Use of lab equipment to conduct experiment

IV. Organizing information:

a. Group information by topic/subtopic
b. Determine relevant and irrelevant information
c. Determine if resource(s) provides sufficient information
d. Organize information into an outline

V. Concluding and testing questions/hypotheses:

   a. Examine questions/hypotheses for support and nonsupport

   b. Suggest conclusions to specific questions

VI. Critiquing:

   a. Verify conclusions

   b. Evaluate research process

VII. Presenting information/product:

   a. Audience
      1. Small group of classmates
      2. Entire class
      3. Students and adults
      4. Mentor

   b. Evaluation
      1. Evaluate through given criteria
      2. Develop criteria or evaluation
      3. Evaluate product of others

   c. Product components
      1. Oral presentation summarizing research
      2. Oral presentation with outline
      3. Select and use ready made visuals
      4. One page summary of research
      5. Research paper with outline
      6. Research paper with bibliography
      7. Oral presentation with audiovisual aid(s)
      8. Support a hypothesis statement in oral or written product

VIII. Future study:

   a. Gather input from audience

   b. Examine project for future study possibilities

Arranging the classroom logistics to provide the flexibility needed to allow for learning environment modifications demands that teachers create environments which are student-centered. Such environments encourage independence, are open, accepting, complex, and permit high mobility (Maker, 1982). They are laboratory-like arrangements providing time for independent inquiry as well as opportunities for shared inquiry with others. Reading period blocks may need to be increased to meet specific reading goals and to utilize discussion and debate experiences.

CONCLUSION

A major factor in the success of a reading program for gifted and talented children is the organization of that program. This chapter has presented three main considerations in organizing such a program: policy issues, assessment procedures, and curriculum modifications. Several suggestions were provided in each area. These suggestions are designed to assist administrators and teachers develop the knowledge, skills, and attitudes that will help gifted and talented children become efficient users of print media. This will empower these children in all their learning challenges and enrich their levels of performance. Such optimal learning should be the goal for all education.

REFERENCES

Adams, I. (1976). Children's books for the remedial reading laboratory. *The Reading Teacher, 30,* 266–70.

Anderson, M.A., Tollefson, N.A., & Gilbert, E.G. (1985). Giftedness and reading: a cross-sectional view of differences in reading attitudes and behaviors. *Gifted Child Quarterly, 32,* 186–189.

Barbe, W. (1961). Reading aspects. *Curriculum planning for the gifted.* Englewood Cliffs, NJ: Prentice Hall.

Barbe, W. (1975). *Barbe Reading Skill Checklist.* Englewood Cliffs, NJ: Prentice-Hall.

Bloom, B. (1956). *Taxonomy of educational objectives: Cognitive domain.* New York: David McKay Co.

Burns, P.C. & Roe, B.D. (1976). *Teaching reading in today's elementary schools.* Chicago: Rand McNally.

Burns, P., Roe, B., & Ross, E. (1984). Teaching reading in today's elementary schools. Dallas: Houghton Mifflin.

Cassidy, J. (1979). What about the talented reader? *Teacher, 21,* 76–79.

Chall, J.S. (1983). *Stages of reading development.* New York: McGraw Hill.

Cushenberry, D. & Howell, H. (1974). *Reading and the gifted child: a guide for teachers.* Springfield, IL: Charles C Thomas.

Dole, J. & Adams, P. (1983). Reading curriculum for gifted readers: a survey. *Gifted Child Quarterly, 27,* 64–72.

Gallagher, J.J. (1985). *Teaching the gifted child.* Boston: Allyn and Bacon.

Gaug, M. (1984). Reading acceleration and enrichment in the elementary grades. *The Reading Teacher, 37,* 372–375.

Harris, A.J. & Sipay, E.R. (1975). *How to increase reading ability.* New York: David McKay.

Maker, J. (1982). *Curriculum development for the gifted.* MD: Aspen.

Malone, C. (1979). Gifted children in early childhood education. *Viewpoints in Teaching and Learning, 34,* 25–28.

Mindell, P. & Stracher, D. (1980). Assessing reading and writing of the gifted: The ways and woof of the language program. *Gifted Child Quarterly, 24,* 72–80.

Oliver, E. (1983). *How do schools meet the needs of gifted readers in 1983.* Paper presented at the annual meeting of the International Reading Association, Anaheim.

Renzulli, J. (1977). *The enrichment triad model: a guide for developing defensive programs for the gifted and talented.* CT: Creative Learning Press.

Ruddell, R.B. (1974). *Reading-language instruction: innovative practices.* Englewood Cliffs, NJ: Prentice-Hall.

Schell, L.M. & Burns, P.C. (1972). *Remedial reading: classroom and clinic.* Boston: Allyn and Bacon.

Swassing, R.H. (1985). *Teaching gifted children and adolescents.* Columbus, OH: Merrill

Switzer, C., & Nourse, M.L. (1979). Reading instruction for the gifted child in first grade. *Gifted Child Quarterly, 54,* 323–336

Terman, L.M. (1925). *Genetic studies of genius: mental and physical traits of a thousand gifted children.* Stanford: Stanford University Press.

Williams, F.E. (1970). *Classroom ideas for encouraging thinking and feeling.* Buffalo, NY: D.O.K. Publishers.

Chapter 9

TEACHING MATHEMATICALLY GIFTED CHILDREN

Dina Tirosh

Mathematics teachers at every grade level come into contact with students who demonstrate high ability in mathematics and indicate a desire to learn more than is being offered in the regular curriculum. These learners usually provide a great deal of satisfaction to their teachers. However, because of the difficulty in meeting the needs of the special enrichment or acceleration in mathematics within the framework of the regular classroom, these learners may constitute a source of frustration for their teachers.

This situation has been formally acknowledged by the National Council of Teachers of Mathematics (NCTM) in the United States. In their Agenda for Action (NCTM, 1980), they described students gifted in mathematics as being seriously neglected, in terms of realizing full potential. They cited outstanding mathematical ability as one of the society's precious resources, essential for maintaining leadership in a technological world, and recommended that increased attention be devoted to identifying and developing the abilities of students gifted in mathematics.

Interest in the nature and characteristics of mathematically gifted children has increased in the last decade. Even the prestigious journal *Educational Studies in Mathematics* recently devoted an entire issue to the topic (Leder, 1986). This interest has been raised for three major reasons. First, recent legislation requires school systems to provide for the needs of exceptional children including gifted, learning disabled, physically handicapped and mentally retarded. Special programs for the gifted are seen as one phase of providing for individual differences in children and not an arrangement giving special privilege or rewards to a select few (Syphers, 1972, p. 21). Second, mathematics education focuses on problem solving, and gifted children are of particular interest because of their potentially unique problem-solving capabilities. Third, today's rapid scientific and technological advances are creating urgent needs in society for people with intellectual, technical, and personal-social skills. They are required to be both producers and consumers of the world's rapid changes. Mathematically-gifted children are likely to be characterized by these requisite abilities.

There is a myth that gifted children can develop their capacities without any kind of special enrichment. Blakers (1983) argued that even some teachers believe this; they claim that investment in special education for gifted students is unnecessary. However, the PRISM survey (NCTM, 1981) has confirmed that it is not true. Mathematically-gifted students tend to underestimate their potential, and many of them perform far below their potential. Therefore, special education for gifted children is essential.

Many types of programs for gifted children are offered in various countries (Larsson, 1986). Despite the proliferation of special education for gifted and talented children, most gifted children are found in regular classes most of the time. More specifically, very few mathematically-gifted learners receive their education in full-time special schools. When they are in special schools for gifted where no differentiation is made by discipline, they may require the same special attention to their mathematical giftedness that they would have required had they remained in their regular classroom. Students who participate in part-time supplementary programs offered to gifted and talented children, also study mathematics in their regular classes. Stanley (1978) noted that parents and teachers sometimes forbid even the most mathematically gifted students to be radically accelerated by, for example, enrolling concurrently in a course of mathematics at a university. Accordingly, the challenge of meeting the needs of mathematically gifted children falls most frequently on the regular classroom teacher.

Teachers in regular classrooms are required to meet the needs of many types of students, their levels of abilities and interests in mathematics and in other disciplines as well. This chapter is designed to help teachers meet the challenge of providing for the needs of the mathematically gifted learners in the regular classrooms more successfully. The chapter is divided into five sections. The first section is devoted to defining mathematical giftedness, the second and third to the teaching-learning processes of acceleration and enrichment, respectively, the fourth, to specific learning projects and activities, and the final section, to classroom organization and management.

1. WHO IS MATHEMATICALLY GIFTED?

In Chapter 1, Milgram described the historical development of our understanding of giftedness from the narrow unidimensional IQ-oriented definition, as represented in the work of Terman (1925), to the broad multidimensional definitions presented in the prestigious Marland report (1972) and in the 4 × 4 Structure of Giftedness conceptualization that she has developed. Milgram cited four categories of gifted behavior (overall intellectual ability, specific intellectual ability, overall original or creative thinking, and specific creative talents) each of which can be manifested at four levels (profoundly, moderately, mildly gifted, and nongifted). This multidimensional view is particularly relevant to understanding mathematically gifted learners.

Ridge and Renzulli (1981) cited the following three clusters of human traits as implicated in mathematical giftedness: above-average general abilities, high levels of task commitment, and high levels of creativity. They defined gifted and talented children as those possessing or being capable of developing this composite set of traits and applying them to any potentially valuable area of human performance" (Ridge and Renzulli, 1981, p. 204). They argued that above-average general ability is necessary but not sufficient for mathematical giftedness. This implies that the general intellectual abilities of all mathematically-gifted children are above average.

On the other hand, Heid (1983), Kissane (1986), Span and Overtoom-Corsmit (1986), and even Ridge and Renzulli (1981), themselves, noted that high scores on achievement tests do not necessarily imply giftedness in mathematics. In marked contrast to the Ridge and Renzulli (1981) view presented above, Heid (1983) claimed that mathematically-gifted children are commonly, but by no means necessarily, generally gifted. If Heid is right then there are two types of mathematically-gifted students, those with high general intellectual ability, and those with average (or even lower) general intellectual ability. This distinction has many practical implications for modification of the curriculum, and should be further investigated.

Most researchers distinguish between ordinary mathematical ability (for mastering information, reproducing it, and using it independently) and creative mathematical ability related to the independent creation of an original product. They also agree that computational ability should not be the only criterion of giftedness in mathematics (Johnson, 1983; Kissane, 1986; Krutetskii, 1976; Stanley, Keating and Fox, 1974; Stanley, 1984; Wagner and Zimmermann, 1986; Wheatly, 1983). They generally agree that cognitive characteristics include the ability to organize data, to perceive patterns and relationships among concepts, to think in mathematical symbols, to form concepts and generalizations, to criticize logical arguments, to think of divergent ideas, and to transfer ideas (Greenes, 1981; Krutetskii, 1969; Wagner and Zimmermann, 1986). Greenes noted that gifted students like problems that call for different types of solutions, and that they prefer complex mathematical problems to simple ones.

Research on mathematically-gifted learners at the elementary level is relatively meager. Ashley (1973) listed such characteristics as exceptional mathematical reasoning, good memory, and persistence. Johnson (1983) claimed that the quality of thinking identifies a child gifted in mathematics. He argued that capable children can proceed quickly from a specific set of instances, eliminate intermediate steps in the thinking process, and switch from a direct to a reverse order.

Most research on mathematically gifted children has been done at the level of middle-school and above. Two systematic, well-documented studies are those by Krutetskii in the Soviet Union and Stanley, Keating, and Fox at Johns Hopkins University in the United States.

Krutetskii's research (1969, 1976) with sixth, seventh, and eighth graders identified the following characteristics of gifted children: (1) The ability to think in curtailed structures, omitting many of the seemingly necessary links in the train of thought. (2) Flexibility of mental processes, that is, switching the direction of mathematical thought, and quickly finding solutions to unfamiliar types of problems. (3) A striving for clarity, simplicity, economy, and rationality. (4) A tendency to deal in the abstract, solving problems on their most general levels. (5) A mathematical cast of mind, inferring mathematical meanings in the world about them. (6) A clear interest in mathematics, and a tendency not to tire when working on mathematics. Krutetskii argued that there are different types of mathematical giftedness and different levels of mathematical abilities.

Far less attention has been devoted to the personal-social characteristics of the mathematically-gifted. Stanley and his colleagues at Johns Hopkins University made a major contribution to our understanding of the personal-social characteristics of mathematically-gifted children. Stanley, Keating, and Fox (1974) studied a highly select group of thirty-five seventh and eighth graders. They reported that mathematically-gifted children displayed a positive self-image, greatly enjoyed mathematics, wanted to study mathematical material more difficult than their usual school work, and were eager to study on their own. Stanley (1978, p. 94) noted that brilliant students are eager to move ahead rapidly. These precocious students also showed a strong verbal ability, which is probably necessary for self-instruction in mathematics.

2. THE TEACHING-LEARNING PROCESS: ACCELERATION

There has been considerable controversy among authorities on gifted education about what form the teaching-learning process should take when offering special education for the mathematically-gifted learner. The views on this question can generally be divided into two categories, those favoring acceleration and those favoring enrichment. Acceleration is the less frequently used of the two approaches and allows the learner to advance rapidly and at his own pace through the regular mathematics curriculum. The pace is determined by the individual's ability, interest, and motivation. This approach has resulted in radical acceleration to such an extent that one can find a very young child studying advanced levels of mathematics with university students. Acceleration enables students to complete a program in less time or at an earlier age than usual. It is used in many high schools, colleges, and universities, and varies from a modest shortening of time to a radical condensing of the entire curriculum into two or three years.

Stanley and his colleagues pioneered radical acceleration in the U.S. (Stanley, Keating, & Fox, 1974; Stanley, 1978). They developed a program that many consider to be the most systematic long-term study of gifted children to be conducted in the U.S. since Terman. The Stanley program, the Study of Mathematically Precocious Youth (SMPY), has been adopted in many parts of the United States and around the world. Stanley reported considerable variation in ability within the highly select group that he studied. They argued that each gifted child should get the special education that he needed, and therefore individual programs should be developed. They devised accelerated programs tailored to each child's abilities, interests, emotional maturity, motivation, and geographical circumstances.

Acceleration programs, which telescope the learning time of students with extremely high mathematical ability and promote early admission to college, are only one of the educational alternatives for the mathematically gifted child. Mathematics educators feel that such programs work for only a small portion of the gifted students. Acceleration is highly controversial; many researchers, teachers, and parents argue that it is an adjustment only in the sense that it makes portions of the standard curriculum available to students sooner than usual.

The authors of the Agenda for Action (NCTM, 1980) recommended that programs be based on enrichment through more ingenious problem-solving opportunities, rather than on acceleration alone.

3. THE TEACHING LEARNING PROCESS: ENRICHMENT

Ellerton (1986), Gallagher (1975), Greenes (1981), Stanley (1978), Stanley, Keating, and Fox (1974), Wavrik (1980), Wheatly (1983) and others claim that mathematically-gifted children are often underserved in their regular classes. Stanley (1978) argued that a typical way of dealing with the brightest students is to give them busy work while the class goes on with its regular work. Busy work usually consists of having them do a great deal more work at the same level as the class they have surpassed. This does not meet the needs of mathematically-gifted students. Enrichment within the regular classrooms, i.e., projects and exercises that will serve to broaden and deepen the learner's understanding of mathematics, should be provided.

Most regular mathematics programs, especially at the elementary school level, are heavily oriented toward computation. The students are expected to be consumers, rather than producers, of mathematics, and to learn mainly by drill and practice. They are seldom challenged with problems that require originality of thought. It seems highly inappropriate for gifted children to study in such a manner.

As classroom teachers, we should not ignore our mathematically-gifted students. We should incorporate enrichment activities that give them a chance to develop their special abilities. Specific examples of such activities are described in the next section.

4. ENRICHMENT AND ACCELERATION ACTIVITIES FOR MATHEMATICALLY GIFTED STUDENTS IN REGULAR CLASSES

As a teacher in a regular class, you have a basic curriculum geared to the nongifted students. You can provide more challenge for gifted students through supplementary materials, that offer enrichment and/or acceleration while keeping the conventional sequence and placement of topics intact.

Enrichment Activities Directly Related to the Topics Being Taught in Class

One type of enrichment consists of extending a topic. This is especially pertinent when a gifted student masters an activity prior to the rest of the class. These activities challenge him and deepen his understanding of the topic. The following are suggested activities of this type for teaching rational numbers.

1. A research activity directly connected to material covered in class involves repeating decimals. Have your students write fractions of the form m/n for $m < n$ (such as 1/3, 2/3, 1/7, 2/7, 3/7) in decimal form. That will lead them to encounter repeating decimals. Then you can guide interested students toward fractions with prime denominators greater than 5. For instance, you may ask them to inquire about simple fractions with a denominator of 7.

$$\text{They will find that } 1/7 = .142857 \quad 4/7 = .571428$$
$$2/7 = .285714 \quad 5/7 = .714285$$
$$3/7 = .428571 \quad 6/7 = .857142$$

The students will probably observe that the cycles of these decimals consist of the same numerals and have the same length. This observation may cause some students to come up with hypotheses such as: there are other repeating decimals that behave in a similar manner, and the length of the cycle is always less than the number of the denominator. The students will probably be eager to check their hypotheses. You can have them work with other fractions, such as with denominators 13 and 17; then they can be encouraged to analyze their results and to examine other properties of repeating decimals.

You can trigger further thought by asking them questions like: What happens when writing decimals in other bases? Is it possible to write all repeating decimals in fraction form? The students should be invited to raise other assumptions about repeating decimals, and to check their correctness.

Hobbs and Burris (1978), Lichtenberg (1978), Ockenga (1984), Seabloom (1967), Sgroi (1977), Trafton and Zawojewski (1984), Wagnes (1979) and Woodburn (1976) provide more activities with repeating decimals.

2. Conventional topics may be extended by investigating their historical origins. Although this is a popular form of supplementary material, it can lack challenge for gifted children. To avoid superficiality, you can

have students tackle problems that lead to the origin of mathematical concepts. Some students might want to find out who used rational numbers in ancient days, and why they were needed. Others may write a dialogue, in the form of Galileo's dialogues, about fractions. Books such as *A History of Mathematics* by Carl Boyer (1968) or *What is Mathematics?* by Courant and Robbins (1943) will expose students to the use of fractions in Egypt, Mesopotamia, China, and Greece. These activities help them understand the relationship between the development of mathematics and the needs of the daily life.

3. A student can pretend that she is an ancient Egyptian who worked with fractions with unit numerators. She can be asked to show her classmates how the Egyptians wrote fractions like $3/4$, $5/8$, $3/7$. In doing this research, she will learn the importance of a convenient system of writing, and the fact that inappropriate symbols can delay the advance of mathematics. Various properties of unit fractions still stimulate mathematical researchers; the student, too, can look for general properties, raise assumptions, and try to verify them. For instance, she may assume that each fraction in the form $2/n$ can be presented as the sum of two unit fractions. Some of her assumptions will be too difficult for her to test; she may leave them until she has a wider mathematical knowledge.

4. If a child is interested in unit fractions, he can work with the harmonic triangle (see Table 9-1). In this triangle, all of the fractions are unit fractions. When a child generates the next row, he will investigate the properties of the triangle, generating a hypothesis, and testing it. He can then read more about the triangle in an article by Stones (1983). This might encourage him to work (independently or with friends who show an interest in the topic) on other special triangles, such as Pascal's triangle: he will encounter a whole new mathematical world.

5. Another project involves the density of rational numbers. Ask the student to generate a method for finding a number between any two rational numbers. After he comes up with one or more methods, you can introduce McKay's theorem along with the story about McKay. As a student in Sherzer's eighth grade class, McKay discovered that "to find a fraction between two fractions, all you have to do is add the tops and the bottoms" (Sherzer, 1973, p. 229).

Have students use this method and try to explain why it works. They can read more about it in Sherzer's paper. This activity is of special importance, because it proves that students like him can contribute to mathematics. Through such activities, he will understand

Table 9-1.
Harmonic triangle

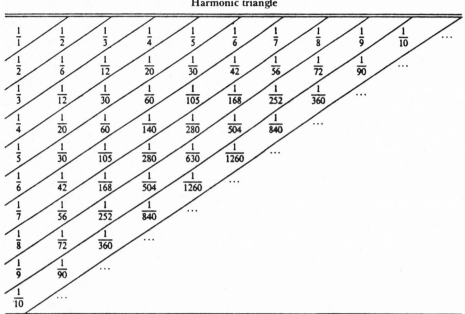

$\frac{1}{1}$	$\frac{1}{2}$	$\frac{1}{3}$	$\frac{1}{4}$	$\frac{1}{5}$	$\frac{1}{6}$	$\frac{1}{7}$	$\frac{1}{8}$	$\frac{1}{9}$	$\frac{1}{10}$	$\cdots$
$\frac{1}{2}$	$\frac{1}{6}$	$\frac{1}{12}$	$\frac{1}{20}$	$\frac{1}{30}$	$\frac{1}{42}$	$\frac{1}{56}$	$\frac{1}{72}$	$\frac{1}{90}$	$\cdots$	
$\frac{1}{3}$	$\frac{1}{12}$	$\frac{1}{30}$	$\frac{1}{60}$	$\frac{1}{105}$	$\frac{1}{168}$	$\frac{1}{252}$	$\frac{1}{360}$	$\cdots$		
$\frac{1}{4}$	$\frac{1}{20}$	$\frac{1}{60}$	$\frac{1}{140}$	$\frac{1}{280}$	$\frac{1}{504}$	$\frac{1}{840}$	$\cdots$			
$\frac{1}{5}$	$\frac{1}{30}$	$\frac{1}{105}$	$\frac{1}{280}$	$\frac{1}{630}$	$\frac{1}{1260}$	$\cdots$				
$\frac{1}{6}$	$\frac{1}{42}$	$\frac{1}{168}$	$\frac{1}{504}$	$\frac{1}{1260}$	$\cdots$					
$\frac{1}{7}$	$\frac{1}{56}$	$\frac{1}{252}$	$\frac{1}{840}$	$\cdots$						
$\frac{1}{8}$	$\frac{1}{72}$	$\frac{1}{360}$	$\cdots$							
$\frac{1}{9}$	$\frac{1}{90}$	$\cdots$								
$\frac{1}{10}$	$\cdots$									

that mathematics is alive and in a continuous process of development.

6. Supplementary projects can also be based on looking at conventional topics from different viewpoints. For instance, what are the gains and losses when extending the realm of numbers from natural to positive rational numbers. This extension offers the possibility of dividing any natural number by any other natural number, because the quotient could be a positive rational number. However, some properties of operations with natural numbers, such as that the product of two numbers is larger than either of the factors, do not hold for positive rational numbers.

The student can show that the fundamental laws of the arithmetic of the natural numbers, such as the commutative and associative laws of addition and multiplication, continue to hold in the domain of rational numbers. This is one aspect of generalization. Thus, the inquiry gives the student an important opportunity to learn the structural nature of mathematics.

7. You can introduce a new definition with new notations taken from other instances in mathematics. Present the students with rational numbers as ordered pairs of natural numbers. Have them make calculations and try to solve addition, subtraction, multiplication, and division problems using the new notation. They can also build the natural numbers in

this system and write the laws of mathematical operations under the new presentation.

In the twentieth century the field of mathematics has been characterized by the development of fundamental concepts such as ordered pairs, sets, and relations. By working with these concepts at a relatively early age, students can enhance their mathematical understanding and gain experience with isomorphous systems.

8. Ask your student to find alternative explanations for the concepts being studied in class; what are rational numbers, how to add them, and so on. This will also help weaker students overcome difficulties in grasping the concept. Thus, this activity will have multiple benefits for gifted students: It will deepen their understanding of the topic, develop their communication abilities, and show them how they can use their abilities to help other people.

9. Give your students problems that lead them to other mathematical theories; for example, "Is it possible to arrange rational numbers in a sequence so that every one appears exactly once?" This may lead to the denumerability of rational numbers, and thus to other parts of the Cantorian Theory of Transfinite Numbers. This theory, which is "the finest product of mathematical genius" (Hilbert, 1964/1923), gives students a better understanding of the concept of infinity, and a broader and more accurate understanding of the concept of numbers. Furthermore, it is important for students to have the challenge of studying by themselves a mathematical theory which is not being taught in schools.

10. Challenge your students to find applications of mathematical concepts to other disciplines as well as in ordinary life. Applications of rational numbers can be found in business and in consumer activities, such as taxation, budgeting, savings and investments; in physical science, there are such functions as measuring quantities, computing volumes, and so on. Some students may come up with the use of the Dewey decimal system in libraries. The metric system, which is based on decimals, is another example of the importance of the mathematical system in our daily life.

The above enrichment activities are directly related to topics being taught in class. Thus, they have the advantage of giving the students a broader, deeper, and flexible extension of the topics while remaining within the mainstream of the class curriculum. They suit the intellectual capabilities of the gifted students, and help them realize what mathematics is all about.

Independent Study of Topics Not Directly Related to Those Being Taught in Class

A second type of enrichment consists of independent study of topics not directly connected to what is being taught in class. You can suggest various topics from Number Theory (such as congruence and modulo number systems), Combinatorics, Group Theory, and so on, and let the students choose their own projects.

Students can also study concepts or problems that cut across topics; for example, the various uses of numbers in mathematics, or the paradoxes of infinity, in geometry, in algebra, in probability and so on. Such activities can teach students a great deal about the need for definitions and formal proofs, and about the history and development of mathematics. Moreover, it gives them opportunities to widen their mathematical horizons.

Solving Real-World Problems Using Mathematics

A third type of enrichment involves real-world problems: city planning, city budget management, and so on. Many problems that have actually arisen are suitable for high school students. Working on these problems (independently, in pairs, or in groups), will encourage the students' interest in mathematics. They will learn to gather new facts, to observe various phenomena, to analyze data, to accumulate mathematical knowledge, and so on. This real-world activity gives students an opportunity to make practical use of mathematical theories, and challenges them to use their special abilities for the benefit of society.

Tutoring

Tutoring is an enrichment activity that, if used carefully, can be very beneficial for both the gifted students and the student who is being tutor. The challenge of explaining a mathematical topic to someone who does not understand it forces the gifted child to review his own thinking, to analyze the components of the topic, and to find other ways of looking at it. Likewise, it helps him to learn how to communicate his ideas in clear and understandable ways. However, the success of tutoring depends greatly on the aptitude of a gifted child for this kind of activity. Not all gifted children enjoy tutoring and they should not be forced to engage in it.

Computer Programming

We agree with Koetke (1983) that gifted students should be encouraged to use the computer as a tool for exploring mathematical problems. The reasoning patterns and the discipline developed in writing computer programs can help gifted students look for patterns, find the most elegant solutions, and apply mathematical learning to other areas.

Wavrik (1980) argued that computer programming is also an excellent place for gifted students to practice coping with failure. Debugging (i.e., finding out why a program does not work as intended, and fixing it) is a prominent function in programming. It teaches students that making mistakes and learning from them are essential parts of the learning process. This is especially important for gifted children, who are accustomed to being right and have a hard time admitting that they are wrong.

Student Presentations

Finally, each student should get a chance to discuss his activities with his teacher, and with students and other people who are interested in mathematics. It is important that he is offered suggestions and criticism so as to help him correct and further develop his ideas. The format of the student's final report should be determined by the teacher and the student according to the type of work, its originality, its application to the prospective audience, and how the student feels about it. The student should also report on at least part of his work to his class, so other students will benefit from the potential tapped by the gifted. The preparation and presentation of a final product based upon her individual projects must be carefully planned and implemented. Teachers should be aware of the potential danger involved in having a gifted child present concepts and materials that are not understood and not appreciated by their less gifted classmates. It is possible and desirable to arrange for gifted children to share their knowledge and the results of their efforts.

The above suggestions for modifying the curriculum help gifted students understand that mathematics is an intellectual creation, not a static collection of facts, methods, and rules. The activities broaden the students' mathematical horizons and develop the capabilities needed by a researchers.

Teachers can find many suggestions for enrichment activities in professional journals and in other sources. Often, however, the real problem is not what to do with gifted children, but how to organize the instruction in order to meet the needs of both the gifted students and the other students in the class. The rest of this chapter deals with some of the aspects of classroom organization and management.

CLASSROOM ORGANIZATION AND MANAGEMENT

A practical problem faced by teachers is identifying the gifted students in their classes; this is particularly difficult in regard to mathematics. Such identification should be made on the basis of quantitative and qualitative information about the child's thinking. However, teachers are not usually given this kind of information. Therefore, it seems that the best policy is to give all students in the class a chance to participate in the enrichment activities. Each student should obtain an opportunity to exercise his own potential, and to get involved in these activities according to his ability and his interest. Moreover, this means that gifted students will be integrated with the class rather than isolated as a select group.

There are many approaches to the individualization of instruction for gifted children. Among the most useful are the Contract Activity Packages (CAPS) developed by Dunn and described in detail in another chapter of this book. Below are two additional models of instruction that permit individual students to engage in enrichment activities within the regular classroom, learning centers and the Renzulli Enrichment Triad Model.

1. Learning centers were designed to individualize learning for students of all ability levels. Well-planned centers allow students to deepen their understanding in topics from inside or outside the regular program. Sirr (1984) highly recommended this method for differentiating the elementary mathematics curriculum for exceptionally able students. She argued that differentiated materials must be prepared by someone well trained in mathematics and in education. However, most elementary teachers are not specialists in mathematics, and therefore need help in finding suitable materials. Parents and high school mathematics teachers can help locate and evaluate supplementary materials.

Sirr noted that plans exist (Connor, Connor, and Joval, 1981) for mathematics learning centers that are being used by gifted children. These centers can be set up by any teacher in his regular class. Other enrichment materials for gifted children that require little or no adaptation for use in learning centers, can be found in mathematical journals, in problem-solving books, and in mathematical recreation books. Games such as the Tower of Hanoi, and books such as *Boxes, Squares, and Other Things* (Walter, 1970) can serve as independent learning centers. Computers can also be used as learning centers (Kraus, 1984).

Parents, volunteers, and students can help prepare learning centers; in fact, this enterprise could be planned as a challenge for the students. Besides, the mathematics teachers in a school can divide the work among their classes, so that each class prepares part of the materials; they can then distribute the materials to the other classes.

Learning centers are merely a model of instruction; their influence on gifted students depends on the mathematical content of the materials. The centers should include activities that develop basic mathematical skills such as locating and processing quantitative data, collecting and organizing data, and estimating measures. They should also include activities that encourage the discovery of mathematical relationships. Problems that require originality and flexibility of thought should be available. The students should be provided with opportunities to pursue mathematical topics independently and in depth.

2. Another way of offering enrichment in regular classes is the Enrichment-Triad Model (Renzulli, 1977). It provides individualization by letting a student pursue his own particular interests to whatever extent he desires, in his preferred style of learning.

Renzulli's model offers three types of enrichment. Type One consists of general exploratory activities to stimulate interest in specific subject areas. The activities should be designed "to bring the students in touch with the kinds of topics or areas of study in which he or she may have a sincere interest" (Renzulli, 1977, p. 17).

Mathematical journals such as *Arithmetic Teacher, Mathematics Teacher, Mathematics in School* and *Mathematics Student* provide ready sources of ideas. Mathematical puzzles, games, and recreation books can introduce various areas to the students. The students should understand that after a given period of time they will have to choose a specific area for in-depth research. The main role of the teacher at this stage is to expose the students to the available areas, to monitor their interests, and to help them formulate solvable problems in the areas they choose.

Type Two enrichment is a group training which intends to develop processes in the areas chosen through Type One activities. This training may include specific skills such as using library systems, and higher-level thinking processes such as hypothesizing and evaluation. It should help students develop the investigative skills needed for solving the types of problems they are interested in.

Good examples of such training are in *The Art of Problem Posing* (Brown and Walter, 1983). This book provides students with opportunities for solving problems, organizing data, creating new ideas derived from various mathematical topics, and generating new problems. The students encounter problems such as: "There are nine Supreme Court Justices. Every year, the Supreme Court session begins with each judge shaking hands with every other judge. How many handshakes are there altogether?" Likewise, they are encouraged to generate other questions about the same situation. These questions can serve as a context for of problems at the Type Three level.

Type Three enrichment consists of individual and small group investigations of real problems; "students become problem finders as well as problem solvers and ... investigate a real problem using methods of inquiry appropriate to the nature of the problem" (Ridge and Renzulli, 1981, p. 221). Students are encouraged to arrive at their own answers in their own ways. The main role of the teacher is to arrange for gifted students to have adequate time, environment, assistance, and support material, and help him find appropriate outlets for his product.

Ridge and Renzulli state that while Type One and Type Two are appropriate for most students in regular classes, Type Three enrichment is suitable mainly for the gifted. Here, students assume responsibility for their own learning. They are free to choose among subject areas and items within a topic, as well as the type of problems and the depth of learning. This type of enrichment allows students to broaden their mathematical horizons, to develop their own tastes, and to act as independent researchers.

Ridge and Renzulli recommend the use of the Enrichment-Triad Model in elementary and secondary schools. They claim that it is appropriate for a teacher who is willing to wrestle with a somewhat different approach for instructing gifted students. Indeed, it is the most widely applied curriculum model for gifted students in the United States (Tannenbaum, 1983).

A teacher who is willing to give his students the freedom to choose their topics should understand that they might encounter problems which neither he nor the students can solve. It is essential that the teacher does not feel threatened in this situation. He should help the students find other sources which can provide the information. He should function more as a resource manager who offers informed encouragement, and less as a giver of answers. He should create an educational environment that encourages gifted students to assume control of their own learning, so that they can acquire the skills needed for independent mathematical activity (and, perhaps, for a future as a professional mathematician).

The teacher is often the only agent in the educational system who has direct contact with gifted children and, thus, the opportunity to provide them with appropriate learning activities. It is possible to serve the needs of both gifted children in your class and those not identified as gifted. This chapter has provided you with a sampling of effective approaches that can be used in teaching mathematically gifted students in a regular classroom. There is no need to wait for future programs and complex identification processes in order to fulfill your responsibilities to these extraordinary students.

REFERENCES

Ashley, R.M. (1973). Ideas for those who are mathematically bright. In R.M. Ashley (Ed.), *Activities for motivating and teaching bright children.* West Nyack, NY: Parker Publishing.

Blakers, A.L. (1983). The gifted child in Australia. In M. Zweng, T. Green, J. Kilpatrick, H. Pollak, & M. Suydam (Eds.), *Proceedings of the Fourth International Congress on Mathematical Education.* Berkeley, CA: Birkhauser Boston.

Boyer, C.B. (1968). *A history of mathematics.* New York: John Wiley & Sons.

Brown, S.I., & Walter, M.I. (1983). *The art of problem posing.* Philadelphia, Pennsylvania: The Franklin Institute Press.

Connor, W., Connor, J.S., & Joval, L. (1978). *Creative math learning centers.* Eau Claire, WI: Department of Education.

Courant, R., & Robbins, H. (1943). *What is mathematics.* New York: Oxford University Press.

Ellerton, N.F. (1986). Children's made-up mathematics problems—a new perspective on talented mathematicians. *Educational Studies in Mathematics, 17,* 261–271.

Gallagher, J.J. (1975). *Teaching the gifted child.* Boston: Allyn and Bacon.

Greenes, C. (1981). Identifying the gifted student in mathematics. *Arithmetic Teacher, 28*(6), 14–17.

Heid, M.K. (1983). Characteristics and special needs of the gifted student in mathematics. *Mathematics Teacher, 76*(4), 221–227.

Hilbert, D. (1964). On the infinite. In P. Benacerraf & H. Putman (Eds.), *Philosophy of mathematics* (pp. 134–151). New Jersey: Prentice-Hall. (Original work published 1923).

Hobbs, B.F., & Burris, L.H. (1978). Minicalculators and repeating decimals. *Arithmetic Teacher, 25*(4), 18–20.

Johnson, M.L. (1983). Identifying and teaching mathematically gifted elementary school children. *Arithmetic Teacher, 30*(5), 25–26 & 55–56.

Kissane, B.V. (1986). Selection of mathematically talented students. *Educational Studies in Mathematics, 17,* 221–241.

Koetke, W. (1983). Computers and the mathematically gifted. *Mathematics Teacher, 76*(4), 270–273.

Kraus, W.H. (1984). The Computer as learning center. In V.P. Hansen, & M.J. Zweng (Eds.), *Computers in mathematics education* (pp. 54–61). Washington, D.C.: National Council of Teachers of Mathematics.

Krutetskii, V.A. (1969). An investigation of mathematical abilities in school children. In J. Kilpatrick & I. Wirszup (Eds.), *The structure of mathematical abilities. Soviet studies in the psychology of learning and teaching mathematics, Vol 2.* Stanford, CA: School Mathematics Study Group.

Krutetskii, V.A. (1976). *The psychology of mathematical abilities in schoolchildren.* Chicago: The University of Chicago Press.

Larsson, Y. (1986). Governmental policies on the education of gifted and talented children: A world view. *Educational Studies in Mathematics, 17,* 213–219.

Leder, G. Editor (1986). *Educational Studies in Mathematics, 17,*

Lichtenberg, D.R. (1978). Minicalculators and repeating decimals. *Mathematics Teacher, 71*(9), 524–529.

Marland, S.P., Jr. (1972). *Education of the gifted and talented: Report to the Congress of the United States by the U.S. Commissioner of Education.* Washington, D.C.: U.S. Government Printing Office.

National Council of Teachers of Mathematics, (1980). *An agenda for action: Recommendations for school mathematics of the 1980s.* Reston, VA: The Author.

National Council of Teachers of Mathematics, (1981). *Priorities in school mathematics: An executive summary.* Reston, VA: The Author.

Ockenga, E. (1984). Chalk up some calculator activities for rational numbers. *Arithmetic Teacher, 31*(6), 51–53.

Renzulli, J.S. (1977). *The enrichment triad model: A guide for developing defensible programs for the gifted and talented.* Mansfield Center, CT: Creative Learning Press.

Ridge, H.L., & Renzulli, J.S. (1981). Teaching mathematics to the talented and gifted: An interdisciplinary approach. In V. J. Glennon (Ed.), *The mathematical education of exceptional children and youth* (pp. 191–266). Reston, VA: National Council of Teachers of Mathematics.

Seabloom, E. (1967). Rapid repeating decimal-fraction interchange. *Mathematics Teacher, 40*(1), 42–44.

Sgroi, J.T. (1977). Patterns of repeating decimals: A subject worth repeating. *Mathematics Teacher, 70*(7), 604–605.

Sherzer, L. (1973). McKay's Theorem. *Mathematics Teacher, 66*(3), 229–230.

Sirr, P.M. (1984). A proposed system for differentiating elementary mathematics for exceptionally able students. *Gifted Child Quarterly, 28*(1), 40–44.

Span, P., & Overtoom-Corsmit, R. (1986). Information processing by intellectually gifted pupils solving mathematical problems. *Educational Studies in Mathematics, 17*, 273–295.

Stanley, J.C. (1978). Rationale of the Study of Mathematically Precocious Youth (SMPY) during its first five years of promoting educational acceleration. In J.C. Stanley, W.C. George, & C.H. Solano (Eds.), *The gifted and the creative: A fifty-year perspective* (pp. 75–112). Baltimore, MD: The Johns Hopkins University Press.

Stanley, J.C. (1984). Use of general and specific aptitude measures in identification: Some principles and certain cautions. *Gifted Child Quarterly, 28*(4), 177–180.

Stanley, J.C., Keating, D.P., & Fox, L.H. (1974). *Mathematical talent: Discovery, description, and development.* Baltimore, MD: The Johns Hopkins University Press.

Stones, I.D. (1983). The Harmonic Triangle: Opportunities for pattern identification and generalization. *Mathematics Teacher, 76*(5), 350–354.

Syphers, D.F. (1972). *Gifted and talented children: Principal programming for teachers and principals.* Arlington, VA: Council for Exceptional Children.

Tannenbaum, A.J. (1983). *Gifted children: Psychological and educational perspectives.* New York: McMillan.

Terman, L.M. (1925). *Genetic studies of genius: mental and physical traits of a thousand gifted children.* Stanford: Stanford University Press.

Torrance, E.P. (1984). *Mentor relationships: How they aid creative achievement, endure, change, and die.* Buffalo, NY: Bearly Limited.

Trafton, P.R., & Zawojewski, J.S. (1984). Teaching rational number division: A special problem. *Arithmetic Teacher, 31*(6), 20–22.

Wagner, H., & Zimmermann, B. (1986). Identification and Fostering of mathematically gifted students. *Educational Studies in Mathematics, 17*, 243–259.

Wagnes, S.S. (1979). Fun with repeating decimals. *Mathematics Teacher, 72*(3), 209–212.

Walter, M. (1970). *Boxes, squares and other things: A teacher's guide to a unit of informal geometry.* Reston, VA: National Council of Teachers of Mathematics.

Wavrik, J.J. (1980). Mathematical education for the gifted elementary school student. *Gifted Child Quarterly, 24*(4), 169–173.

Wheatly, G.H. (1983). A mathematics curriculum for the gifted and talented. *Gifted Child Quarterly, 27*(2), 77–80.

Woodburn, D. (1976). Can you predict the repetend? *Mathematics Teacher, 69*(8), 675–678.

Chapter 10

TEACHING SCIENCE TO GIFTED SCIENCE STUDENTS

Robert E. Yager

In every classroom we find students whose interest and ability in science far exceeds that of their classmates. In this chapter we will consider methods and materials that can help teachers meet the challenge of providing special education for gifted science students within the framework of the regular classroom. The chapter is divided into three sections. The first section deals with the question of who is the gifted science student and the second with what kind of education will best contribute to the realization of his/her potential. In the third section we present several real-world examples of exemplary science teaching units that meet the needs of science-gifted children of different ages.

I. WHO IS THE SCIENCE-GIFTED STUDENT?

This question is in effect two questions, i.e., what is science and what are the characteristics of a student gifted in science?

What is science? A major problem in science education is to agree upon a definition of science—both in terms of philosophy and practice. Science is not a simple human enterprise. Certainly it is easier to define and to evaluate enterprises such as reading, writing, computing, physical skills, reviewing, and interpreting history, art, music, and the practical arts. The total enterprise called science involves skills and knowledge from many of these fields.

Some attempts at defining science in attractive, meaningful, and thought-provoking ways illustrate the problem. Feynman (1966) has defined science as the belief in the ignorance of experts. Roller (1970) has defined it as the continuing quest for knowledge. Campbell (1957) has defined it as the current explanations and theories for which experts in a given field agree. To many, science is reasoning that includes all the so-called higher-order thinking skills.

A particularly useful definition of science is the following one offered by George Gaylord Simpson (Pittendrigh & Tiffany, 1957):

> Science is an exploration of the material universe in order to seek orderly explanations (generalizable knowledge) of objects and events: but these explanations must be testable.

This definition provides a useful framework within which to consider science education for the gifted because it identifies the three essential ingredients of science. The first is *exploration* —observing and examining the objects and events in the material universe that surrounds us. Exploration is motivated by curiosity, a natural commodity in the makeup of human beings. Curiosity is not merely a desirable personality characteristic. It is a need that the organism has that must be satisfied in order to function normally, one that exists in abundance in most students, especially at the younger age levels (Vidler, 1977).

The second ingredient of science is *explanation* —formulating possible explanations of the objects and events encountered during the process of exploring the universe. Basic science is based upon the desire of people to attempt to explain the things they see or wonder about and their skill in doing so.

The third ingredient of science is the process of *testing explanations* that are formulated. Developing and using tests to check the validity of explanations are important components of the process of basic science.

What are the characteristics of a student gifted in science? Renzulli (1977) identified the following three basic attributes of gifted students: (1) above average intelligence, (2) high level of motivation or commitment to the task, and (3) high level of creativity. Numerous investigators have suggested identifying characteristics of gifted science students—though often without referring to Simpson's three basic ingredients of science (Gear, 1976; Phillips, 1976; Stanley, 1976). In addition to the characteristics cited by Renzulli for all gifted children, there are a number of characteristics specific to science-gifted children. It is probably useful to use Simpson's approach and to define gifted science students in behavioral terms as those who *demonstrate;* (1) a high level of curiosity about objects and events that surround them, (2) strong motivation to explore and to investigate the phenomena encountered while exploring about which he/she is curious, (3) high ability to generate a large number of creative and valid, that is, unusual and high quality, explanations relevant to the questions under investigation, and (4) high ability to develop and use empirical tests of explanations generated.

Paul Brandwein (1955) has been interested in gifted students in science for many years and has studied some of the most highly gifted from Forest Hills High School in New York. Brandwein continues to report about his 35-year-old longitudinal study of gifted science students. He hypothesized three broad factors or categories of characteristics useful in identifying students with special gifts in science. The school can do little regarding two factors but can be the primary agent for providing the third.

Brandwein has suggested the *genetic factor* as the first influencing giftedness in science. Indeed abilities such as high general intelligence as reflected in verbal and mathematics ability, although influenced by the environment, probably have a strong basis in heredity. Brandwein includes certain other neuromuscular features in this general area.

Brandwein next cited a *predisposing* factor. This factor may be divided into two major categories, persistence, and questing. *Persistence* is a student's willingness to spend great amounts of time, to withstand discomfort, and to face failure. *Questing* means a general dissatisfaction with present explanations of the universe. Questing will not permit a person to say "so what"; it causes a person to question authority; it is reflected in the curiosity exhibited by science-gifted students. Both the school and home environments should create an atmosphere which fosters asking questions. It should be recognized that questioning probably reflects curiosity, a motive that is inherent in one's personal make-up.

The school and the curriculum are probably not the primary means for developing either the genetic or the predisposing factors. However, the school can be of critical importance in the third factor cited by Brandwein, i.e., *the activating factor,* the effect of an inspirational teacher and/or peak experience. It is common for persons who realize their potential giftedness to a large degree to attribute critical roles to specific people, situations, and experiences, and to express their indebtedness to them publicly. It is important that regular classroom teachers and school counselors be aware of genetic and predisposing traits that characterize students with special gifts in science; however, it is equally important for them to activate science giftedness. Teachers should not remain tied to their courses of study—to the task of preparing students for college courses by providing only traditional content which characterizes the various disciplines of science. They should strive to develop alternative means that provide the activating experiences essential for full development of potential abilities in science for all students but especially for the science-gifted.

In a major position paper the National Science Teachers Association (NSTA, 1984) listed 13 cognitive and affective characteristics of a successful science student. He/she is a learner who:

1. uses science concepts, process skills, and values in making responsible everyday decisions;
2. understands how society influences science and technology as well as how science and technology influence society;
3. understands that society controls science and technology through the allocation of resources;
4. recognizes the limitations as well as the usefulness of science and technology in advancing human welfare;
5. knows the major concepts, hypotheses, and theories of science and is able to use them;
6. appreciates science and technology for the intellectual stimulus they provide;
7. understands that the generation of scientific knowledge depends upon the inquiry process and upon conceptual theories;
8. distinguishes between scientific evidence and personal opinion;
9. recognizes the origin of science and understands that scientific knowledge is tentative, and subject to change as evidence accumulates;
10. understands the applications of technology and the decisions entailed in the use of technology;
11. has sufficient knowledge and experience to appreciate the worthiness of research and technological development;
12. has a richer and more exciting view of the world as the result of science education; and
13. knows reliable sources of scientific and technological information and uses these sources in the process of decision making.

The *gifted* science student is one who excels in such traits and who performs in an exemplary manner in many if not all of the 13 areas.

II. WHAT KIND OF SCIENCE EDUCATION IS BEST FOR THE SCIENCE-GIFTED STUDENT?

What are the desirable features of science education for the science-gifted student? The National Science Teachers Association defined the major purpose for a quality science program in the following statement included in a 1984 position paper (NSTA, 1984):

> The goal of science education during the 1980's is to develop scientifically literate individuals who understand how science, technology, and society influence one another and who are able to use this knowledge in their everyday decision-making. Such individuals both appreciate the value of science and technology in society and understand their limitations.

Science education should provide opportunities for students to perfect skills in the three dimensions considered to be essential ingredients of basic science cited by Simpson above (Pittendrigh & Tiffany, 1957). Science classrooms should provide students with the opportunity to develop and to practice skills in (1) observing and exploring the world around them systematically, (2) examining phenomena and formulating explanations for discrepant events observed, things that interest them, or questions that occur to them, and (3) developing tests of the validity of explanations generated.

Gifted students must experience all three dimensions of basic science and be evaluated in terms of their performance in each. When all dimensions are stressed, the kind of student described by the NSTA Position Paper is more likely to emerge.

Gifted students require assistance and direction as they experience science in its most complete form. Effective teachers of the gifted are those who present a model of scientific attitude. In their daily interaction with students they demonstrate the process of basic science. They constantly explore, explain, and test the world around them, thus inspiring their students to adopt a similar approach to life and assisting them in perfecting skills in all three areas.

McCormack and Yager (in press) have classified the three Simpson dimensions into five domains. These domains and examples of each are outlined as follows:

Domain I—Knowing and Understanding (knowledge domain)

Science aims to categorize the observable universe into manageable units for study, and to describe physical and biological relationships. Ultimately, science aims to provide reasonable explanations for observed relationships. Part of any science instruction always involves students learning some of the information developed through science.

The *Knowing and Understanding Domain* includes:

Facts
Information
Concepts
Laws (Principles)
Existing explanations and theories being used by scientists
Internalized knowledge which can be used

This vast amount of information is usually classified into such manageable topics as: matter, energy, motion, animal behavior, plant development.

Domain II—Exploring and Discovering (process of science domain)

How scientists think and work provides another dimension of science. There are specific and definable processes that characterize human actions that result in new knowledge of the universe. Generally, these processes are embodied in the terms "exploring and discovering." Some processes of science which can be used in science instruction illustrate goals and outcomes in this domain:

Observing and describing
Classifying and organizing
Measuring and charting
Communicating and understanding communications of others
Predicting and inferring
Hypothesizing
Testing
Identifying and controlling variables
Interpreting data
Constructing instruments, simple devices, and physical models

Domain III—Imagining and Creating (creativity domain)

Much research has been done on developing and enhancing students' abilities in the domain of original or creative thinking (Barron & Harrington, 1981; Kogan, 1983; Wallach, 1970). Unfortunately, little of the knowledge that has accumulated about creativity over the years has been systematically incorporated into science education programs. The heavy emphasis in most science programs is on learning a given body of information. Little formal attention has been given in science programs to developing imagination and creative thinking. Here are some of the human abilities important in this domain:

Visualizing — producing mental images
Combining objects and ideas in new ways
Producing alternate or unusual uses for objects
Solving problems and puzzles
Fantasizing
Pretending
Dreaming
Designing devices and machines
Producing unusual ideas
Identifying
Isolating
Merging
Diverging
Converging

Domain IV—Feeling and Valuing (attitudinal domain)

In these times of increasingly complex social and political institutions, environmental and energy problems, and general concern about the future, scientific content, processes, and even attention to creativity are not sufficient parameters for a science program. Human feelings, values, and decision-making skills need to be addressed. This domain includes:

Developing positive attitudes toward science in general, science in school, and science teachers
Developing positive attitudes toward oneself (an "I can do it" attitude)
Exploring human emotions
Developing sensitivity to, and respect for, the feelings of other people
Expressing personal feelings in a constructive way
Making decisions about personal values
Making decisions about social environmental issues
Exploring arguments on either side of an issue

Domain V—Using and Applying (applications and connections domain)

It seems pointless to have any science program if the program does not include some substantial amount of information, skills, and attitudes that can be transferred and used in students' everyday lives. Also, it seems inappropriate to divorce "pure" or "academic" science from technology. Students need to become sensitized to those experiences they encounter which reflect ideas they have learned in school science. Some dimensions of this domain are:

Seeing instances of scientific concepts in everyday life experiences

Applying learned science concepts and skills to everyday technological problems

Understanding scientific and technological principles involved in household technological devices

Using scientific processes in solving problems that occur in everyday life

Making decisions related to personal health, nutrition, and life style based on knowledge of scientific concepts rather than on "hear-say" or emotions

Integrating science with other subjects

Taking specific actions designed to resolve problems and/or to improve a local, regional, national, and/or international problem

Becoming involved in community-action projects; extending school experiences beyond the classroom

Emphasizing the interrelationships and interconnectedness of science to other human enterprises

The Yager and McCormack (in press) description presented above represents a major contribution in that it replaces general statements of lofty goals with specific measurable behavioral objectives. It is important for science teachers to devote ample time to the systematic assessment of the progress of their students in each domain. Many instruments of varying degrees of reliability and validity are available for the task. Some of the most common instruments that are being used to measure accomplishment in each domain include:

Domain I—Knowing and Understanding (knowledge domain)

1. Science Subtest, Iowa Tests of Basic Skills (Hieronymus et al.)
2. Science Subtests, Iowa Tests of Educational Development (Feldt et al.)
3. Science Subtest, Metropolitan Achievement Tests (Prescott)
4. Stanford Achievement Test (Madden, et al.)
5. ACS/NSTA Cooperative Chemistry Test (ACS–NSTA)
6. Physics Achievement Examination (AAPT–NSTA)
7. High School Biology Examination, Version 1987 A (NABT–NSTA)

Domain II—Exploring and Discovering (process of science domain)

1. The Methods and Procedures of Science: An Examination (Woodburn)
2. Test of Enquiry Skills (Fraser)
3. Wisconsin Inventory of Science Processes (Welch)
4. Cedar Rapids Schools Science Process Measure (Phillips)
5. Scientific Curiosity Inventory (Campbell)
6. Assessment Model for Science Process Domain (Binadja)

Domain III—Imagining and Creating (creativity domain)

1. Purdue Creativity Test (Lawshe and Harris)
2. Torrance Tests of Creative Thinking (Torrance)
3. Modes of Thinking in Young Children (Wallach et al.)
4. How Do You Really Feel About Yourself (Williams)
5. Thinking Beyond (Dagher)
6. Assessing Aspects of Creativity (Sanchez)
7. Creativity Via One's Imagination (Lindquist)

Domain IV—Feeling and Valuing (attitudinal domain)

1. Student Preferences and Understandings (NAEP)
2. Scientific Attitude Scale (Moore and Sutman)
3. Attitude Toward Study of Science (Yager)
4. Test of Attitudes on Technology-Society Interaction (Piel)
5. Attitudes Toward Science and Technology (Temple University)
6. Test of Science-Related Attitudes (Fraser)

Domain V—Using and Applying (applications and connections domain)

1. Science and Society (Dagher)
2. Views on Science-Technology-Society (Aikenhead)
3. Test on the Social Aspects of Science (Korth)
4. STS Examination Items for Science in a Social Context (ASE)
5. Applying Science Concepts (NAEP)

Figure 10-1 provides a model of the domains and indicates a desirable direction for approaching science in all five domains. The real world of the student is closest to the application and connections domain. This is the domain which includes the immediate environment of all people; it can provide access and entree to the other domains. Or, it can provide for practical and real problems where some students may elect to remain.

However, the most gifted in science will develop positive attitudes concerning basic science; they will develop creatively as their curiosity, explanations, and tests of the validity of such explanations advance, improve, and become more original.

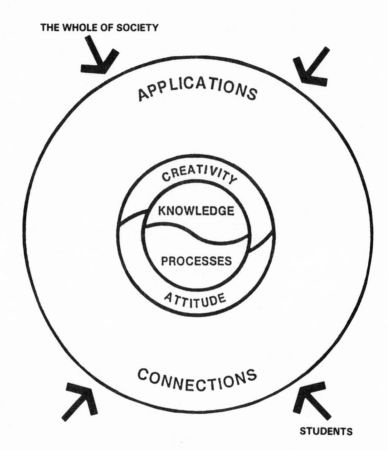

Figure 10-1. Five domains of basic science

Science education as it currently exists: Textbooks, examinations, laboratories. In 1978, the National Science Foundation in the U.S. funded three large studies to determine the status of science in schools (Helgeson, Blosser, & Howe, 1977; Weiss, 1978; Stake and Easley, 1978). After spending over three million dollars and much time in reviewing research reports, the results of several surveys, and information gained directly by observers who spent significant time in a few randomly selected districts, it was concluded that science for most students could be described and defined by content that was included in the relatively few textbooks used at a given grade level. In fact, it was observed that 90 percent of all science teachers use a textbook in excess of 90 percent of the time (Harms and Yager, 1981). This generalization applies to examinations, laboratory manuals, accompanying audiovisual material, and exercises. It seems that in the real world of schools, science is the information, exercises, and teacher strategies described and elaborated by science textbooks.

Few people would be comfortable with defining science as being the material found in science textbooks, yet it becomes just that for nearly all students who study science in schools. The examination of course outlines and textbooks provides no indication that students are permitted, or expected, to test their own ideas or those of others. On the basis of the findings cited above, we are forced to accept the painful conclusion that few students experience science as exploration, explanation, and testing explanations. Science as it is currently being taught in many if not most schools ignores the three basic ingredients of science.

Most teachers are quick to agree to more lofty goals and espouse definitions that emphasize dimensions that go beyond the information/content level in textbooks. In fact most textbooks are criticized because they do little other than present information in some organized way and seem to imply that knowing science is to know the information that is offered on the pages of a book. Nevertheless, despite abundant pious pronouncements to the contrary, in the final analysis, skill in science is defined as knowing more than other students of the material presented. The skills required are memorization, recall, and information acquisition.

Recent critiques of standardized examinations in science reveal that most items deal with mastery of information and with the ability to perform certain skills. These skills usually require basic information before they can be performed; most relate to mathematical skills. When factor analyses are undertaken, most science exams factor into verbal and computational skills (Lindquist, 1964). Such skills coincide with typical instruction in school science. There is great emphasis upon mastery of vocabulary (Hurd, Robinson, McConnell, & Ross, 1981; Yager, 1983). There are more new words and terms in the typical science textbook than would be encountered in studying a foreign language for two or three years. Science examinations stress vocabulary. Teacher-made as well as textbook examinations often focus upon vocabulary—often half of the items.

Razali (1986) has recently reported that the Chemistry Achievement Examination distributed by the American Chemical Society consists of half content/concept items and half of these are vocabulary items. The other half of the test focuses on skill items with half related to simple mathematical manipulations.

Laboratories often play a prominent role of science courses. In fact many refer to the college preparatory courses (i.e., those appropriate for gifted students) as "laboratory science." Unfortunately, when one looks at the so-called laboratories that accompany typical courses, it is disappointing to observe that here as well there is a lack of any of the basic ingredients of science (Simpson's definition). Fuhrman, Lunetta, and Novick (1982) have reported that most laboratories are exercises in verifying what is already known. The Project Synthesis Report, a National Science Foundation-supported research effort (Harms & Yager, 1981), indicated that 90 percent of the laboratories used in typical schools require little more than the ability to follow directions. Most of the desired results were known before the laboratory activities began.

In summary, science-gifted students are not receiving school experiences that are likely to contribute to full realization of their potential ability. The process of science education, in many instances, is almost totally textbook oriented. Examinations and laboratory exercises generally reflect this limited orientation as well.

Exemplary programs of science education. The National Science Teachers Association (NSTA) Search for Excellence program has existed for five years. A total of 150 programs have been identified as exemplary. They are each described in the NSTA publication series *Focus on Excellence* (1983). In examining the Search for Excellence programs Penick and Yager (1983) concluded that the following principal features characterize exemplary science programs:

1. These programs were all designed to be excellent, rather than simply relying on routine textbook selection. From the descriptive data about each program, it was possible to deduce some similarities in their origins, development, and goals.
2. Many of the programs were initially designed by someone in the central administration or by a science teacher acting in the role of science supervisor or master teacher. These leaders usually brought about the desired change by stimulating the active participation of the science faculty—and frequently by consulting with state-level science supervisors, university faculty members, and community leaders.
3. Many teachers received released time to develop the curriculum, and virtually all exemplary programs report extensive inservice efforts to develop their ideas. These inservice efforts are neither of the one-day-a-week nor even the one-workshop-in-a-summer variety. Most exemplary programs report several years of inservice effort, including extensive summer sessions.

4. The curricula that result from these efforts are almost entirely locally developed. Textbooks are not usually very visible; where they are visible, they usually play a secondary role, as resources and references.

5. Considerable time has been spent in these exemplary programs on developing the curriculum, on organizing how it will be presented, and on encouraging teachers to work as teams. Considerably less attention has been paid to the use of appropriate teaching strategies. This is identified as an area of continuing need.

6. Little attention has been paid to evaluation of programs or of teachers within programs. In most cases the developers view these programs as still evolving and do not feel that they have reached their final state. They do, however, base changes and improvements on actual research evidence.

7. The programs are recognized in the school and community at large; faculty from other departments and community groups are actively involved and assume some ownership for the program. The result is that the exemplary science programs are in evidence well beyond the science classroom and department.

8. Teachers in the exemplary programs are different from average teachers. They are older; they are more experienced; they are active professionally in the school, community, and organizations. Teachers of exemplary science programs seek out professional activities, including in-service offerings.

Of particular importance when considering the science-gifted is the evidence that has accumulated demonstrating that exemplary science education programs improve students attitudes concerning some of the central attributes of science. Some of the most interesting data have resulted from the 1977 Assessment of Science by the National Assessment of Educational Progress (NAEP, 1978). Many of the same items were included in the Fourth Assessment of Science in 1982 (Hueftle, Rakow, & Welch; 1983). The assessment items were administered to random samples of 9, 13, and 17-year-old students from the total population in the U.S. A total of 2,500 students responded to each item at each age level. It is possible to generalize about the total 9, 13, and 17-year-old populations with such techniques.

Yager and Penick (1986) have tabulated results from 9, 13, and 17-year-old samples from the Third and Fourth Assessments of Science (NAEP) and from follow-up studies conducted at the University of Iowa. Following are some data from a study by Simmons and Yager (in press) comparing attitudes toward science in students in schools selected at random from the national assessments of science cited above with students in exemplary programs designed to meet the needs of all students. Each column is identified as follows:

A = Percent of students with positive response from Third Assessment of Science (NAEP)
B = Percent of students with positive response from Fourth Assessment of Science (NAEP)
C = Percent of students with positive response from NSTA Exemplary Programs

Student Views of Science Classes

	9 Year Olds			13 Year Olds			17 Year Olds		
	A	B	C	A	B	C	A	B	C
Fun	62	61	93	33	40	84	27	26	59
Interesting	85	84	84	42	49	86	39	43	74
Exciting	50	53	80	43	42	76	48	46	51
Boring	4	5	7	31	29	10	39	41	21

Student Feelings Concerning Science Classes

	9 Year Olds			13 Year Olds			17 Year Olds		
Makes Me Feel:	A	B	C	A	B	C	A	B	C
Uncomfortable	5	6	8	36	21	10	43	31	20
Successful	56	57	61	42	37	58	30	29	37
Curious	43	46	80	36	29	76	31	24	64
Able to Make Decisions	49	51	64	44	48	76	43	49	68

Student Views of Their Science Teacher

	9 Year Olds			13 Year Olds			17 Year Olds		
	A	B	C	A	B	C	A	B	C
Makes Science Exciting	90	90	73	58	54	78	41	44	61
Admits to Not Knowing	45	46	68	30	23	73	17	16	66
Really Likes Science	37	33	32	76	77	85	81	82	87
Encourages Students to Share Experiences	66	64	76	52	46	84	44	45	86
Encourages Student Questions	52	54	80	52	54	86	51	52	77
Asks Questions Frequently	61	63	92	55	66	91	45	61	86
Knows Much Science	57	60	59	55	65	88	79	81	86

Shulman and Tamir (1973) observed that motivating students to learn is more important than getting them to "seem-to-learn" based upon recall-type examinations. The NAEP (1978, 1982) reports demonstrate that much science education is failing to realize this goal. On the contrary, the typical program seems to result in students becoming less curious, less interested, and less able to apply information.

It is heartening to note that exemplary programs and teachers alleviate many of the negative affective outcomes of instruction. Whether or not these exemplary programs offer special advantages for science-gifted students remains to be empirically investigated. Anecdotal information suggests that such programs are especially good for the gifted since they are free to plan, to try, to exercise their interest and creativity.

The confounding of high verbal/math achievement, general giftedness, and specific giftedness in science. One frequently occurring problem has become a focus of concern for science educators. As science programs improve and move toward meeting the criteria for excellence established by the National Science Teachers Association (NSTA, 1987), problems increase for high school students who have been judged as extremely successful in the standard nonexemplary programs. Students recognized for their high achievement in science because of their excellent performance in textbook-oriented programs where they learned as directed and received high grades on standard evaluation instruments found themselves unable to meet the new and in many ways more stringent standards of the exemplary programs. Let us look for a moment at a possible explanation for this seemingly incongruous situation.

Typical programs for the science-gifted student are programs of acceleration. The most successful students are encouraged to explore a particular discipline or topic in more depth. Senior level courses are offered one to three years sooner. It is not uncommon to find advanced high school students enrolled in university science courses. Such programs of acceleration generally emphasize greater mastery (in terms of depth as well as breadth) of information. Accordingly, students in many of the textbook-oriented classes described above who are characterized by verbal fluency and the ability to manipulate numbers, perform well on textbook-oriented examinations and are consequently viewed as gifted in science. This is unfortunate, because only one domain is being considered rather than the whole enterprise of science. They do not acquire knowledge or experience in the other four domains of science cited above, that is, exploring and discovering imagining and creating, feeling and valuing, using and applying (Yager & McCormack, in press).

Alfred North Whitehead has asked: What is knowledge if it is not useful? If we accept this definition of knowledge then we are forced to recognize a major problem in science education by concluding that very few people, gifted and nongifted, develop any real knowledge of the science they study. Probably an even more painful realization is that it may well be that we are providing special education to nongifted science students and denying it to the gifted.

How can schools find science-gifted students in order to increase their interest and to help them advance in science according to their abilities? Can teachers, perhaps, be counted on to identify science-gifted students and help them to realize their potential? The research concerning teacher identification of gifted science students indicates that this is most unlikely since the subjective assessment by teachers of gifted children is often inaccurate (Callow, 1980; Endean and George, 1982; Gallagher, 1964; Tempest, 1974). These investigators report that teacher identification of science-giftedness is often based on student cooperativeness, high interest and/or motivation in subject matter. Moreover, teachers often confound general giftedness with more specific and possibly nonoverlapping science-giftedness. Some students who get labeled as gifted in science are not gifted at all. They excel at nonscience actions such as recall, repeating information from textbooks and/or teacher lectures, following directions, and performance on standard tests. It is rare to see a student who excels in any area other than mastery of information. All too often the most successful science student is the one who remembers the most the best.

To sum up, the skills mentioned above, although highly valued by teachers, are not the only or most important skills that characterize a science-gifted student and do not reflect the various attributes that indicate success in the five domains of science. Since vocabulary, recall of information, and mathematical skills are not the primary goals in science education, measures of achievement on these dimensions are inappropriate for assessing achievement in science for gifted students.

Can cognitive science contribute to the improvement of science education for the science-gifted student? Cognitive science is an active research area in psychology and one which needs to be considered as one considers the gifted science student. Some cognitive psychologists are concerned with the misconceptions and naive theories that students have. Champagne and Klopfer (1984) have reviewed much of the cognitive science research including their own seminal work with university physics students. It is amazing to note that those students regarded as the most gifted in science (i.e., those completing high school physics, performing well with it, deciding to pursue collegiate study of physics) should have so many misconceptions and naive theories. The work illustrates dramatically a major problem with school science and special problems in developing programs for the gifted in science and even in identifying science-gifted students.

Often there is great temptation to reteach basic concepts as a means of correcting the misconceptions and naive theories. Unfortunately there is little evidence that redoing the same science a second or third time will correct the problems. There is every indication that the misconception has arisen from a real-world experience; repeating school exercises does not alter the actual experience students have had. Students can be coaxed into repeating what teachers want to hear. But, when given a chance they return to their own explanations and interpretations based upon their own experiences and observations. Programs for the gifted in science should emphasize direct student experiences rather than the passive absorption of information presented.

Summary and conclusions. All students should have ample opportunity to experience science—all three aspects as outlined by George Gaylord Simpson (Pittendrigh & Tiffany, 1957), exploration, explanation, and testing explanations. Exemplary programs provide educational experiences and assess student progress in all of the five the domains of science cited by Yager and McCormack (in press). They are not limited by information in course outlines, curriculum guides, or textbooks. They focus only upon direct real-world experiences for students rather than on the typical review of concepts presented in textbooks, performance of verification laboratories, and examinations requiring recall. These ideas are not new. John Dewey (1983) argued many decades ago that real learning occurs only when students have a direct (real-world) experience.

The best program for science-gifted students will have similar attributes to improved programs for all students. The gifted student in science will be able to apply and connect the facts, theories, and information to the real world. Such students will have positive attitudes and will be more creative, especially in terms of number and quality of questions, identification, and distinction between cause and effect, and uniqueness of explanations offered and tests devised.

A science program for gifted science students is one with the following features (Yager, 1983):

1. A focus on social problems and issues. Science cannot be separated from the society which spawns it. It was a mistake trying to make science into an enterprise free of humans—free of societal issues—free of the real environment of life. For many, science has meaning only when it is presented in a real setting.

2. Practice with decision making strategies. All persons must use information as evidence to reach decisions—decisions about daily living as well as decisions about the future of society. Without practice in using information for making decisions students are left with the feeling that science is unimportant and without use.

3. Concern for career awareness. If we live in a technological scientific society, the careers related to science and technology are central to that society. A good science education for all must help with an awareness of such opportunities for a lifetime of work. This does not mean a focus upon careers as only top rate scientists and engineers.

4. Local and community relevance. Science must be based in each community; it must have meaning for students in a given locale. Science study must be concerned with events and objects that can be seen, considered, and studied locally. Meaningful science cannot be textbook science.

5. Emphasis on applications of science. Such applications/technologies can be a means to a consideration of pure science. Technology has more relevance and is more easily seen and understood than the unifying ideas of pure science. Once motivated, once involved, once interested, students can be led to a consideration of deeper meanings and ideas. A consideration of basic science can be an outcome—a result—as opposed to a frontline goal or an organizational scheme.

6. Focus on cooperative work on real problems. Contrived exercises, individual work on verification activities, and textbook problems do not help students grow as cooperative citizens ready to tackle the societal problems of our time. A community concept is needed. A focus on problem resolution rather than problem solution is more realistic and a more desirable goal.

7. Emphasis upon multiple dimensions of science. For many students historical, philosophical, sociological dimensions of science may be more valuable than a content/discipline dimension. The process dimension is important, especially if it deals with practical situations such as decision-making. Surely the applications, i.e., technological dimensions, are more meaningful and viable for many. Political, economic, psychological, and creative dimensions are important views of science for others.

8. Evaluation based on ability to get and to use information. Nearly all evaluation in older models of science education focuses upon definition of terms and concepts and upon verification skills. Evaluation should be viewed as a part of the scientific continuum and hence basic to

any study of science. Finding information and using it are two indispensable skills that must be practiced and valued in K–12 science education.

Appropriate science for gifted students should mirror basic science to a greater degree. We should not be content merely to offer to science-gifted high school students college level courses. Science courses for those with special abilities in science will help them not only to acquire information but also to develop the attitudes and skills required to realize their full potential in science. Science-gifted students will be encouraged to delve into their own curiosities, to expand them, and to find new ones. It will engage them in formulating possible explanations of the things they encounter. It will involve them intimately in testing the validity of their own ideas.

Growth in all domains continues when there are teachers and programs which encourage such growth and which provide experiences that are designed to enhance it. Perhaps the high school is an inappropriate place to redefine basic science and to require different skills and behaviors for students to exhibit success. The problems are fewer when students start their study of basic science in the elementary school.

III. WHAT ARE SOME EXAMPLES OF EXEMPLARY PROGRAMS THAT HAVE SERVED GIFTED STUDENTS WELL?

The National Science Teachers Association initiated a search for excellence program in 1982 which now provides information about some of the most exciting programs in the U.S. Follow-up studies are now revealing how the goals are being realized and how gifted students are performing in domains other than acquisition of information. Students who identify problems, who seek knowledge that responds to such problems, who propose solutions based on the knowledge found, who test such proposed solutions, who move to corrective action based on results with tested ideas, are found to have better process skills, better attitudes, characteristics that are defined as more creative, and the ability to apply and connect their interpretations/solutions to the everyday situation.

Robbi Jaffe and Gary Appel have developed such a program in the Green Acres School in Santa Cruz, California. The whole program is organized around a garden which was established in a parking lot on the school property with the help of students, teachers, and parents. Learning about proper soils and other environmental factors that affect plant growth is central to the effort. The ideas central to sound conservation practices and good ecological procedures are also explored. Community groups such as the local 4-H clubs helped with facilities that are used by the students as well as for their own special after-school programs. Nutrition is a major strand with a third of each class dealing with preparation of food on a daily basis. When students are not actually engaged in some aspect of the garden itself (usually a third of a class on a given day) or in the nutrition strand, they look at some basic science arising from their garden and their nutrition experiences. The instructional team includes a garden staff, unpaid environmental interns from the University, community leaders, and the regular elementary school teachers. The most gifted students become active in every aspect of the work and excel in all activities. Their giftedness is especially valued as all the students gain from their special abilities in a variety of science domains.

Joan McShane (Jefferson Elementary School, Davenport, Iowa) has organized a basic science unit around a special toilet that she has installed in an upper elementary classroom. The toilet is hooked up to a sump pump which provides an entire system for analyzing toilet tissue in terms of its disintegration, the impurities some contain, cost, advertising claims, effect on the environment. The unit—originally planned for three weeks—now comprises two months of science study where numerous facets of the printed curriculum for the school system are moved to the realm of direct experience and analysis instead of the more common and more direct approach of studying concepts for their own sake and merely mentioning the application and possible connection after formal study. As in the case of Santa Cruz, Ms. McShane's gifted students are clamoring for more involvement, more testing, more information, more questions. Her students are experiencing science in a real world way; they are not merely acquiring more information and at a faster rate than other students.

Harold Pratt and a large instructional team at Jefferson County Schools in Lakewood, Colorado, have structured an exceptional junior high school program that focuses on a variety of correct problems and topics which require personal involvement and action. They utilize cooperation learning strategies when the gifted students are often leaders in a host of group efforts. Giftedness is seen as an important strength in a total society as solutions to problems are sought. Ideas of the most able students are welcomed and utilized; they enrich the total class experience. Some of the most impressive activities involve energy, i.e., its sources, its use, its conservation. Students investigate problems in their own homes, their school, their community, and their state. They become involved with professionals, with custodial staff, with political leaders. They learn much about electricity, light, common appliances, consumerism, applied mathematics as they work on current problems. The students have set national records in terms of positive attitudes toward sciences, science study, science as a career, and science teachers. The most gifted students are seen as school and community resources as they lead other students to question, to propose solutions to problems, to test ideas, to take action to resolve problems.

Morgan Masters, junior high teacher in Chariton, Iowa, has changed his whole program into a science/technology/society experience as he attempts to meet the needs of all his students to a higher degree. One of his new units is concerned with the problems of flight. He has utilized staff at a local airport, some of the officials of a local grocery distributing company who are the town's leading users of the airport, parents who are aviation buffs, including one who is an ultralite enthusiast (unbeknownst to anyone else in the town). The students use rockets, model planes, and living organisms to study flight—what is involved and how it occurs. Student questions are sought and used to determine where the study goes. Other teachers including those in art, social studies, and language arts become involved. Some of the most gifted are able to delve more deeply into problems, information that could be used to investigate them, actions to be taken to resolve them. The flight module last year resulted in great parental involvement, major repair and support for the local airport, and students anxious to experience more science.

Dick McWilliams, biology teacher of Grandview Park Baptist School in Des Moines, Iowa, has used the production of videotapes as a means of involving his students in data collection, searching for information, and organizing and interpreting it. In a recent unit on light and vision, he visited the medical facilities of the University Hospitals with his entire biology class. They interviewed ophthalmologists, visited operating rooms, talked with patients. They learned about laser technology and what it meant. Dick McWilliams' students practiced making lenses and worked with school employees, parents, and others in the community concerning problems of sight and normal vision. Their first hand exploration led to questions and investigation that could not have been anticipated in advance. The most gifted were once again the most active, the most productive, the ones who helped the most as the unit unfolded.

They learned much themselves while they helped others with their questions and their understanding.

Arthur Lebatsky and Wayne Browning have developed an exciting course they call "mankind" for high school students in South High School in Clarkstown, New York. This course is structured around a few basic themes, including humankind and society, order in man's world (including biological, social, and aesthetic), reality of disorder, technology and humankind, and change and the future of humankind. In this course students shoulder much of the responsibility for doing, for finding, for analyzing, for debating, for taking action. The teachers adopt many roles, including interventionist, facilitator, group leader, bureaucratic leader, lecturer, inquisitor, role model, antagonist, prober, arbitrator. Student viewpoints are explained; students are encouraged to sharpen such views, to change them in light of new information, to support them, to compare them with others identified as experts. Every attempt is made to stretch the thinking of the students and to have the students offer similar stimulation to the teachers. Experts in the community are identified and frequently used as new ideas and avenues are explained. As in the case of other exemplary programs, the gifted students became thoroughly enmeshed in the activities, in the exploration, in the thinking/ analyzing processes. The most gifted often become the most involved; their ideas are used as they think and explore further. There is no end as to what they might do and what their actions could mean.

These examples illustrate well how Simpson's view of science can be used to advantage in planning and implementing programs for gifted students in science. Science for these students is not information to be mastered more thoroughly and faster than their peers. Instead, science is a grand adventure—one where their own interests, their own explanations, and their own tests of the validity of their ideas are the basic ingredients of science. Gifted students who experience science in such ways invariably are more interested; their experience base is broadened; they advance through a science program with more realistic visions of what science is really like and their own abilities to deal with it.

Typical programs that mean acceleration through a prescribed sequence of courses or a given course outline rob gifted students of real experience with science. Science programs that measure success in science with the quantity of information a student seems to have mastered are common. And, what seem to be the most gifted can excel in such courses. There is only one problem—mastery of this information is not science. Further, most who seem to know it (can repeat it on examination) do not know it at all. They cannot use the information they seem to possess.

REFERENCES

Aikenhead, G. (in press). Student beliefs about science-technology-society: Four different modes of assessment, and sources of students' viewpoints. *Journal of Research in Science Teaching.*

American Association of Physics Teachers and National Science Teachers Association (1983). *Physics Achievement Examination.* Washington, DC: Author.

American Chemical Society & National Science Teachers Association (1987). *ACS/NSTA Cooperative Chemistry Test.* Tampa, FL: Author.

Science Education Center (1986). *Applying science concepts.* Iowa City, IA: Author.

Association for Science Education (1986). *STS Examination Items for science in a social context.* College Lane, Hatfield, Herts AL109AA, United Kingdom.

Institute for Survey Research (1979). *Attitudes toward science and technology.* Temple University, Philadelphia, PA: Author.

Barron, F., & Harrington, D.M. (1981). Creativity, intelligence and personality. *Annual Review of Psychology, 32,* 439–476.

Binadja, A. (1987). *Assessment model for science process domain* (from *National assessment of educational progress*). Iowa City, IA: Science Education Center, University of Iowa.

Biological Science Curriculum Study (1966). *Biology Comprehensive Final Test: Part 1 and Part 2.* Englewood Cliffs, NJ: Prentice Hall.

Bonnstetter, R.J., Penick, J.E., & Yager, R.E. (1983). *Teachers in exemplary programs: How do they compare?* Washington, DC: National Science Teachers Association.

Brandwein, P.F. (1955). *The gifted student as future scientist: The high school student and his commitment to science.* New York: Harcourt and Brace.

Callow, R. (1980). Recognizing the gifted child. In R. Povey (Ed.), *Educating the gifted child.* London: Harper and Row.

Campbell, N.R. (1957). *Foundations of science.* New York: Dover Publications.

Campbell, J.R. (1971). Cognitive and affective process development and its relation to a teacher's interaction ratio. *Journal of Research in Science Teaching, 8,* 317–323.

Champagne, A., & Klopfer, L. (1984). Research in science education: The cognitive perspective. In D. Holdzkom & P.B. Lutz (Eds.), *Research within reach: Science education.* Washington, DC: National Institute of Education, Department of Education.

Dagher, Z. (1986). *Science and society.* Iowa City, IA: Science Education Center, The University of Iowa.

Dagher, Z. (1987). *Thinking beyond.* Iowa City, Iowa: Science Education Center, The University of Iowa.

Dewey, J. (1983). *Experience and education.* New York: Macmillan.

Endean, L., & George, D.R. (1982). Observing 30 able youngsters at a science enrichment course. *School Science Review, 64,* 213–224.

Feldt, L.S., Forsyth, R.A., & Lindquist, E.F. (1979). *Iowa Tests of Educational Development (ITED), Grades 9-12, Science Subtest.* Iowa City, IA: Iowa Testing Programs, The University of Iowa.

Feynman, R.P. (1966). What is Science? Keynote Speech, 15th Annual Meeting, National Science Teachers Association, San Francisco.

Fraser, B.J. (1979). *Test of Enquiry Skills (TOES), Parts B and C.* Victoria, Australia: The Australian Council for Educational Research.

Fraser, B.J. (1981). *Test of Science-Related Attitudes.* Victoria, Australia: The Australian Council for Educational Research.

Fuhrman, M., Lunetta, V.N., & Novick, S. (1982). Do secondary school laboratory texts reflect the goals of 'New' Science curricula? *Journal of Chemical Education, 59,* 563-565.

Gallagher, J.J. (1964). *Teaching the gifted child.* Boston, MA: Allyn and Bacon.

Gear, G.H. (1976). Accuracy of teacher judgement in identifying intellectually gifted children: A review of the literature. *The Gifted Child Quarterly, 20,* 478-490.

Harms, N.C., & Yager, R.E. (1981) (Eds.). *What research says to the science teacher, Volume Three.* Washington, DC: National Science Teachers Association.

Helgeson, S.L., Blosser, P.E., & Howe, R.W. (1977). *The status of pre-college science, mathematics, and social science education: 1955-75.* Columbus, Ohio: The Center for Science and Mathematics Education, The Ohio State University (Washington, DC: U.S. Government Printing Office, Stock No. 038-000-00362-3).

Hieronymus, A.N., Hoover, H.D., & Lindquist, E.F. (1986). *Iowa Tests of Basic Skills (ITBS) Science Subtest.* Chicago: Riverside.

Hueftle, S.J., Rakow, S.J., & Welch, W.W. (1983). *Images of science: A summary of results from the 1981-82 National Assessment in Science.* Minneapolis, MN: Minnesota Research and Evaluation Center, University of Minnesota.

Hurd, P.D., Robinson, J.T., McConnell, M.C., & Ross, N.M., Jr. (1981). *The status of middle school and junior high school science, Volume Two.* Technical Report. Louisville, CO: Center for Educational Research & Evaluation.

Kogan, N. (1983). Stylistic variation in childhood and adolescence: Creativity, metaphor, and cognitive styles. In J.H. Flavell & E. Markham (Eds.). *Handbook of child psychology, Vol. Three. Cognitive development* (4th ed.) (pp. 630-706). New York: Wiley.

Korth, S.W. (1968). *The use of the history of science to promote student understanding of the social aspects of science.* Unpublished Doctoral Dissertation, Stanford University.

Lawshe, C.H., & Harris, D.H. (1957). *Purdue Creativity Test.* Lafayette, IN: Purdue Research Foundation.

Lindquist, E.F. (1964). *Equating scores on non-parallel tests.* Presented at the annual meeting of the American Educational Research Association, Chicago.

Madden, R., Gardner, E., Rudman, H., Karlsen, B. & Merwin, J. (1972). *Stanford Achievement Test.* New York: The Psychological Corporation.

McCormack, A.J. & Yager, R.E. (in press). *Toward a taxonomy for science education.*

Moore, R.W., & Sutman, F.X. (1970). The development, field test, and validation of an Inventory of Scientific Attitudes. *Journal of Research in Science Teaching, 7,* 85-94.

National Association of Biology Teachers & National Science Teachers Association (1987). *High School Biology Examination, Version A* (1987). Washington, DC: Author.

National Assessment of Education Progress (1980). *Student preferences and understandings.* Iowa City, IA: Science Education Center, The University of Iowa.

National Assessment of Educational Progress (1978). *The third assessment of science, 1976–77.* Denver, CO: Author.

National Science Teachers Association (1984). Recommended standards for the preparation and certification of secondary school teachers of science: An NSTA position statement. *The Science Teacher, 51,* 57–62.

National Science Teachers Association (1987). *Criteria for excellence.* Washington, DC: Author.

National Science Teachers Association (1983). *Focus on excellence series.* Washington, DC: Author.

Penick, J.R., & Yager, R.E. (1983). The search for excellence in science education. *Phi Delta Kappan, 64,* 621–623.

Phillips, D.R. (1977). *Cedar Rapids Schools Science Process Measure.* (From the Science Assessment Project). Iowa City, IA: Science Education Center, The University of Iowa.

Phillips, M. (1976). Confluent education, the hidden curriculum, and the gifted child. *Phi Delta Kappan, 58,* 238–240.

Piel, E.J. (1984). *Test of Attitudes on Technology-Society Interaction.* Stony Brook, New York: Author, Department of Technology and Society, State University of New York.

Pittendrigh, C.S., & Tiffany, L.H. (1957). *Life: An introduction to biology.* New York: Harcourt, Brace & Jovanovich.

Prescott, G.A., Balow, I.H., Hogan, T.P., & Farr, R.C. (1985). *Metropolitan Achievement Test.* New York: The Psychological Corporation.

Razali, S. (1986). *Comparison of perceptions of the importance of high school chemistry among various instructors and students in the United States and Malaysia.* Doctoral Dissertation, The University of Iowa.

Renzulli, J.F. (1977). *The enrichment triad model.* Connecticut: Creative Learning Press.

Roller, D. (1970). Has Science a climate? *Sunday Oklahoman,* February, p. 23.

Sanchez, L. (1987). *Assessing aspects of creativity.* Iowa City, IA: Science Education Center, University of Iowa.

Simmons, P.E., & Yager, R.E. (in press). *Comparison of student attitudes about school science in a district with multiple exemplary programs with those found generally.*

Shulman, L.S., & Tamir, P. (1973). Research on teaching in the natural sciences. In R.M.W. Travers (Ed.), *Second handbook of research on teaching.* Chicago, IL: Rand McNally.

Stake, R.E., & Easley, J. (1978). *Case studies in science education, Volumes I and II.* Urbana, IL: Center for Instructional Research and Curriculum Evaluation, University of Illinois (Washington, DC: U.S. Government Printing Office, Stock No. 038-000-00376-3).

Stanley, J.C. (1976). Identifying and nurturing the intellectually gifted. *Phi Delta Kappan, 58,* 234–237.

Tempest, N.R. (1974). *Teaching clever children 7–11.* London: Routledge and Kegan Paul.

The Scientific Literacy Research Center (1967). *Wisconsin Inventory of Science Processes (WISP).* Madison, WI: The University of Wisconsin.

Torrance, P.E. (1966). *Torrance Tests of Creative Thinking.* Princeton, NJ: Personnel Press.

Vidler, D.C. Curiosity. In S. Ball (Ed.), *Motivation in education.* New York: Academic Press.

Wallach, M.A. (1970). Creativity. In P.H. Mussen (Ed.), *Carmichael's manual of child psychology, Vol. 1,* (3rd ed) (pp. 1211–1272). New York: Wiley.

Wallach, M. & Kogan, N. (1965). Wallach and Kogan Creativity Battery. In M. Wallach & N. Kogan, *Modes of thinking in young children.* New York: Holt, Rinehart, & Winston.

Weiss, I.R. (1978). *Report of the 1977 national survey of science, mathematics, and social studies evaluation.* Research Triangle Park, North Carolina (Washington, DC: U.S. Government Printing Office, Stock No. 038-000-00364).

Williams, F. (1972). How Do You Really Feel About Yourself? Inventory. In *Total creativity program for individualizing and humanizing the learning process.* Englewood Cliffs, NJ: Educational Technology Publications.

Woodburn, J.H. (1967). *The methods and procedures of science: An examination.* Rockville, Maryland.

Yager, R.E. (1980). *Attitude toward study of science.* Iowa City, IA: Science Education Center, The University of Iowa.

Yager, R.E. (Ed. 1983). *Centers of excellence: Portrayals of six districts.* Washington, DC: National Science Teachers Association.

Yager, R.E. (1983) (Ed.). *Exemplary programs in physics, chemistry, biology, and earth science.* Washington, DC: National Science Teachers Association.

Yager, R.E. (1983). The importance of terminology in teaching K–12 science. *Journal of Research in Science Teaching, 20,* 577–588.

Yager, R.E. (1983). *Towards a new model for K–12 science education.* Presented at the American Association for the Advancement of Science, May.

Yager, R.E., & McCormack, A.J. (in press). *Assessing teaching/learning successes in multiple domains of science and science education.*

Yager, R.E. and Penick. J.E. (1986). Perceptions of four age groups toward science classes, teachers, and the value of science. *Science Education, 70,* 355–363.

Chapter 11

TEACHING STUDENTS GIFTED IN SOCIAL STUDIES

S. SAMUEL SHERMIS

Teachers often wonder how they can meet the special needs of students in the class who are gifted in social studies without cheating other learners and without ignoring the regularly prescribed curriculum. Many teachers assume (1) that there is a fixed curriculum that must be covered carefully, omitting nothing, (2) that curriculum should be taught in the same way to all students, and (3) that learning should be evaluated in all students in exactly the same way. These assumptions result in a classroom situation in which gifted learners will not be given the enrichment and/or acceleration that they require, on the one hand, and will not be taught and evaluated with strategies appropriate to their abilities and interests, on the other.

By the same token, these misconceptions make it almost impossible to deal with slow learners, some minority children, students with learning deficits—and a good many others within a regular classroom. In order to teach learners with special needs in the regular classroom, teachers must adopt a different set of educational concepts. This chapter is designed to clarify these alternative concepts and to examine their implications for curriculum content, the teaching-learning process, and the evaluation of student progress.

The overall alternative concept that will be discussed in the chapter that follows is that many aspects of the teaching-learning process should be differentiated for gifted learners in the regular classroom. In social studies, this would take the form of giving them the opportunity to identify important real-world problems, read about them, reflect on them, and discuss them. The chapter deals with the following six fundamental questions: (1) What is social studies and what are the agreed-upon goals? (2) What does it mean to talk about children who are "gifted" in social studies? (3) What content is most appropriate for these children and how is it selected? (4) Which teaching strategies are most useful? (5)

249

How does one evaluate the results of such teaching? (6) What are the practical considerations involved in modifying a regular classroom for gifted learners?

I. DEFINITION AND RATIONALE FOR THE SOCIAL STUDIES

Social studies does not consist of an agreed-upon and time-honored organization of content. The definition of what social studies is and what it is for, is a topic of continuing controversy. It is not like mathematics and other similar disciplines where teachers can argue that unless students learn the four basic mathematical processes, they will be both unfit for future work in mathematics and lack the computational skills necessary for real life. In social studies, although published research on the question has increased dramatically in the last ten years (Barr, Barth, & Shermis, 1977; Dougan, 1985; Rooze, unpublished manuscript), no such consensus on content and aims obtains.

Social studies came into existence in about 1921 to prepare young people for citizenship in a society that was experiencing severe dislocations as the result of immigration, industrialism, and urbanization (Shermis, unpublished manuscript). However, there has never been agreement about what constituted citizenship or what knowledge and experiences are essential components in school programs preparing for it (Barr, Barth & Shermis, 1977, 1978). In their recent work, Shermis and Longstreet (personal communication) argue that when the social studies movement came into existence in the early part of the century for the avowed purpose of teaching citizenship, there was no consistent understanding of what citizenship implied. Then as now citizenship may be defined as or equated with: display of and attachment to patriotic symbols; selected attitudes; selected values; decision-making; knowledge of certain concepts; social participation; being "well informed"; and membership in organizations. Thus, any content could be taught in the name of citizenship.

In the 1920s the social studies took shape and began to acquire content from history, political science, sociology, geography, and other social science disciplines. The content was suitably simplified by reducing the amount of data and by lowering the level of abstraction of the concepts. In the 1930s, social studies educator Edgar Bruce Wesley defined social studies as the social sciences simplified for pedagogical purposes (Wesley, 1937). This definition was widely accepted for many years. Toward the end of his long life Wesley regretted the definition of social studies that he had contributed to the literature and its usual interpretation (Shermis & Barth, 1978; Wesley, 1950). Social studies continued to include practices and content from the 19th century: memorization of state capitals and geographic place-names; indoctrination into what was taken to be the canons of American political democracy; laissez faire capitalism and the Protestant work ethic and "covering" traditional concepts in such courses as American history and civics (Atwood, 1980, 1982; Wronski & Bragaw, 1986). Since knowledge gained from social studies courses could never be persuasively demonstrated as essential to citizenship and since social studies appeared to lack the intellectual rigor thought inherent in other disciplines such as English literature or mathematics, it has always occupied a stepchild existence.

In recent years, the author and his colleagues redefined social studies as " . . . an integration of experience and knowledge from the social sciences and the humanities for the purpose of citizenship education" (Barr, Barth & Shermis, 1977, 1978). Moreover, we specified three distinct, historical traditions, i.e., Reflective Inquiry, Social Science, and Citizenship Transmission. This redefinition of social studies has special significance for teaching students gifted in social studies in regular classrooms. The new approach provides an excellent theoretical basis for the enrichment and/or acceleration required by gifted learners.

The focus on Reflective Inquiry is especially relevant to the teaching of students gifted in the social studies. Reflective inquiry seems to have developed in the late 1930s from the theories of John Dewey and his followers, especially their emphasis upon problem-solving and decision-making (Engle, 1960). Social studies was perceived as an attempt to teach young people to become increasingly reflective about the problems which they will be expected to solve as adults (Bayles, 1960; Hunt & Metcalf, 1968). The newer Barr, Barth, and Shermis approach has by no means supplanted the earlier Wesley definition cited above and is currently the subject of considerable controversy, research, and discussion (Stanley, 1985).

The implications of the new approach would lead to dramatic changes in educational practice. For example, the focus of the teaching-learning process in social studies would be on the selection of topics which are related to long-standing social problems and which lend themselves to interdisciplinary, in-depth research and analysis. Memorization of "mind-disciplining" content, and teaching prearranged content for the purpose of indoctrinating citizens in particular cultural values would no longer be part of the social studies.

II. WHAT IS GIFTEDNESS IN SOCIAL STUDIES?

Lists of traits of gifted children appear frequently in the literature. Kennedy (1987) has sharply criticized such listings in that, according to her findings, neither the traits nor the language employed in describing them is uniform. She argues that the trait listings are derived from empirical research and personal experience and not from a clear theoretical framework. Similarly, curriculum implications derived from the trait lists are atheoretical, largely intuitive, based upon "common sense," and not necessarily self-consistent. Nevertheless, over the years, there has been some partial consensus in the literature about the characteristics of students who do well in social studies and humanities (Colangelo & Zaffran, 1979; Feldhusen & Baska, 1985; Renzulli & Reis, 1985; Renzulli, Reis, & Smith, 1981).

1. They learned to read early, are good readers and enjoy reading. Consequently, they have both an extensive vocabulary and a good fund of knowledge that can be recalled easily.

2. They are relatively adept at problem-solving. They can deal with abstractions easily. They are able to engage in high level cognitive processes, e.g., they can extrapolate, identify missing premises, spot logical lapses, inconsistencies and contradictions, generalize and marshall support for a proposition.

3. They are intellectually curious. This is often accompanied by a tendency to be critical of received wisdom.

4. They willingly participate in the give-and-take of an open discussion.

In addition to the positive characteristics cited above, the following negative traits have been noted as well:

1. Their thinking may not be disciplined.

2. They can identify lapses, inconsistencies, contradictions, and unsupported generalizations in the thinking of others, but may not do the same in themselves.

3. Some gifted children are underachievers, i.e., their academic achievement does not reflect their academic ability.

The traits listed above can serve as general guidelines in our efforts to understand and to provide special education for learners gifted in the social sciences as a group. Please, bear in mind, however, that they do not give us the more complete information needed to provide for the needs of an individual child.

Because of the importance of underachievement in gifted learners, we will conclude this section with a few comments on the topic. There is reason to believe that a disturbingly large number of dropouts in the United States are gifted underachievers. The precise number of gifted dropouts is unknown; it is probably not as high as Marland Report (1971) estimate of 18%, but it is probably distressingly high.

Some gifted students may become bored with school, make no effort to learn, and become abrasive and disturbing in class. This kind of behavior often leads to resentment from teachers. Since in many classes, high grades are used as a reward for conformity and good deportment, the grades of the gifted child may decline. For example, one child, now an adult, began to read adult literature at age eight and a half (Barth & Shermis, 1981). In the third grade his achievement test scores were all in the 90th percentile or above, with a composite score of 98 percent. From about the sixth grade his schoolwork gradually declined and at the age of 16 he became a dropout. After leaving school he taught himself a variety of skills, e.g., electronics, carpentry, electricity, plumbing, and auto mechanics. Nevertheless, he continually refused to return to school or even to consider pursuing an alternative method of getting a high school diploma. Recently, at the age of 20, he supervised the construction of a five million dollar housing project.

The wide variety of reasons for underachievement in gifted learners and strategies that parents, teachers, and counselors can use to help in such situations are discussed in some detail in a recent book by Milgram (in press), Griggs (see Chapter 4), Karnes (see Chapter 10), and Meckstroth (see Chapter 6). Moreover, in an earlier chapter of the current volume (see Chapter 3), Dunn reports data demonstrating the efficacy of matching teaching style with individual learning style in teaching dropouts who were persuaded to return to school.

III. WHAT CONTENT IS MOST APPROPRIATE?

The growing awareness of the need for special education for the gifted and talented in the United States and the legislation in most states providing funding for it spurred a proliferation of new programs and curriculum materials. Unfortunately, curriculum materials presented for gifted learners are often basically regular materials cosmetically redecorated or perhaps slightly revised and equipped with a manual. In order to meet the special needs of gifted learners, the curriculum content of social studies must be differentiated from that offered to their nongifted peers. In this section we will present principles designed to guide the differentiation of curriculum content for gifted students with the discussion of real-world social problems as the focus.

Numerous investigators have given attention to social studies curriculum content (Roeper Review, 1981; Shermis & Clinkenbeard, 1981; Subotnik, 1984; Voss, 1986). A few years after the concept "social problem" was introduced by Dunn in his well-known report (1916), the first textbooks with social problems as the focus of curriculum content in the social studies began to appear. However, without a definition of the term "social problem," each text author defined "problem" in his/her own way and basically continued to simplify the research data of sociologists and to lower the level of abstraction. The content of social studies curriculum tended to become rigid and to rapidly assume an almost immutable shape. A close examination of the table of contents and treatment of 1916–1925 high school social problems textbooks reveals content and treatment strikingly similar to texts published today. On this subject, see also Shermis and Barth (1979).

The Barr, Barth, and Shermis definition (1977, 1978) of social studies as an integration of knowledge and experience from the social sciences and the humanities for the purpose of citizenship education provides the theoretical framework to guide the selection of curriculum content for the social studies for gifted learners. Two important concepts relevant to questions of curriculum content emanate from this approach. First, the teaching-learning process should emphasize *integration,* a higher level cognitive process which requires synthesis of information and ideas. Such integration/synthesis requires curriculum content that consists of a large amount of relevant data from as many sources as possible.

Second, one of the major purposes of the teaching-learning process in social studies is citizenship education. This refers to participation at any level in the governance process. The implication is that students should be trained in the central activity of governance: the making of decisions on matters of social policy in which the issues and content are always complex, morally ambiguous and rife with missing data, irrationality, and unsupported generalizations.

In place of the traditional curriculum content, many educators think that the most appropriate content for gifted students consists of specific real-world social problems. For the purpose of this discussion, problems refer to persistent and unsolved social issues which exist on two dimensions: located in our society as objective behavior which society commonly identifies as problematic; perceived subjectively by individuals as problematic. The approach of using real-world problems as the main curriculum content of citizenship education in social studies was developed by Griffin and his students (Engle, 1982), by Hunt (1975), and Hunt and Metcalf (1955, 1968). Not all researchers in social studies education agreed with the problem-centered approach (Cox, 1985). Nevertheless, Metcalf (1985) was able to answer the criticism convincingly.

Defining "problem" has not been a simple matter. The concept of "perceived threat to socially important values," for example, was part of the original definition of "social problem." Many still consider this part of the original definition valid. Readers interested in a more thorough discussion of the history of the concept "problem" and "social problem" are referred to Shermis and Barth (1979).

A partial list of appropriate problems to be used as curriculum content for gifted learners might include:

• changing sex roles and practices in our society: the distance between socially approved morality and actual practice.

• the conflict between natural resource exploitation for profit and destruction of ecological balance.

• the difficulty inherent in worldwide arms reduction.

• control of destructive economic cycles versus preservation of the free-market system.

• religious, ethnic and racial conflict: its sources; attempts at amelioration.

• the rise of anomie, that is, lawlessness and alienation in our political democracy.

• the First Amendment, pornography, and censorship.

• those arising out of technology, i.e., in vitro fertilization, genetic engineering, the use of enormously expensive life-support systems for the terminally ill, availability of experimental drugs (e.g., anticancer medications, AZT for those with AIDS), body part transplants, and disposal of industrial pollution.

Problems such as these are appropriate for gifted students because:

1. They are perceived as sources of threat to socially important values.
2. Each of them carries a good many (usually unidentified implications)

for young people; and because of this they may rather easily be identified as real, substantive problems by young people.

3. They are persistent, have hitherto resisted solution and, therefore, are accompanied by conflictual and strongly held emotions.

4. They are inherently interesting and with but slight encouragement, students enjoy discussing them.

5. They can be approached in an interdisciplinary fashion, that is, they require content from many sources for even a partial understanding.

6. A wide variety of data is available from many sources, magazines, liberal intellectual journals, government publications, newspapers, television.

7. While textbooks may include discussion of such problems, treatment is shallow, fragmentary, and rife with covert and unidentified biases (Engle, 1982; Hunt, 1975; Hunt & Metcalf, 1955, 1968). This situation may provide an opportunity for students to engage in criticism of a source, usually considered sacrosanct, i.e., textbooks.

8. Published materials provide opportunity for students to engage in higher level thought processes under teacher guidance. That is, students can distinguish different kinds of evidence, explore sources of information, trace the development of a thought-line historically, identify assumptions, compare conceptual frameworks, analyze philosophical support, compare different treatments of one issue, distinguish between extrapolation and prediction, and suggest public policy, to mention only a few.

9. The well never runs dry, i.e., inquiry into one problem leads to perceived connections with another.

Many problems such as those listed above are made intractible by the tendency of adults to keep them "off limits" to young people. Such problems are designated as Closed Areas (Engle, 1982; Hunt, 1975; Hunt & Metcalf, 1955), closed in the sense that they are not open to objective inquiry by the young. The reason why young people are kept away from certain kinds of disturbing topics is probably because their teachers are themselves in conflict about the problematic issues involved.

In considering the approach being recommended here, many questions come to mind. How can one deal with community members who wish to keep certain ideas off limits to students? How does one protect the process of academic freedom from censors of one kind of another? How does one protect teachers who use such an approach from hostility emanating from other teachers as well as from administrators and parents? How does one protect learners from undue pressure to accept the teachers' ideas? These issues are important but beyond the scope of this chapter. Those interested in information on these questions are referred to Bayles (1960) and Shermis (1983). In the sections that follow, we will deal with strategies for problem-solving centered teaching and evaluation. We will conclude with some practical suggestions including how to obtain, store, and manage the large amount of data that are the curriculum materials required by the approach.

IV. STRATEGIES FOR TEACHING LEARNERS GIFTED IN SOCIAL STUDIES

Not only curriculum content, but also teaching strategies should be differentiated for gifted learners. Social studies classes often take the form of traditional recitations. They are based on one text in which reading assignments are made. In class, students answer memory-level questions, teachers explain material presented in the text, and give multiple-choice examinations. Sometimes teachers try to provide for the needs of learners gifted in social studies by giving them more after-the-chapter questions, heavier home work assignments, and occasional special term reports. The recitation approach and superficial attempts to provide enrichment for the gifted are, to say the least, not conducive to reasoned in-depth consideration of important issues. They might even generate boredom and poor behavior in some students.

If the problem-oriented approach to curriculum content discussed above is adopted, one of the most effective strategy for teaching social studies to gifted learners is probably discussion. A discussion should be a mutual sharing of viewpoints. The teacher's role becomes that of discussion leader rather than primary provider of information. The teacher may at times explain and clarify, but more often will raise questions, contrast different student positions, suggest resources to be consulted, probe for support, play devil's advocate, encourage the shy or self-conscious child, ask for summaries, and use a wide variety of other discussion strategies. Social studies teachers should encourage candid, vigorous and uninhibited discussion. On the other hand, a classroom discussion should not become a bull session in which anyone can say anything, no matter how irrelevant or unsupported.

It is by no means simple to conduct discussions that are open yet controlled and directed. Discussions require more language sophistication and greater knowledge than conventional recitation classes. Evidence suggests that most social studies teachers tend to confine their discussion-leading to the asking of memory-level who, what, when, and where questions. The usual procedure is that a teacher asks such a question, then uses a student's correct answer as a jumping off point to a brief lecture on formal content. Teachers require special training and experience in order to sharpen the essential skills of discussion-leading and questioning. Readers interested in a more thorough treatment of these topics are referred to the following sources: Beyer (1971), Cartledge and Milburn (1986), Feldhusen and Treffinger (1984), Friedman (1984) and Gallegher (1985). One problem that sometimes arises in social studies classes is that learners who are encouraged to be critical rather than blindly accepting of the views of others may criticize the teacher's views, as well. Teachers must learn to cope with these situations in a positive and productive manner.

The Bloom Taxonomy of Educational Objectives (1956)

In order to design instruction for gifted learners it is important to understand how they think. A number of theories of cognition have contributed concepts that teachers will find very useful in designing instruction for gifted learners. Guilford (1967) developed a theoretical model of the structure of intelligence, and Meeker (1969) applied the concepts to classroom instruction. Gagne (1970) stressed the hierarchical complexity of cognition. In his widely used model of gifted education, Renzulli (1977) stressed the importance of matching curriculum content and teaching strategies to the higher level cognitive abilities of gifted learners.

Benjamin S. Bloom's Taxonomy of Educational Objectives: Cognitive Domain (1956), in particular, has proven to be an extremely useful tool to teachers in their efforts to differentiate curriculum content and teaching strategies. He described a hierarchy of the following six increasingly complex levels of cognitive processing, each consisting of a varying number of cognitive skills:

(1). Knowledge

"Includes those behaviors and test situations which emphasize the remembering, either by recognition or recall, of ideas, material, or phenomena" (p. 62).

(2). Comprehension

"Includes those objectives, behaviors, or responses, which represent an understanding of the literal message contained in a communication" (p. 89).

(3). Application

A demonstration of comprehension shows that the student can use the abstraction when its use is specified. A demonstration of application shows that he will use it correctly, given an appropriate situation in which no mode of solution is specified" (p. 120).

(4). Analysis

"Comprehension emphasizes the grasp of the meaning and intent of learning content, and application denotes bringing to bear appropriate generalizations and principles to further understanding. Analysis involves the breakdown of the material into its constituent parts and detection of the relationship of the parts and of the way they are organized" (p. 144).

(5) Synthesis

"This is a process of working with elements, parts, et cetera, and in combining them in such a way as to constitute a pattern or structure not clearly there before" (p. 162).

(6) Evaluation

"Making of judgements about the value, for some purpose, of ideas, work, solutions, methods, material, et cetera, It involves the use of criteria as well as standards for appraising the extent to which particulars are accurate, effective, economical, or satisfying" (p. 185).

Teachers should become familiar with the Bloom model. They should learn to identify verbal statements at different levels of abstraction. Knowing the difference between a memory level question (called "knowledge" in Bloom's language) and an application question or knowing what is implied by the term "analysis" or "evaluation" will probably provide teachers with a basis for asking questions, making assignments, and evaluating responses. The kind of cognitive activities that are included in "synthesis" require that both teachers and students become adept at all preceding levels of thought processes, because synthesis, as defined by Bloom (1956), is built upon all lower processes, i.e., knowledge, understanding, application, and analysis.

Resources Required by the Teaching-Learning Process: Expanding the Data Base

In the preponderance of classrooms, the most important resource is the textbook. However, one clear implication of the concepts presented in previous sections about the definition and goals of the social studies, the characteristics of gifted learners, curriculum content and instructional strategies, is that the data base used in the teaching-learning process must be expanded. Two observations are relevant here. First, one frequently ignored or discounted source of data is the students themselves. Much of what young people say or think is, admittedly, not well grounded. However, what students bring to a discussion, presentation, or assignment must, nevertheless, be considered data. Second, in a social studies discussion, data from any source—not simply text material—must be admitted. Data or evidence are defined as whatever bears upon the truth, validity, or meaning of a proposition. This means that students and teachers can submit literally whatever data seem reasonable.

This approach implies that a great deal of data ought to be located in the classroom, or available close by in a social studies depository or in the media center or library. Indeed, social studies classrooms should evolve into social studies library resource centers. It is possible for teachers, preferably a number of teachers or even the entire social studies department, to cooperate in order to create such a resource center.

A resource center would contain:

Magazines and Journals. Within any community, individuals subscribe to magazines and journals. In many instances, they are routinely discarded immediately after reading or collected first in a pile in the garage and thrown out later. Enterprising teachers may simply ask students to collect used magazines, e.g., news magazines, both liberal and conservative intellectual journals, publications of a variety of organizations that espouse causes ranging from resource conservation and ecology through civil rights, military preparedness, disarmament and peace, "pro choice" or "Right to Life." These may be organized on shelves and used as a student resource.

Multi-Media Resources. These offer opportunities for a wide variety of "hands-on" experiences and can be ordered from commercial sources or from catalogues that list "free and inexpensive" materials. These resources constitute almost unlimited possibilities for the expansion of the classroom data base.

Fictional Literature. For example, books like *Seven Days in May, 1984, Les Miserables, The Octopus, The Jungle, Grapes of Wrath,* and many others that deal with social themes, conflict, and unresolved social problems should be made available to learners.

Computer Links. Teachers can arrange computer links with various data bases and resource services, and even with other schools and/or universities all over the world. Although such possibilities boggle the imagination, they are not inconceivable given the state of computer-assisted-instruction and computer technology and their availability to educational institutions.

Television and Video-Cassette Recorders. Films and videotapes of Public Television specials, and high-level news reporting are another excellent resource for classroom data.

Audiotape Recordings. A tape deck capable of playing the different varieties of audiotapes can be used for playing speeches, National Public Radio broadcasts, and commercial audiocassettes on a wide variety of topics.

A File of Clippings of Newspaper Stories. This file can, for example, include feature stories or editorials taken from the *New York Times Sunday Supplement, Time, Commentary, or The New Republic.*

While some affluent school libraries or media centers may contain some of these resources, most do not. In any event, it is better to have such data bases readily on hand in the classroom so that students have instant access to the material as needed. The organization of such data is time-consuming. Teachers working together can reduce the labor. Students can also help, as can parents, especially parents participating in groups whose goals include support and advocacy for gifted and talented children.

Other Teaching Strategies

In addition to the questioning and discussion strategies mentioned above, there are many other teaching strategies that are useful to the regular classroom teacher in providing for the needs of gifted learners. Many of the guiding principles for customizing curriculum content for gifted and talented learners in regular classrooms presented in the first section of the current volume are applicable to social studies. Individualization of instruction and the use of computers in a variety of ways are especially promising approaches (see Chapters 3 and 5).

Detailed suggestions to guide regular classroom teachers in modifying the social studies curriculum to create a more challenging program for gifted learners are provided by Barth and Shermis (1981). Specific units on topics for each grade level, kindergarten through grade 12, are presented. Each unit includes learning objectives, learning activities, materials, and duration of time required.

Mentor programs have also grown and have proven extremely helpful to classroom teachers in expanding the horizons of gifted students (Bellflower, 1982; Runions, 1980; Torrance, 1984). Individuals with expertise or specialized knowledge can act as mentors—guides, informal teachers, confidantes, resources—for able students who wish to explore a particular (possibly even prevocational) topic or who wish to know more about a subject. For instance, mentors may be adults with knowledge of a particular geographical area, those who have experience in such areas as labor mediation or foreign service, or retired or active professors in social science or humanities departments.

V. EVALUATING STUDENT PROGRESS

Teachers often respond with enthusiasm to the ideas about curriculum content and teaching strategies discussed above. They agree that such teaching may be desirable, should prove stimulating, and think that they would enjoy it. On the other hand, they frequently express a great deal of concern about evaluating the results of such a teaching-learning process. The legitimate concerns that teachers entertain about the complexities of evaluation should not deter them from selecting appropriate content, leading discussions on significant, controversial issues, and asking higher level questions.

When one is asking Bloom-Level I or Bloom-Level II questions, there is no real problem with evaluation. The best performance is that which comes closest to the textbook or to the teacher's understanding of the text. The problems arise in evaluating students' capacity to analyze, synthesize, and especially, to render judgments. How can teachers evaluate the responses of students objectively when higher level questions, especially at the Bloom Level VI are used in class discussions and in essay-type examinations, and when agreement with the text author's language or the teacher's opinion is irrelevant?

One highly recommended approach is to use predetermined criteria, or standards of judgment. The criteria should be presented to students and interpreted for them. Adoption of criteria does not necessarily guarantee objectivity or fairness in evaluation. However, it is one way that can help teachers to reduce the subjectivity that very frequently characterizes evaluation of high level cognitive processes. Criteria will vary from class to class and from age to age. I have used the criteria suggested below to make judgments in classroom discussions and as formal criteria for judging essay-type answers. They are intended as an example and are not to be considered either exhaustive or definitive.

1. Does the student grasp the point and is the answer relevant?

Verbally gifted students can frequently simply take a teacher's question, turn it into a declarative sentence, add a few intuitive judgments, and produce responses that satisfy the teachers. The student may not have grasped the point and there may be no evidence of thought. If the teacher's approval is the point, this technique works. Teachers can prevent this by asking "probing" questions, i.e., questions which are designed to elicit more than simple information or a rephrasing of the question. Questions which ask students to provide a rationale, an illustration for a generalization, or a generalization to fit one or several examples will test understanding. The criteria listed below are designed for the evaluation of Comprehension, Bloom Level II. For the evaluation of higher levels, other criteria are needed.

2. Is the evidence adequate and accurate?

Evidence is defined here as data that bear upon the question, topic, issue, or problem. The central question, then, becomes: Allowing for age and sophistication, and considering how much data are available, does a student bring to bear evidence which is *accurate, sufficient* to support a generalization and *relevant* to the proposition that is being discussed? The important criterion is, Does the student defend or support an answer in terms either of logic or fact?

3. Does the answer have structure, logic, and organization?

Students—especially able ones who are also glib—can "talk a question to death" by simply saying whatever comes to mind, in the hope that sooner or later they will say something right or hit on a phrase of which the teacher approves. Both in classroom discussions and in essays, students should be asked to refrain from rambling, incoherent, repetitive, and irrelevant answers. Teachers should help students grasp a point and express the answer logically and succinctly. This process requires teachers to pay attention to a number of logical constructs, e.g., Are students aware of the assumptions they make? Can they cite a particular premise or is it simply implicit and unconsciously taken for granted? Do students extend a generalization beyond what it can carry?

4. Is the writing or verbal expression effective, clear, intelligible?

Part of this criterion involves formal correctness which refers to matters of syntax, grammar, clarity of expression, word choice, spelling and the like. Although students are not prone to like this criterion, it is valid. In the real world inept, clumsy, verbose arguments, no matter how valid they may seem to the one making them, are not acceptable.

Essay-type test answers and students' participation in classroom discussions are difficult to evaluate. One difficulty is deciding the relative weight of sophisticated evaluation criteria such as those cited above. The weights assigned to these criteria should not be fixed. They require constant consideration and reconsideration and must be continuously modified with experience.

VI. PRACTICAL CONSIDERATIONS AND CONCLUSION

In this section we will discuss a number of practical considerations that are often quite important in determining the success or failure of efforts by classroom teachers to meet the needs of gifted learners in their classrooms.

A Coordinator. Contact with other programs for the gifted and talented within a single school and with other schools in the system is highly desirable. One social studies teacher with a special interest in gifted and talented children, should be appointed to shoulder this extra responsibility. The roles and responsibilities of the coordinator of a schoolwide enrichment program were described in detail by Renzulli and Reis (1985).

Special Funding. Funds are becoming increasingly available in many states. In order for a particular school system to receive these funds, a funding proposal is ordinarily required. Preparation of such a proposal is best done by an ad hoc group of teachers who can do the necessary research, writing, budget planning, evaluation, etc. The coordinator of social studies for the gifted and talented described above would probably also act as coordinator for a proposal writing team. Since applying for special funding is a complex undertaking, a broadly-based community planning committee is recommended. Some parents may be quite helpful in preparing a request for funding.

Public Relations. It is important to enlist the support and cooperation of curriculum coordinators, principals, superintendents, and members of local boards of education. Renzulli and Reis (1985) stressed the importance of communication with these prime interest groups. Some people in key positions hold attitudes that are not positive toward special education for the gifted (Stewart, 1972: Wiener & O'Shea, 1963). These persons should be informed of philosophy and rationale guiding the gifted and talented program, and kept up-to-date on all aspects of the program—its successes and problems. Although, opposition to gifted education seems to be fading in the United States, some administrators and board members are still hostile to programs for the gifted. They believe them to be inherently elitist and to benefit a few children at the expense of the others. They prefer to see funds allocated to educational programs that offer clear benefits to all of the children.

In many communities parents have organized in order to support programs for the gifted and talented. These groups have proven useful in many ways. They help by raising funds for special materials and for field trips and excursions. Of even greater importance is the role of parents as advocates for special education for gifted children and as sources of ideas and strategies.

CONCLUSION

In order to teach learners gifted in the social studies in regular classrooms effectively, teachers must be willing to adjust curriculum content and teaching strategies for the special needs of these learners. They must individualize instruction wherever possible. They must expand their use of discussion. They must be willing to collect and to organize a wide array of resources.

Students who are gifted in the social sciences are interested in social arrangements, attitudes, and practices. They should be encouraged to inquire into a wide variety of topics, problems, and issues. Their questions should be regarded with respect rather than with suspicion.

The dominant educational goal in our society is to provide equal educational opportunity for *all* children. It should be clearly understood, that when gifted learners receive the same education as their less gifted peers, they are being denied their right to equal educational opportunity.

REFERENCES

Atwood, V.A. (1980) (Ed.). The history of social studies. *Theory and Research in Social Education, 8, Special Issue.*

Atwood, V.A. (1982). Historical foundations of social studies education. *Journal of Thought, 17, Special Topic Issue.*

Barr, R.D., Barth, J.L. & Shermis, S.S. (1977). *Defining the Social Studies, Bulletin 51.* Washington: National Council for the Social Studies.

Barr, R.D., Barth, J.L. & Shermis, S.S. (1978). *The nature of the social studies.* Palm Springs: ETC.

Barth, J.L. & Shermis, S.S. (1980). Nineteenth century origins of the social studies movement: Understanding the continuity between older and contemporary civics and U.S. history textbooks. *Theory and Research in Social Education, 8,* 29–50.

Barth, J.L. & Shermis, S.S. (1981). *Teaching social studies to the gifted and talented.* Indianapolis: Indiana Department of Public Instruction.

Bayles, E.E. (1960). *Democratic educational theory.* New York: Harper and Row.

Bellflower, D.K. (1982). Developing a mentor relationship. *Roeper Review, 5,* 45–46.

Beyer, B. *Inquiry in the social studies classroom: A strategy for teaching.* Columbus, OH: Charles E. Merrill.

Bloom, B.S. (1956). (Ed.). *Taxonomy of educational objectives: Cognitive domain.* New York: David McKay.

Cartledge, G. & Milburn, J.F. (•••) (Eds.). *Teaching social skills to children: Innovative approaches.* Second Edition. New York: Pergamon Press.

Colangelo, N. & Zaffrann, R.T. (1979) Identification. in N. Colangelo & R.T. Zaffrann (Eds.), *New voices in counseling the gifted,* Dubuque, IA: Kendall/Hunt.

Cox, C.B. (1985). Lawrence E. Metcalf: An Annotated Signature, Founders of the social studies. *Indiana Social Studies Quarterly, 38,* 58–71.

Dougan, A.M. (1985). *The search for a definition of the social studies: A historical overview.* Chicago: National Council for the Social Studies.

Dunn, W.A. (1916). *Bulletin 28, The Social Studies in Secondary Education.* Washington, D.C.: U.S. Government Printing Office.

Engle, S.H. (1960). Decision making: The heart of the social studies instruction. *Social Education, 24,* 301–304, 306.

Engle, S.H. (1982). Alan Griffin 1907–1964. In V.A. Atwood, (Ed.), *Journal of Thought, Special Topic Edition, 17,.*

Feldhusen, J. & Baska, L. (1985). Identification and assessment of the gifted and talented. In J. Feldhusen (Ed.), *Toward excellence in gifted education.* Denver: Love.

Feldhusen, J. & Treffinger, D. (1984). *Teaching creative thinking and problem-solving.* Dubuque, IA: Kendall-Hunt.

Friedman, M. (1984). *Teaching higher order thinking skills to gifted students. A systematic approach.* Springfield, IL: Charles C Thomas.

Gagne, R.M. (1970). *The conditions of learning* (Second Edition). New York: Holt, Rinehart, & Winston.

Gallegher, J.J. (1985). *Teaching the gifted child* (Third Edition). Boston: Allyn and Bacon.

Guilford, J.P. (1967). *The nature of human intelligence.* New York: McGraw-Hill.

Hunt, M.P. (1975) *Foundations of education: Social and cultural perspectives.* New York: Holt, Rinehart and Winston.

Hunt, M.P. & Metcalf, L.E. (1955). *Teaching high school social studies.* New York: Harper and Row.

Hunt, M.P. & Metcalf, L.E. (1968). *Teaching high school social studies* (Second Edition). New York: Harper and Row.

Kennedy, D. (1987). *Curriculum theory in gifted education: Trait lists are not enough.* Unpublished manuscript, Purdue University, West Lafayette, Indiana.

Marland, S.P., Jr. (1971). *Education of the gifted and talented.* 2 vols. Washington, DC: U.S. Government Printing Office.

Meeker, M. (1969). *The SOI: Its interpretation and uses.* Columbus, OH: Charles E. Merrill.

Metcalf, L.E. (1985). A response. *Indiana Social Studies Quarterly, 38,.*

Renzulli, J.S., Reis, S.M. & Smith, L.H. (1981). *The revolving door identification model,* Mansfield Center, Connecticut: Creative Learning Press.

Renzulli, J.S. & Reis, S.M. (1985). *The schoolwide enrichment model: A comprehensive plan for educational excellence.* Mansfield Center, Connecticut: Creative Learning Press.

Roeper Review. (1981) Social studies curricula for the gifted. Special Issue, Volume 4.

Rooze, G.E. (•••). *An Analysis of the conceptions of social studies education.* Unpublished manuscript.

Runions, T. (1980). The Mentor Academy Program: Educating the gifted/talented for the 80's. *Gifted Child Quarterly, 24,* 152–157.

Shermis, S.S. (•••). *The birth of the social studies: A study in cultural conflict.* Unpublished manuscript, Purdue University, West Lafayette, Indiana.

Shermis, S.S. (1983). Criteria for selecting controversial curricula. *The Indiana Social Studies Quarterly, 36,* 33–39.

Shermis, S.S. & Barth, J.L. (1978). Social studies and the problem of knowledge: A re-Examination of Edgar Bruce Wesley's classic definition of the social studies. *Theory and Research in Social Education, 6,* 31–43.

Shermis, S.S. & Barth, J.L. (1979) Defining social problems, *Theory and Research in Social Education, 7,* 1–19.

Shermis, S.S. & Clinkenbeard, P.R. (1981). History texts for the gifted: A look at the past century. *Roeper Review,* 19–21.

Shermis, S.S. & Longstreet, W. (personal communication).

Stanley, W.B. (1985) Recent research in the foundations of social education: 1976–1983.

In W.B. Stanley (Ed.), *Review of research in social studies education: 1976–1983, Bulletin 75,* Washington and Boulder: National Council for the Social Studies and ERIC Clearinghouse for Social Studies/Social Science Education.

Stewart, J.C. (December, 1972). A survey of attitudes of superintendents toward educational programs for gifted children. *Dissertation Abstracts International 33A,* No. 2794.

Subotnik, R.F. (1984). Emphasis on the creative dimension: Social studies curriculum modification for gifted intermediate and secondary students. *Roeper Review,* 7, 7–10.

Torrance, E.P. (1984). *Mentor relationships: How they aid creative achievement, endure, change, and die.* Buffalo: Bearly Limited.

Voss, J.F. (1986). Social studies. In R.F. Dillon & R.J. Steinberg, R.J. (Eds.). *Cognition and instruction.* Orlando, FL: Academic Press.

Wiener, J.L. & O'Shea, H.E. (1963). Attitudes of university faculty, administrators, teachers, supervisors, and university students toward the gifted. *Exceptional Children, 30,* 163–165.

Wesley, E.B. (1937). *Teaching social studies: Theory and practice* (Third Edition). Boston: D.C. Heath.

Wesley, E.B. (1950). *Teaching social studies in high schools* (Third Edition). Boston: D.C. Heath. (See Chapter 2, Social studies defined and delimited).

Wronski, S.P. & Bragaw, D.H. (1986) (Eds.). *Social studies and social sciences: A fifty-year perspective, Bulletin 78.* Washington DC: National Council for the Social Studies.

Chapter 12

CHALLENGING LINGUISTICALLY GIFTED STUDENTS IN THE REGULAR FOREIGN LANGUAGE CLASSROOM

JUDITH L. SHRUM

Foreign language teachers generally consider themselves capable of recognizing linguistically superior students on the basis of student performance in the target language. The ease with which a student manipulates the language is one of the signs that indicates ability unrelated to the number of years the student has studied the language. Linguistically-gifted students are able to use the language for communication in a variety of linguistic contexts, and with a high level of accuracy, although mistakes may still occur. However, once identified, meeting the needs of these learners for enrichment and/or acceleration presents a formidable challenge to the teacher in the regular classroom. Public recognition of linguistic superiority can sometimes be counterproductive to the development of a gifted student's ability and to the progress of other students in the same class.

Nearly every foreign language teacher has had a student like Bob who studied Spanish VI in his junior year of high school in a school that officially offered Spanish only through Spanish IV. He eagerly participated in the combined Spanish III–IV class every day, even though his listening and speaking abilities far exceeded those of the rest of the students. He was able to absorb full-length unedited Spanish plays and novels, and he wrote social correspondence in Spanish as easily as full-length term papers. He held first chair violin in the local symphony, was a frequent soloist in statewide classical violin concerts, and was often the highest scorer on Algebra tests. In 1973, neither the teacher nor the student were yet aware of the relationships Myer (1985) would show between musical ability (tonal and meter skills), math skills, and language-learning skills (sound/symbol association, syllable discrimination, spelling ability).

The learning experiences Bob's teacher planned for him were inspired more by the student's giftedness than informed about how to challenge and encourage the use of his gifts. The teacher made some serious errors. For instance, when Bob suggested that he'd like to investigate the relationship between the land of Spain and a composer and his music that he was studying for his violin class, his teacher agreed to the plan, hoping that Bob's newly-acquired understanding would enlighten other class members. The teacher asked Bob to tell the class about his investigation and to play his recital music for the class. On the day of his class performance, Bob played flawlessly, wringing every emotive drop of culture from the instrument and the music. As hauntingly beautiful strains floated from Bob's violin across the classroom, his fellow classmates wriggled, squirmed, wrote notes, and whispered annoyingly. Bob recognized that his peers were not only unappreciative, but downright deprecating in their behavior toward his well-prepared and heartfelt presentation. For months, perhaps years, he had hidden his developing talents from his peers in order to gain some modicum of acceptance from them (see Barbe, 1954; Sisk, 1987). In a brief uninformed gesture, a teacher had allowed that fragile relationship to shatter.

It is the image of a discouraged young man walking to his school bus the afternoon after his presentation, shuffling his feet and dragging his violin case in one hand and his Spanish novels in the other that inspires this chapter. It is written for linguistically-gifted students and their teachers, and for other professionals who wrestle with the challenges presented by superior language learners.

All students should have the opportunity to study foreign languages. The learning of a second, third, or fourth language is not a privilege extended only to the brightest of human beings. In Europe, Asia, India, the Middle East, and South America, where several languages are spoken within a geographic space equivalent to the size of Pennsylvania, it is evident that language learning is no respector of intellectual levels or socioeconomic classes. People of the poorest and wealthiest classes function daily in two or more languages. That the study of languages has been restricted in some countries to only those who demonstrate mastery of their native language is a limitation of human intelligence without basis. According to Garfinkel and Prentice (1985), foreign language teachers are willing to include any learner in their classes. They state that today's foreign language teachers "have no quarrel with including a large range of talents in their classes to be sure that no one is denied a chance" (p. 3). If observation of this phenomenon is insufficient to convince us, the work of linguists (Chomsky, 1972; Krashen, 1981; Vygotsky, 1934/1986) points to the Language Acquisition Device (LAD) and the language "monitor" (Krashen, 1982, 1983) that constitute part of the brain function of all humans. Brain researchers (Heilman, 1978; Levy, 1977; Sperry, 1974; Wittrock, 1980) have located the physical places in the human brain where language functions reside.

The benefits of second language study for all students are beyond question. Masciantonio (1977) reports case after case in which students classified as below-average learners in socioeconomically disadvantaged circumstances surpassed peers in academic achievement as a result of exposure to foreign language study, particularly Latin. Landry (1973a & b, 1974) reports improved divergent thinking, figural and verbal creativity among students who study foreign languages at the elementary school level. Jarvis (1980) summarizes the political, sociological, and intellectual benefits derived from the study of second languages. Herron (1982) explodes the myth that second language study is for the intellectual or economically elite, presenting a solid case for the study of second languages in the curriculum of all students. Limiting access to programs of foreign language study is a policy without basis in human individual variation that can have serious consequences (see, for example, Perkins, 1979). Although the remainder of this chapter is written with linguistically gifted learners in mind, one should not conclude that only children with special language acquisition abilities should have the opportunity to study foreign languages.

Linguistically gifted students require special provisions within the regular foreign language classroom. Given the diversity of ability and interests held by students in any second language classroom, contemporary foreign language teaching methods appropriately encourage the use of the target language for individual expression and for communicating about topics that interest individual students. Savignon (1983) described communicative competence as "the ability to convey meaning, to successfully combine a knowledge of linguistic and sociolinguistic rules in communicative interactions" (p. v, cited in Savignon, 1972). It is the exchange of information between people that is important. Language teachers began to move, as a profession, away from repetitive drills based on the exchange of obvious information between the teacher and the students toward the meaningful exchange of real information. Participants in the exchange of information changed too. Instead of talking to students in a lecture format, today's second language teachers spend more time finding ways students can speak with each other in the target language. Foreign language teachers who have embraced the ideals of helping their students become competent in communication must pay particular attention to and draw upon the individual interests of each student.

This chapter is divided into three sections. In the first section a definition of linguistic giftedness that reflects important recent theoretical developments in the field of foreign language teaching/learning is presented. In the second section, additional characteristics of gifted second language learners are mentioned, and authoritative guidelines for assessing proficiency are discussed. In the third section, the understandings of what linguistically-gifted learners *are* and the descriptions of what they can *do* with language are combined and demonstrated in examples of classroom activities designed to improve student proficiency in language use. The activities permit linguistically-gifted students to capitalize on their greater initial understanding and to progress more rapidly than their peers. These activities also represent examples of how enrichment/acceleration provided for the linguistically-gifted can "radiate" and provide benefit to them and to their less linguistically-gifted peers as well. The instructional strategies cited here are not limited to a specific age or curriculum level. They can be used in an intellectually honest manner with students in any year of language study.

I. WHO IS LINGUISTICALLY GIFTED?

Foreign language teachers are learning to teach toward the intellectual capabilities of each student. Many incorporate Krashen's (1982) input hypothesis into their instruction and emphasize the importance of the formula "$i + 1$." Although the "$i + 1$" portion of Krashen's theory of language learning/acquisition relates more to what happens when a learner is immersed in the target language by, for instance, visiting the country where it is spoken, the input hypothesis has implications for the language classroom as well. In this hypothesis, "i" is the level of comprehensible input from another speaker that the student understands. The phrase "$i + 1$" means that acquisition of language occurs at that point where the student's understanding (comprehensible input, or "i") is challenged by input just one notch beyond the present level of understanding, represented by the symbols "+ 1." Each learner's *"i"* could be above, below, or at the same level as any other learner's *"i."* Moreover, it is conceivable that each language learner could have a different *"i"* for any given grammatical point, syntactical structure, or verbal utterance. The level of comprehensible input could vary according to the function and the context in which the language is used. Krashen's (1982) concept of *"i* + 1" adds new perspectives to definitions of the linguistically gifted. The linguistically gifted could be those whose level of comprehensible input is generally higher than that of their peers. Indeed, the ability to manipulate symbol systems, like languages, has long been an important part of giftedness.

Clark (1983) cites several case studies of children whose verbal virtuosity earned them identification as "gifted." When considered in light of evidence of the biological basis of giftedness, this definition of linguistically gifted appears promising. Clark (1983) points to a more rapid speed of processing due to an increased number of dendrites, synapses, and an increased quantity of myelin that speeds electrical and chemical impulses through the brain. She lists these recent findings about the measurable biological basis for giftedness:

1. Accelerated synaptic activity that allows for more rapid thought processing (Thompson, Berger & Berry, 1980).
2. Biochemically richer neurons, allowing for more complex thought patterns (Krech, 1970; Rosenzweig, 1966).
3. More use of the prefrontal cortex of the brain, allowing for more future planning, insightful thinking, and intuitive experiences (MacLean, 1978; Restak, 1979).
4. More use of alpha wave activity allowing for more relaxed and concentrated learning (Lozanov, 1977; Martindale, 1975).
5. More coherence and synchronicity of brain rhythms more often, allowing heightened concentration, focused attention, and in-depth probing and inquiry (Millay, 1981, pp. 29–30).

The information added by Clark (1983) on the more rapid speed of processing suggests yet another modification to the definition of linguistically-gifted proposed earlier. The second digit in the formula of *"i* + 1" ought to be to be modified so that you would have *"i* + 2" or *"i* + 3," or perhaps a higher number indicating both a higher level of comprehensible input and an ability to think in larger steps and at a more rapid rate than their peers.

In summary, the working definition of linguistically-gifted students of—fered here, is that they are those whose levels of comprehensible input are higher than that of their peers, and whose speed of mental processing is more rapid and thus proceeds in larger leaps beyond the level of comprehensible input.

Most school divisions that incorporate the study of foreign languages in their programming for gifted students identify participants at the end of the first or the second year of foreign language study, using definitions of gifted that are based on IQ tests, and scholastic performance in first- or second-year language classes. Though perhaps well-intentioned, this approach is fallacious since linguistic gifts do not wait until the end of first- or second-year of foreign language learning to manifest themselves. Further, the nurturance of linguistic ability should not be postponed until the completion of a specified number of years of language study. Comprehensible input is confronted daily in language classes of all levels, and the "+1, 2, 3, or more" of advanced understanding that follows must be facilitated immediately, not when the student is accepted to "accelerated Spanish" or "Spanish III–TAG." Accordingly, linguistic talents are best nurtured in regular classrooms rather than through programming modifications.

Each student's level of comprehensible input should be challenged with her/his own "+1 or more" once the regular classroom teacher has been able to recognize what the student is capable of understanding. The definition of linguistic giftedness offered here relies on the professional judgment of the teacher as one knowledgeable in the accurate use of the target language and as one who is capable of identifying a given student's level of comprehensible input and supplying appropriate additional linguistic stimuli ("+2 or more"). Although some teachers will require training and practice in sharpening these skills, the need for complex psychometric identification procedures is diminished when linguistically gifted students are taught in a regular foreign language classroom.

Within the regular foreign language classroom, the teacher is faced with a dilemma: how to nurture the linguistically gifted learner, providing "i + 2 or more" when every additional increment of comprehensible input to able students widens the gap between them and their peers. Fenstermacher (1982) takes an entitlement approach to the resolution of this dilemma, arguing that teachers and administrators should formulate the gifted student's entitlements in ways that ensure both their good treatment and the good treatment of other learners. The strategies for differentiating instruction presented here provide appropriate nurturance and intellectual stimulation for linguistically gifted learners as well as benefits to their classmates.

II. ASSESSING LINGUISTIC GIFTEDNESS

The recent theoretical developments cited above cast doubt upon some earlier descriptions of linguistically-gifted students that focused on measurements of students' innate ability (Bartz, 1982; Gordon, 1981). In a more current description of characteristics of linguistically-gifted learners the National Council of State Supervisors of Foreign Languages (Bartz, 1982), cited an IQ in the top 3–5 percent of the student population with reference to scores on intelligence tests and scores 500–600 on the SAT exam. Of even greater importance, however, was their listing of the following additional set of descriptors that focus on how gifted students function in their language use:

1. Field independence: the student can select appropriate linguistic stimuli and ignore inappropriate ones.
2. Ambiguity tolerance: the learner's ability to cope better with that which is new, different, paradoxical in a given task.
3. Balanced generalization: the second language learner can classify linguistic data in neither too wide nor too narrow a manner, and use the target language as a separate reference system independent of the native language.
4. Extroversion: successful language learners usually possess a degree of aggressiveness and daring.
5. Good second language learners know something about their learning style and can integrate things into their own cognitive styles, regardless of the teacher's style or the style of the materials.
6. Risk taking: good second language learners feel comfortable taking risks and they do so often.
7. Seek arenas in which to use the language.
8. Guessing: good language learners manipulate the language based on linguistic clues to form hypotheses that are then tested and evaluated in the learners' mind.
9. Attention to form as well as meaning, in order to learn about underlying patterns of rule-governed relationships: students monitor their own language use.
10. Adjust to the new target language early.
11. Empathy and sensitivity to other people's feelings. (p. 330)

Foreign language teachers agree that grades earned or number of years of language study are insufficient descriptors of the level of proficiency that can be expected from students at various points along the continuum of language acquisition. Instead of saying that a student is a "straight A student in Spanish I," meaning that the student could probably use the language as well as a B student in the middle of Spanish II, student proficiency can be described as "intermediate high." According to Omaggio (1986), proficiency is performance that implies a high degree of competence through training (p. 2). The American Council on Teaching Foreign Language and the Educational Testing Service (ACTFL/ETS) compiled proficiency guidelines that describe a student's performance in the target language in each of four skills (listening, reading, writing, speaking) and cultural understanding.

Proficiency is measured on the ACTFL/ETS scale in terms of the kinds of contexts in which the student is able to perform, the level of accuracy, and the kind of communicative function the student can use, that is, the task for which the student is using the language. The scale consists of these descriptors of performance: Novice (low, middle, and high), Intermediate (low, middle, and high), Advanced and Advanced Plus, and Superior. The scale descriptors are several paragraphs in length and outline the type of language function, context, and level of accuracy that can be expected of a learner performing at a given level. Further, they describe the kinds of typical errors that occur, and indicate patterns of language use that differentiate a given level from the next. For instance, a student performing at the novice-high level in speaking would be able to manipulate the target language in these ways:

• Able to satisfy partially the requirements of basic communicative exchanges by relying heavily on learned utterances but occasionally expanding these through simple recombinations of their elements. Can ask questions or make statements involving learned materials. Shows signs of spontaneity although this falls short of real autonomy of expression. Speech continues to consist of learned utterances rather than of personalized, situationally adapted ones. Vocabulary centers on areas such as basic objects, places, and most common kinship terms. Pronunciation may still be strongly influenced by first language. Errors are frequent and, in spite of repetition, some novice-high speakers will have difficulty being understood even by sympathetic interlocutors (Omaggio, 1986, p. 434).

III. DIFFERENTIATING INSTRUCTION FOR INDIVIDUAL LINGUISTICALLY GIFTED LEARNERS: TEACHING STRATEGIES THAT WORK

The outstanding ability displayed by linguistically gifted learners can be described in terms of language traits, conceptualization traits, socialization traits, and productivity traits (Bartz, 1982). In the remaining pages of this chapter, these four sets of traits will be meshed with the approach of proficiency accomplishments described in the previous section in order to transform descriptions of human abilities into descriptions of performance. Moreover, classroom strategies enabling teachers to differentiate instruction for linguistically gifted learners will be presented. In each instance, classroom activities suitable for students performing at a given proficiency level will be modified for the linguistically-gifted learner, who is performing at a more advanced level of proficiency. Modification is accomplished through changing the context, function, or accuracy expectation of the activity.

Language Traits. The linguistically-gifted language learner is highly verbal, able to manipulate the language easily and creatively. The proficiency guidelines enable teachers and learners to describe the progress of each learner along a language-acquisition continuum. The gifted learner's ability to move more rapidly along this continuum and to learn in greater depth at each level of the proficiency scale can be nurtured. Appropriate reading materials, creative writing, and the strengthening of research skills are three needs identified by Bartz (1982) for linguistically gifted learners. When working with gifted learners, the term "need" must be interpreted less as a deficiency to be filled and more as an opportunity to be developed. The need or opportunity for creative writing is explored here for a student who performs at an intermediate level but who is in a first-year class where most students are performing at the novice level. Bartz (1982) described the need in this way:

> Highly controlled fill-in-the-blank writing exercises should be kept to a minimum. More emphasis should be put on open-ended, free expression, communicative-type exercises. Rote drilling in writing may be necessary but should not be imposed to the same extent as may be necessary for the average student (p. 331).

An activity suggested for novice learners who are developing proficiency in writing consists of using a picture or a line drawing of a house, a classroom, or a student's bedroom (Omaggio, 1986):

Content: Description of a house

Functions: Description, using prepositions of place

Student Task: Based on the drawing (Appendix A), students fill in the description of Oliver's house, using the appropriate preposition from the box at the bottom and adding the appropriate article in the second blank before each noun.

Passage: Olivers Haus steht _____ _____ Ecke Bauerstrase. Es ist ein grosses Haus mit drei Stockwerken. _____ _____ Haus ist die Garage. Das Das Auto steht _____ _____ Garage. Der Garten ist _____ _____ Haus. Am Zaun, _____ _____ Gartentür, hängt das Schild. Der Dachboden ist _____ _____ Wohning. Wenn es regnet, hängt Olivers Mutter die Wäsche _____ _____ Boden.

/   an auf hinter in neben über   /

/ _____ / (pp. 237–239)

This activity can be modified for a linguistically gifted student performing at an intermediate-middle level in writing who is placed in a regular foreign language class where peers are performing at the novice level by changing the context, the expectation of accuracy, or the function for which the student uses the language. Modification includes the expansion of novice-level contexts such as the student's immediate surroundings, home and classroom to include intermediate-level contexts such as lodging in hotels, and restaurants. Simply change the context to a hotel in Germany, provide another line drawing with necessary additional vocabulary, and ask the student to write a postcard home describing his/her hotel. The activity could be structured in this way:

Content: Description of a hotel

Functions: Description, using prepositions of place

Student Task: Based on the drawing in Appendix B, the student will write a postcard to a friend at home describing the room and the hotel in which s/he is spending the night.

Instructions to the Student: Imagine that you are spending the night in a Bavarian hotel as you tour Germany. Write home to your friend and describe the room and the hotel. Use the drawing your teacher attached as a guide.

The activity, as now presented to the student, allows for free expression in terms of what to describe first, and which spatial relationships to select for inclusion in the post card. The student could be encouraged to go beyond the use of prepositions of place and include other descriptive terms, such as what each room is used for, the principal colors found there, the clients who usually lodge in that hotel, etc. The linguistically-gifted student finds it more challenging to make the description in the postcard as rich as possible. Note, too, that the use of the postcard or the letter home to a friend meets the standards set by Renzulli (1977) that gifted children should present their work to "real audiences," and the recommendations of language specialists that classroom language be used for "real" communication in life-like situations (Omaggio, 1986; Savignon, 1983).

Conceptualization Traits. According to Bartz (1982), linguistically-gifted learners have keen insight into cause and effect relationships and can rapidly master facts and manipulate symbols in creative ways. He suggests, as does Gordon (1981), that the use of drill be minimized, though not entirely eliminated from the classroom experiences of linguistically-gifted learners. Further, he suggests that the value of the learner's uniqueness be paramount and that learning for these students be self-directed. Developing the linguistically-gifted learner's capacities offers opportunities for contributions to the learning of the rest of the class members. For instance, a linguistically-gifted youngster may be able to skim a reading passage, or use prereading clues such as guessing the topic of the story from its title. S/He may be able to determine the nature of the story from the patterns of conversational interaction printed on the page, in Spanish indicated by a long dash whenever a new speaker begins; or from the lengthy paragraphs of narrative prose on each page, the linguistically-gifted learner may hypothesize that the reading selection is an essay instead of a fast-paced detective tale. The hypotheses generated by the gifted learners can be shared with the class, and they, too, can learn the strategies of recognizing relationships and making educated guesses about implications.

Implementation of these strategies in the regular classroom is a daily matter. For instance, while students are completing a practice exercise, the linguistically-gifted student, who has demonstrated understanding already or who has rapidly completed the assignment, is often left with nothing to do. A teacher wishing to involve the student could easily err and give the student another set of exercises to complete that represents basically more of the same materials the student has already mastered. Instead, the student's ability to manipulate language symbols and to hypothesize about relationships could be made productive for the student and his/her classmates. Suppose the teacher knows that the class will encounter a reading assignment the next day, and asks that the linguistically-gifted student describe the story, without reading it. The teacher suggests that the student look at the pictures, the title, the shape of the paragraphs, and quickly scan the selection to see which words are recognizable. From that information the student composes five sentences to describe the selection. These are presented as hypotheses to the rest of the class, who, when assigned the reading, are to determine the accuracy of the hypotheses. Students who are reading at the advanced level and whose classmates are intermediate-level readers will find that this activity relieves them of the boredom of having nothing productive to do, and integrates their abilities for the benefit of the class and for their own further intellectual growth.

Socialization Traits. According to Bartz (1982), linguistically-gifted language learners are outgoing and friendly, have a well-developed sense of humor, and are open to others. They need to assume various roles in group interaction and should be exposed to people of varied backgrounds; these experiences should encourage them to understand themselves and others, and should enable them to accept nonconformity. Many gifted learners struggle to gain acceptance among their peers. The foreign language classroom affords them the opportunity to step aside from themselves and to be someone or something else for a while through role-playing. Many teachers use a small group activity in which pairs of students daily converse using the dialogue or grammar point of the day. The activity enables learners to view the environment, geographic location and role of a person in a foreign country by pretending to be that person.

Shallcross and Sisk (1985) recommend that the gifted learner be given opportunities to develop self awareness by interacting with others while involved in various activities. Activities in which all students participate but which also allow the gifted student to explore and assume differing roles are most valuable for teaching culture in a regular classroom containing students with a wide range of linguistic abilities.

According to the ACTFL/ETS Provisional Guidelines for proficiency in cultural behavior, student performance at the novice level can be described as:

Limited interaction. Behaves with considerateness. Is resourceful in nonverbal communication, but is unreliable in interpretation of non-verbal cues. Lacks generally the knowledge of culture patterns requisite for survival situations. (p. 458)

The linguistically gifted learner, because of heightened sensivity to personal interactions and because of an ability to process language more rapidly, may perform at the intermediate level in cross-cultural encounters:

Survival competence. Can deal with familiar survival situations and interact with a culture bearer accustomed to foreigners. Uses behavior acquired for the purpose of greeting and leave-taking, expressing wants, asking directions, buying food, using transportation, tipping. Comprehends the response. Makes errors as the result of misunderstanding; miscommunicates, and misapplies assumptions about the culture. (p. 458)

A classroom strategy suitable for use at a variety of levels is one in which the teacher converts the classroom floor into a map of the target country (Hammers, 1985a & b), designating certain student desks as key cities or villages. For instance, a Spanish teacher may delineate, on the classroom floor with masking tape, the borders of Spain, designating student seat locations as the cities of Santiago de Compostela, Barcelona, Madrid, Granada, and Sevilla. Most workbooks and contemporary textbooks are set in contexts that are consistent for a whole chapter. When students study the chapter in which a family visits Barcelona, they have a real place in their classroom that is associated with the location of that city. Opportunities abound for practicing the very real communicative function of asking and giving directions by having the students whose seats are near Granada in which direction they would travel to get to Barcelona. The question can be expanded in breadth and depth by students who wish to investigate the modes of transportation available to get from their city or village to Barcelona.

Much can be learned from assuming the identity of a person in another land. Over several years of teaching, Hammers (1985a & b) has compiled file folders representing the complete lives of individuals of varying ages, personalities, and lifestyles in Germany for use by his students. The file for a German teenager, for instance, might contain the teen's name, hair color, eye color, and a sample identification card; sample school grade cards for several years; perhaps some pen pal letters; descriptions of favorite music and activities; statements of career goals and personal interests; some photographs of the neighborhood in which the teen lives, and some family photos. Some of the information may be real, and some of it manufactured by a creative teacher, or former students.

The key feature for all the information in the file is that it will be used as a student assumes that identity for a specified period of time, perhaps a semester, or a year. When the students answer questions in class, they answer them in the character they have assumed. When discussing dating behavior in Germany, students speak from the point of view of their assumed character. A meek linguistically-gifted teen may assume the identity of an assertive Spanish physician, directing the activities of the emergency room, using the dialogue context that occurs in the text. The same physician could describe personal views of euthanasia as part of a debate held later in the lesson.

The linguistic gifts that are employed in presentations of this sort are thought by classmates to belong to the assumed identity, not to the classmate giving the presentation. A solution to the dilemma presented in the introduction of this chapter might have been found if all students in Bob's class had assumed identities. He could have expressed his musical talent as a member of the Granada Symphony Orchestra, and could have spoken about his life in southern Spain, and shared the historical and personal significance of his land to his music. His contribution would have been made over the length of a school year, and his superior accomplishments would not have seemed to his classmates to be showcased. Each of his peers would have had opportunities to speak from their alter-identities possibly as auto mechanics in Santiago de Compostela, living in the shadow of the shrine of the patron saint of Spain and speaking Gallego, French and Spanish (Castellano); or as elderly sisters in Madrid whose family supported the monarchists in the Spanish Civil War and who spent a year in a hideous war prison for women.

The key to this strategy is its flexibility to allow the gifted language learner to pursue indepth exploration of an assumed character representing the target culture. The context described in this strategy presents numerous opportunities for modification appropriate to each student's proficiency level. In this way, the learner could achieve what Hanvey (1979) calls the greatest level of crosscultural awareness, the level at which one understands "how another culture feels from the standpoint of the insider" (p. 53). The learner finds the new culture believable and subjectively familiar.

Productivity Traits. Linguistically-gifted learners generally operate at high energy and intellectual levels, are self-motivated, and set high standards for their work. One of the academic needs, or opportunities to learn for gifted language learners includes learning activities that allow for "the sharpening of technical skills, research and communication skills" (Bartz, 1982, p. 332). Perhaps the most challenging task for the foreign language teacher who attempts to differentiate instruction for gifted learners is to find ways to sharpen technical and research skills, such as speaking and listening in the target language, for novice or intermediate learners. The oral production of a novice-mid language learner consists primarily of learned phrases, two or three words in length, and expressing very basic needs in limited daily circumstances. Students at this level are able to say such things as "Buenos dias." If asked a question that is similar to the memorized material they have studied, they can give answers, such as: "Me llamo Carolina," or "Estudio español."

In a classroom of students performing at novice level, there are likely to be some students who perform at the intermediate level. Their oral production differs from that of their novice peers because they can initiate, minimally sustain, and close a basic communicative task, can ask and answer questions, and can create with the language (Omaggio, 1986, p. 434). A teacher can offer challenges to these linguistically-gifted learners, helping them to improve their listening and speaking skills and their research skills, by providing structured interview opportunities with advanced, superior, or native speakers of the target language. To prepare the gifted learner for the interview, the teacher can use some of the same classroom materials used for the novice students. For instance, the intermediate performers and their novice peers can use this activity in class:

  Objective: Students listen to a passage to identify family members and family relationships.
  Directions: Teacher reads passage once while students listen. The passage is read a second time, with pauses between sentences, to allow students to fill in the initials of the family members on the family tree (Appendix C). One more reading can be provided to allow students to check their work.
  Student Task: Initials completed under the faces in the illustration in Appendix C results in the word *compris* (understood) spelled on their papers. (Omaggio, 1986, p. 137)

Modification of the task requires adjustments in context, function or level of accuracy expected. The teacher may expect the intermediate performers to use the third reading to begin their puzzle sheets, finish them sooner, and begin to compose a set of perhaps five narrative statements about their own families. Use of these statements could follow immediately during the same class period as a second listening paragraph for the novice students, but read aloud to them by the teacher from the narrative statements of the intermediate students. The listening task for the novice students this time is to identify the student whose family the teacher is describing.

Sharpening research skills can be combined with sharpening language skills by asking students to find out some information that can only be learned through interviews with speakers of the target language. Most readily one thinks of interviews with native speakers from the school's community. For instance, after viewing the film *El Espíritu de la Colmena* (*The Spirit of the Beehive*), students could interview a native of Cataluña now living in the United States who had experienced the Spanish Civil War, the setting and subject for the film. Since the film presents challenges to student interpretation without an understanding of censorship, and of the War and its time, students must focus their interviews on the elements they did not understand, and ask questions that will elicit responses from their respondent that will help them in their interpretation of the film. The rules of the interview are that students may not refer to the film directly and they must use Spanish. Two sample interviews follow, the first that might be developed by intermediate students, and the second by linguistically-gifted students performing at the advanced level of proficiency:

Interview 1

¿Cómo se llama Ud? ¿Ud. vivi durante la Guerra Civil? ¿Cuando empezo la Guerra? ¿Qué hizo Ud. durante la guerra? ¿Lucho con qué grupo de soldados? ¿Dónde lucho? ¿Recibio unas heridas? ¿Qué hizo su familia durante la Guerra? ¿Qué paso con el dinero de su familia? (What is your name? Did you live during the Civil War of Spain (1936–1040)? When did the War begin? What did you do during the War? With which group of soldiers did you fight? Where? Did you get wounded? What did your family do during the War? What happened to the family posessions?)

Interview 2

¿Puede Ud. describirme, por favor, su vida antes de la Guerra Civil? ¿Y como fue su vida en los años despé de la Guerra? ¿Puede describir un dia tipica de un soldado durante la Guerra? ¿Cómo es recibir o dar una herida? Qué opinion tiene sobre las causas de la Guerra? ¿Como le afecto a su familia la Guerra? (Please describe for me your life before the Civil War. What was your life like in the years after the War? Can you describe a typical day of a soldier during the War? What's it like to get or give a wound? What opinion do you have about the causes of the War?)

Though interview 2 is three questions shorter than interview 1, the kinds of questions asked are designed to elicit more information that is likely to help students interpret the film. Interview 1 consists of choppy lower cognitive level questions designed to elicit information and facts, but not facts that are likely to help with interpretation. In adapting this activity for linguistically-gifted language learners, the context and the communicative function of the student task has remained constant. The linguistically-gifted students were perhaps a bit more accurate in their use of simple phrases, but since they attempted higher levels of thought in their questions and in the responses they will have to interpret, they may risk even lower levels of language accuracy overall than their less capable peers. What has made this a successful strategy is the flexibility contained in it for students to match their own abilities to the task. If no native speakers are available in the local community, novice-level students can conduct similar interviews with advanced-level students who may be studying the Spanish Civil War.

In summary, taking the position that foreign languages are for everyone, and that there will be a wide range of abilities represented in any given foreign language class, this chapter has presented a new definition of the term linguistically-gifted: those students who comprehend more linguistic input and who acquire language more rapidly and in larger steps than their peers. The definition combines knowledge recently acquired about the speed of mental processing in gifted individuals with Krashen's (1982) input hypothesis of language acquisition. The definition is relevant to the second language classroom environment as teachers offer students differentiated instruction designed to develop proficiency in the use of the target language.

Teachers can successfully work with linguistically gifted learners by recognizing what they comprehend (i) and by offering additional input at the "+2, 3, 4 or more" level. The ACTFL/ETS Proficiency Guidelines offer descriptions of the performance that can be expected by language learners at various stages along the continuum of language acquisition. By consulting the Guidelines, teachers can avoid the errors of holding unrealistic expectations for linguistically-gifted learners. By modifying the linguistic function, the context, or the expectation of accuracy for any given activity, teachers can adjust daily class activities to match and challenge their linguistically-gifted learners. The activities proposed in this chapter avoid singling out the superior abilities of one or several students. These are activities that keep all students involved on the day's tasks, but differentiate instruction by providing linguistically gifted learners with higher levels of comprehensible input and additional challenges. In this manner, the negative social interactions experienced by some gifted children in regular classrooms can probably be minimized without diminishing the academic challenge that they require.

ENDNOTE

1. The author gratefully acknowledges the assistance of Alexander M. Cuthbert for reading and commenting upon earlier drafts of this manuscript.

REFERENCES

American Council on Teaching Foreign Language/Educational Testing Service Provisional Proficiency Guidelines. (1984). *Foreign Language Annals, 17,* 453–459.

Barbe, W. (1954). Differentiated guidance for the gifted. *Education, 74,* 306–311.

Bartz, W. (1982). The role of foreign language education for gifted and talented students. *Foreign Language Annals, 15,* 329–334.

Carlson, N. (1981). An exploratory study of the characteristics of gifted and talented foreign language learners. *Foreign Language Annals, 14,* 385–394.

Clark, B. (1983). *Growing up gifted.* Columbus, OH: Charles E. Merrill.

Chomsky, N. (1972). *Language and mind.* New York: Harcourt, Brace, & Jovanovich.

Garfinkel, A. & Prentice, M. (1985). Foreign language for the gifted: Extending cognitive dimensions. Lincolnwood, IL: National Textbook Co. (ERIC Document Rperoduction Service No. ED 262 641)

Fenstermacher, G. D. (1982). To be or not to be gifted: What is the question? *Elementary School Journal, 82,* 299–303.

Gordon, F. W. (1981). *Foreign Languages for the Gifted and Talented.* Harrisburg, PA: Pennsylvania State Department of Education. (ERIC Document Reproduction Service No. ED 233 608)

Hammers, J. (1985a). Culture and language: The individual approach. *Foreign Language Annals, 18,* 53–58.

Hammers, J. (1985b). *Personalizing and individualizing culture learning.* Presentation at annual meeting of American Council on teaching Foreign Languages. Chicago, IL.

Hanvey, R. (1979). Cross-cultural awareness. In E. C. Smith and L. F. Luce (Eds.), *Toward Internationalism: Readings in cross-cultural communication* (pp. 46–56). Rowley, MA: Newbury House.

Heilman, K. M. (1978). Language and the brain: relationship and localization of language function to the acquisition and loss of various aspects of language. In J. S. Chall & A. F. Mirsky (Eds.), *Education and the Brain: The Seventy-seventh Yearbook of the National Society for the Study of Education* (Part II, pp. 143–168). Chicago, IL: University of Chicago Press.

Herron, C. (1982). Who should study foreign language? The myth of elitism. *Foreign Language Annals, 15,* 441–449.

Jarvis, G. A. (1980). The value of second-language learning. In F. M. Grittner (Ed.), *Learning a second language: The Seventy-ninth Yearbook of the National Society for the Study of Education* (Part II, pp. 26–43). Chicago, IL: University of Chicago Press.

Krashen, S. (1981). *Second language acquisition and second language learning.* London: Pergamon Press.

Krashen, S. (1982). *Principles and practice in second language acquisition.* New York: Pergamon Press.

Krashen, S. (1983). The din in the head and the Language Acquisition Device. *Foreign Language Annals, 16,* 41–44.

Krech, D. (1970). Don't use the kitchen sink approach to enrichment. *Today's Education, 59,* 30–32.

Landry, R. G. (1973a). The enhancement of figural creativity through second language learning at the elementary school level. *Foreign Language Annals, 7,* 111–115.

Landry, R. G. (1973b). The relationship of second language learning and verbal creativity. *Modern Language Journal, 57,* 110–113.

Landry, R. G. (1974). A comparison of second language learners and monolinguals on divergent thinking tasks at the elementary school level. *Modern Language Journal, 58,* 10–15.

Levy, J. (1977). The mammalian brain and the adoptive advantage of cerebral asymmetry. *Annals of New York Academy of Science, 299,* 264–277.

Lozanov, G. (1977). A general theory of suggestion in the communication process and the activation of the total reserves of the learner's personality. *Suggestopaedia-Canada, 1,* 1–4.

MacLean, P. (1978). A mind of three minds: Educating the triune brain. In J. S. Chall & A. F. Mirsky (Eds.), *Education and the Brain: The Seventy-seventh Yearbook of the National Society for the Study of Education* (Part II, pp. 308–342). Chicago, IL: University of Chicago Press.

Martindale, C. (1976). What makes creative people different. *Psychology Today, 9* (2), 44–50.

Masciantonio, R. Tangible benefits of the study of Latin: A review of research. *Foreign Language Annals, 10,* 375–382.

Millay, J. (1981). Bilateral synch: Key to intuition? *Brain/Mind Bulletin, 6,* 1–3.

Myer, Bettye J. (1985). Relationships among selected measures of auditory foreign language aptitude and achievement, musical aptitude and experience, prior academic achievement, sex, and handedness factors at the secondary school level. *Dissertation Abstracts International, 46,* 1546A. University microfilms No. DA 8518996.

Omaggio, A. (1986). *Teaching language in context: Proficiency-oriented instruction.* Boston: Heinle and Heinle.

Perkins, J. A. (1979). Strength through wisdom: Report of the President's Commission on Foreign Languages and International Studies. *Foreign Language Annals, 12,* 457–464.

Renzulli, J. (1977). *The enrichment triad model: A guide for developing defensible programs for the gifted and talented.* Mansfield Center, CN: Creative Learning Press.

Restak, K. (1979). *The brain: The last frontier.* New York: Doubleday.

Rosenzweig, M. (1966). Environmental complexity, cerebral change and behavior. *American Psychologist, 21,* 321–332.

Savignon, S. J. (1972). *Communicative competence: An experiment in foreign language teaching.* Philadelphia: Center for Curriculum Development.

Savignon, S. J. (1983). *Communicative competence: Theory and classroom practice.* Reading, MA: Addison-Wesley.

Shallcross, D. & Sisk, D. (1985). *The growing person.* Buffalo, NY: Bearly Limited.

Sisk, D. (1987). *Creative teaching of the gifted.* New York: McGraw-Hill.

Sperry, R. W. (1974). Lateral specialization in the surgically separated hemisphere. In F. O. Schmitt & R. C. Worden (Eds.), *The neurosciences third study program* (pp. 5–20). Cambridge, MA: MIT Press.

Thompson, R., Berger, T., & Berry, S. (1980). An introduction to the anatomy, physiology, and chemistry of the brain. In M. Wittrock (Ed.), *The brain and psychology* (pp. 4–32). New York: Academic Press.

Wittrock, M. (1980). *The brain and psychology.* New York: Academic Press.

Vygotsky, L. S. (1986). *Thought and language.* (A. Kozulin, Trans.). Cambridge, MA: The MIT Press. (Original work published in 1934)

Appendix A

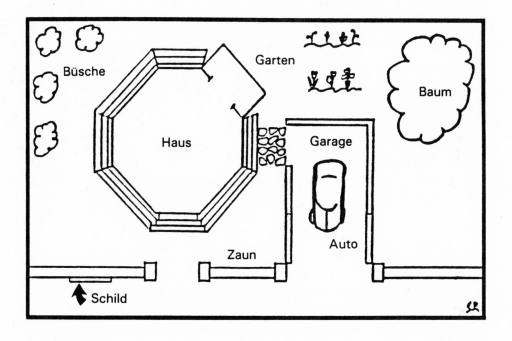

GERMAN HOTEL ROOM

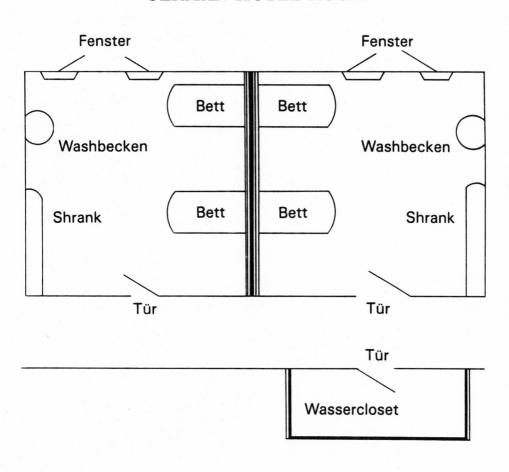

Appendix C

Complete the diagram by placing in the blanks the *initial* of the name of each of the family members, according to the information in the passage.

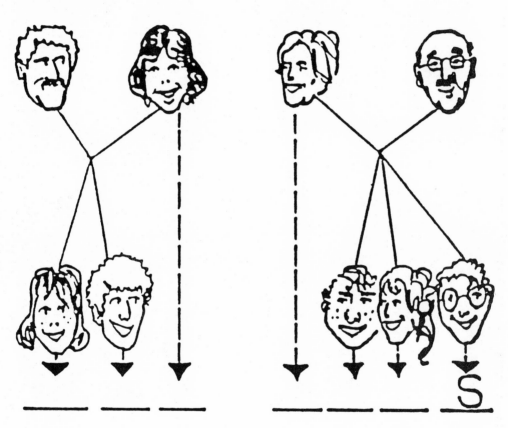

AUTHOR INDEX

A

Adams, I., 188, 202
Adams, P., 198, 202
Aikenhead, G., 231, 245
Albert, R.S., 15, 19, 20, 21, 22, 29
Amabile, T.M., 16, 29
Anderson, M.A. xiii, 179, 180, 202
Arad, R., 16, 30
Ashley, R.M., 208, 220
Atwood, V.A., 251, 266
Austin, A.W., 26, 30

B

Balow, I.H., 230, 247
Barbe, W., 185, 188, 202, 270, 286
Bareford, K., xiii, 5, 129, 143, 145
Barr, R.D., 250, 251, 254, 266
Barron, F., 12, 16, 29, 115, 126, 228, 245
Barth, J.L., 250, 251, 252, 254, 255, 262, 266
Bartz, W., 275, 277, 279, 280, 283, 286
Baska, L., 252, 266
Bayles, E.E., 251, 257, 266
Bellflower, D.K., 262, 266
Berger, T., 273, 288
Berry, S., 273, 288
Beyer, B., 258, 266
Binadja, A., 231, 245
Blakers, A.L., 206, 220
Bloom, B.S., 13, 15, 18, 20, 22, 29, 36, 60, 189, 202, 258, 260, 266
Blosser, P.A., 232, 246
Boston, B.O., 7, 20, 22, 29, 147, 148, 166
Boyer, C., 212, 220
Bragaw, D.H., 251, 268
Brandwein, P.F., 225, 245
Brennan, P., 64, 88, 89, 104, 106
Brown, S.I., 219, 220

Bruner, J.S., 36, 60
Bruno, J., 89, 94, 96, 106
Bull, K.S., 115, 126
Burks, B.S., 18, 29
Burns, P. C., 181, 189, 202, 203
Burr, S., 147, 166
Burton, E., 80, 104
Burris, L.H., 211, 221

C

Callow, R., 238, 245
Caley, M., 143, 145
Campbell, N.R., 223, 245
Campbell, J.R., 231, 245
Carbo, M., 78, 79, 80, 81, 88, 96, 100, 104, 106
Carruthers, S.A., 83, 104
Cartledge, G., 258, 266
Cassidy, J., 179, 202
Cavanaugh, D., 69, 89, 92, 94, 106
Chall, J.S., 182, 202
Champagne, A., 238, 245
Chomsky, N., 271, 286
Clark, B., 273, 286
Clay, J.E., 95, 105
Cody, C., 66, 89, 93, 94, 105
Colangelon, N., 252, 266
Conner, W., 217, 220
Conner, J.S., 217, 220
Cornell, D., 21, 29
Cox, C.B., 255, 266
Cox, J., 7, 20, 22, 29, 147, 148, 166
Courant, R., 212, 220
Crabbe, A. 122, 124, 126
Cross, J.A., 92, 94, 105
Curry, L., 66, 105
Cushenberry, D., 185, 202

D

Dagher, Z., 231, 245
Daniel, N., 7, 20, 22, 29, 147, 148, 166
Daniels, P.R., 189, 202
Davis, G.A., xiii, 4, 5, 113, 115, 116, 117, 118,
    119, 121, 126, 127
Davidson, 23, 31
Dean, W.L., 105
Debello, T., 64, 68, 96, 105, 106
DeBono, E., 122, 126
DeGregoris, C.N., 69, 105
DeLeon, P.H., 22, 29
DellaValle, J., 68, 87, 105
Dewey, J., 239, 245
Dole, J., 198, 202
Dougan, A.M., 250, 266
Douglas, D.B., 76, 88, 105
Dunn, K. S., 63, 64, 65, 66, 67, 75, 79, 81, 88,
    92, 94, 96, 100, 104, 106, 109
Dunn, R., xiii, 4, 5, 63, 64, 65, 66, 67, 69, 72,
    73, 75, 76, 79, 80, 81, 88, 89, 92, 94, 95,
    96, 100, 104, 105, 106, 107, 109, 111
Dunn, W.A., 254, 266

E

Easley, J., 232, 247
Eberle, B., 69, 89, 92, 94, 106, 118, 122, 126
Ellerton, N.F., 210, 220
Endean, L., 238, 245
Engle, S.H., 251, 255, 256, 266

F

Farr, R.C., 230, 247
Feingold, S., 16, 30
Feldhusen, J., 252, 258, 266, 267
Feldman, D.H., 15, 29
Feldt, L.S., 230, 246
Fenstermacher, G.D., 274, 286
Feuerstein, R., 122, 126
Feynman, R.P., 223, 246
Firestien, R.L., 118, 127
Forsyth, R.A., 230, 246
Fox, L.H., 208, 209, 210
Fraser, B.J., 231, 246
Freeley, M.E., 72, 82, 106

F

Friedman, M., 258, 267
Fu, V., 16, 31
Furhman, M., 234, 246

G

Gadwa, K., 64, 74, 76, 95, 106
Gagne, R.M., 258, 267
Gallegher, J.J., 22, 29, 42, 60, 189, 202, 210, 238,
    246, 258, 267
Galton, F., 20, 29
Gardiner, B., 96, 106
Gardner, E., 230, 246
Garfinkel, A., 270, 286
Gaug, M., 189, 202
Gear, G.H., 224, 246
George, D.R., 238, 245
Gilbert, E.G., 180, 202
Goertzel, M., 20, 30
Goertzel, V., 20, 30
Gold, M.J., 177, 178
Goldring, E., 18, 20, 29
Gordon, F.W., 275, 279, 286
Gordon, J., 117, 120, 126
Gourley, T.J., 147, 166
Greenes, C., 208, 210
Griggs, S.A., 63, 64, 72, 73, 74, 75, 76, 92, 95,
    106, 107, 109
Grobman, H. 42, 60
Greenacre, P., 20, 30
Guilford, J.P., 9, 12, 30, 36, 60, 258, 267

H

Hammers, J., 281, 286,
Hanvey, R., 282, 286
Harms, N.C., 233, 234, 246
Harrington, D.M., 12, 16, 29, 115, 126, 228,
    245
Harris, A.J., 189, 203
Harris, D.H., 231, 246
Heid, M.K., 207, 220
Heilman, M., 271, 287
Helgeson, S.L., 232, 246
Hieronymus, A.N., 230, 246
Herron, C., 271, 287
Hilbert, D., 214, 220
Hobbes, B.F., 211, 221
Hodges, H., 68, 71, 95, 107

Hogan, T.P., 230, 247
Holland, J.L. 13, 16, 26, 30, 31
Hollingworth, L.S., 15, 30
Hoover, H.D., 230, 246
Howe, R.W., 232, 246
Howell, H., 185, 202
Hueftle, S.J., 235, 246
Humphreys, L., 16, 30
Hunt, D.E., 76, 107
Hunt, M.P., 251, 255, 256, 267
Hurd, P.D., 233, 246

I

Isaksen, S. G., 118, 127

J

Jarsonbeck, S., 94, 107
Jarvis, G.A., 271, 287
Jensen, D.W., 18, 29
Johnson, C.D., 95, 107
Johnson, M.L., 208, 221
Joval, L., 217, 220

K

Kaley, S.B., 76, 107
Kaplan, S.N., xiii, 169, 178
Karlsen, B., 230, 246
Keating, D.P., 208, 209, 210
Keefe, J.W., 67, 80, 107
Kennedy, D., 252, 267
Kirby, P., 68, 107
Kissane, B.V., 207, 208
Klopfer, L., 238, 245
Koetke, W., 216, 221
Kogan, N. 16, 30, 228, 231, 246, 248
Korth, S.W., 231, 246
Krech, ., 273, 287
Kreitner, K.R., 92, 93, 94, 107
Krashen, S., 271, 272, 273, 287
Kraus, W.H., 218, 221
Krimsky, J., 68, 69, 106, 107
Kroon, D., 68, 78, 80, 82, 108
Krutetskii, V.A., 208

L

Laband, D.N., 20, 30
Landry, R.G., 271, 287
Larsson, Y., 206, 221
Lawshe, C.H., 231, 246
Leder, G., 205, 221
Lemmon, P., 72, 84, 108
Leder, G., 16, 30
Lentz, B.F., 20, 30
Levy, J., 271, 287
Lichtenberg, D.R., 211, 221
Lindquist, E.F., 230, 231, 233, 246
Lipman, M., 122, 126
Lowman, L.M., 42, 61
Lozanov, G., 273, 287
Lunetta, V.N., 234, 246
Lutz, S.W., 26, 31
Lynch, P.K., 68, 108
Lyne, N.A., 92, 108

M

MacKinnon, D.W., 20, 30
MacMurren, H., 68, 85, 108
MacClean, P., 273, 287
Madden, R., 230, 246
Maker, C.J., xiii, 4, 33, 35, 50, 61, 189, 201, 203
Malone, C., 180, 203
Marland, S.P., 9, 28, 30, 207, 253, 267
Martindale, C., 273, 287
Martini, M., 68, 78, 80, 108
Masciantonio, R., 271, 287
Maslow, A.H., 125, 126
Matarrazo, J.D., 18, 25, 30
McClelland, D.C., 8, 25, 30
McConnell, M.C., 233, 246
McCormack, A.J., 227, 230, 237, 239, 246, 248
McCurdy, H.G., 20, 30
Meckstroth, E.A., 20, 32
Mednick, S.A., 12, 30
Meeker, M., 258, 267
Merwin, J., 230, 246
Metcalf, L.E., 251, 255, 256, 267
Micklus, S., 122, 125, 126, 147, 166
Milburn, J.F., 258, 266
Miles, B., 68, 96, 108
Milgram, N.C., xiii, 147, 166
Milgram, N.A., 13, 16, 26, 31

Milgram, R.M., xiii, 3, 7, 13, 16, 23, 26, 30, 31, 34, 253, 267
Millay, J., 273, 287
Miller, S., 143, 145
Mindell, P., 185, 203
Moore, R.W., 231, 246
Moran, J. D., III., 16, 31
Murrain, P.G., 64, 68, 70, 106, 108
Murray, C.A., 66, 69, 95, 106, 108
Myer, B.J., 269, 287

N

Naisbitt, J., 47, 61
Nichols, R.C., 26, 30
Nourse, M.L., 180, 203
Novick, S., 234, 246

O

Ockenga, E., 211, 221
Oden, M.H., 9, 18, 25, 32
Oliver, E., 188, 203
Omaggio, A., 276, 277, 279, 28, 288
Osborn, A.F., 120, 127
Oscanyan, F.S., 122, 126
O'Shea, H.E., 265, 268
Overtoom-Corsmit, R., 207, 222

P

Pacigia, A., 143, 145
Parnes, S.J., 115, 118, 127
Peck, E., 153, 166
Pederson, J.K., 66, 95, 108
Pennick, J.R., 234, 235, 247, 248
Perkins, J.A., 271, 288
Perrin, J., 66, 67, 77, 92, 93, 96, 109
Phillips, D.R., 231, 247
Phillips, M., 224, 247
Piel, E.J., 231, 247
Pittendrigh, S., 224, 227, 239, 247
Pizzo, J., 69, 109
Poze, T., 120, 126
Prentice, M., 270, 286
Prescott, G.A., 230, 247
Price, G.E., 63, 64, 65, 66, 67, 70, 75, 76, 77, 80, 82, 92, 94, 106, 107, 109
Primavera, L., 95, 109

Q

Quinn, P., 69, 106

R

Rabkin, L., 16, 31
Rakow, S.J., 235, 246
Razali, S., 233, 247
Reiss, S.M., 252, 258, 265, 267
Renzulli, J.S., 16, 25, 31, 189, 203, 218, 224, 247, 252, 258, 265, 267, 279, 288
Restak, K., 273, 288
Restak, R., 64, 78, 109
Ricca, J., 66, 91, 92, 93, 94, 109
Richards, J.M., Jr., 26, 31
Ridge, H.L., 16, 31, 207, 219
Rimm, S.B., 119, 121, 126, 127
Robbins, 212, 220
Robinson, J.T., 233, 246
Roe, A.E., 20, 31
Roe, B.D., 181, 189, 202
Rogers, C.R., 114, 125, 127
Roller, D., 223, 247
Rooze, G.E., 250, 267
Rosenbloom, G., 16, 31
Rosenzweig, M., 273, 288
Ross, E., 181, 202
Ross, N.M., Jr., 233, 246
Ruddell, R.B., 189, 203
Rudman, H., 230, 246
Rudmanis, I., 116, 126
Runco, M.A., 15, 19, 20, 21, 22, 29
Runions, T., 262, 267

S

Sanchez, L., 231, 247
Savignon, S.J., 271, 279, 288
Sawyers, J.K., 16, 31
Scarr, S., 20, 31
Schell, L.M., 189, 203
Seabloom, E., 211
Sgroi, J.T., 211, 221
Shallcross, D., 280, 288
Shallcross, D.J., 120, 127
Sharp, A.M., 122, 126
Shea, T.C., 69, 71, 72, 109

Shermis, S.S., xiv, 249, 250, 251, 252, 254, 255, 257, 262, 266, 267
Shertzer, L., 212, 221
Shillenburg, P.M., 143, 145
Shrum, J.L., xiv, 269
Shulman, L.S., 236, 247
Simmons, P.E., 236, 247
Sinatra, R., 95, 109
Sipay, E.R., 189, 203
Sirr, P. M., 212, 221
Sisk, D., 270, 280, 288
Smith, E., 121, 127
Smith, J.M., 116, 127
Smith, L.H., 252, 267
Span, P., 207, 222
Sperry, R. W., 271, 288
Stake, R.E., 232, 247
Stanish, B., 118, 120, 126, 127
Stanley, J.C., 224, 248
Stanley, J.L., 12, 15, 31, 206, 208, 209, 210
Stanley, W.B., 251, 267
Sternberg, J.E., 23, 31
Stewart, E.D., 92, 93, 94, 109
Stones, I.D., 212, 222
Stracher, D., 185, 203
Stewart, J.C., 265, 268
Subotnik, R.F., 254, 268
Sutman, F.X., 231, 246
Swassing, R.H., 181, 203
Switzer, C., 180, 203
Syphers, D.F., 205, 222

T

Taba, H., 42, 61
Tamir, P., 236, 247
Tanenbaum, R., 76, 109
Tannenbaum, A.J., 15, 18, 22, 25, 28, 31, 165, 166, 219
Tempest, N.R., 238, 248
Terman, L.M., 9, 13, 18, 25, 29, 31, 32, 181, 203, 207
Thies, A., 64, 110
Thomas, M.A., xiii, 4, 5, 113
Thompson, R., 273, 288
Tiffany, L.H., 224, 227, 239, 247
Tirosh, D., xiv, 16, 205
Tolan, S.S., 20, 32

Tollefson, N.A., 180, 202
Torrance, E.P., 116, 119, 127, 231, 248, 262, 268
Townsend, J.L., 143, 145
Trafton, P.R., 211, 222
Trautman, P., 76, 88, 110
Treffinger, D.J., 118, 121, 127, 258, 267

U

Urbschat, K., 78, 80, 110

V

VandenBos, G.R., 22, 29
Vidler, D.C., 224, 248
Vignia, R.A., 66, 110
Vigotsky, L.S., 271, 288
Virostko, J., 68, 83, 110
Von Dech, R., 115, 127
Voss, J.F., 254, 268

W

Wagner, H., 208, 222
Wagnes, S.S., 211, 222
Waked, W., 95, 109
Wallas, G., 118, 127
Wallace, W.L., 42, 61
Wallach, M.A., 12, 16, 25, 26, 32, 228, 231, 248
Walter, M., 218, 222
Walter, M.I., 219, 220
Wasson, F., 92, 93, 110
Wavrik, J.J., 210, 216, 222
Webb, J.T., 20, 32
Webber, P.L., 20, 31
Weinberg, F., 78, 110
Weinberg, R.A., 20, 31
Weiner, J.L., 265, 268
Weiss, I.R., 232, 248
Welsh, W.W., 235, 246
Wesley, E.B., 250, 251, 268
Wheatley, G.H., 208, 210, 222
Wheeler, R., 78, 80, 82, 110
White, R., 68, 75, 110, 111
Williams, F.E., 192, 203, 231, 248
Wing, C. W., Jr., 16, 25, 26, 32
Wittig, C., 66, 111
Wittig, M., 20, 31
Wittrock, M., 271, 288

Woodburn, D., 211, 222
Woodburn, J.H., 231, 248
Wronski, S.P., 251, 268

Y

Yager, R.E., xiv, 16, 22, 227, 230, 231, 233, 234,
    235, 236, 237, 239, 246, 247, 248
Yitzhak, V., 13, 23, 31

Young, A., 83, 104

Z

Zaffran, R.T., 252, 266
Zawojewski, J.S., 211, 222
Zenhausern, R., 69, 75, 89, 92, 94, 106,
    111
Zimmerman, B., 208

SUBJECT INDEX*

B

Bloom's Taxonomy of Educational Objectives,
190, 258

C

Chall's Stages of the Development of Reading,
182
Classroom management, 170, 179, 217,
Computers
application programs, 129
classroom equipment, 140
integration with curriculum, 135
Curriculum content for gifted
acceleration, 177
in mathematics, 209
enrichment, 177
in mathematics, 210
principles of customization, 33,
Creative growth
teaching for, 113–114
classroom atmosphere, 114
Creative thinking techniques, 119

D

Differentiation of curriculum for gifted
learners, 33
foreign languages, 269, 277
language arts, 169
teaching strategies, 176
science, 227
mathematics, 211
social studies, 249

E

Evaluating student progress
social studies, 262

G

Giftedness
definition, 9
linguistically, 272
mathematical, 209
science-gifted, 233
social studies, 252
identification, 24
assessing linguistic giftedness, 275
in regular classrooms, 7
reading and library skills, 179
assessment, 181
curriculum modifications, 188
Williams, 192

I

Individualizing instruction, 63
Contract Activity Packages, 96

L

Learning style, 64, 66
elements of, 68–90
of gifted, 91
Learning Style Inventory, 66

---

*The first page reference for a given subject in a given chapter is cited in this index. The reader will find additional references to the subject in subsequent pages of the chapter in many instances.

M

McCormack and Yager domains, 227
Milgram's 4 × 4 Structure of Giftedness
    Model, 9

P

Pull-out programs, 7, 147

S

SEEK (Summit Educational Enrichment for
    Kids), 147

T

Teaching gifted in regular classrooms, 3